# VICTORIA CROSS at TAKROUNA:
# The Haane Manahi Story

# VICTORIA CROSS at TAKROUNA:
# The Haane Manahi Story

Paul Moon

*First published in 2010 by Huia Publishers*
*39 Pipitea Street, PO Box 17–335*
*Wellington, Aotearoa New Zealand*
*www.huia.co.nz*

*ISBN 978-1-86969-420-3*



*Front cover images: Sergeant Haane Manahi at Maadi, Egypt, taken by George Bull;*
*Alexander Turnbull Library, Wellington, New Zealand; DA-04139*
*Takrouna Pinnacle and fortification, Norman Bennett*
*Back cover image: War Graves Commission cemetery at Enfidaville, Norman Bennett*



*National Library of New Zealand Cataloguing-in-Publication Data*
*Paul Moon.*
*Victoria Cross at Takrouna : the Haane Manahi story / Paul Moon.*
*ISBN 978-1-869694-20-3*
*1. Manahi, Haane, 1913-1986. 2. Manahi, Haane, 1913-1986*
*—Medals. 3. Enfidaville, Battle of, Tunisia, 1943. 4. Soldiers—New*
*Zealand—Biography. [1. Kōrero nehe. reo 2. Pakanga. reo 3.*
*Kōrero taumata. reo] 1. Title.*
*940.540092—dc 22*
*Printed in Thailand by Sirivatana Interprint PCL.*

*Published with the support of the Ngāti Whakaue Education Endowment Trust Board*

# CONTENTS

# ACKNOWLEDGEMENTS

This book would not have come into existence without the assistance of a great number of people to whom I am deeply grateful. I should like to thank all those for their help and participation:

**Rauawa [Rau] Manahi,** *who was extremely generous with his time, and in sharing a wealth of material relating to his father's life.*

**Geoff Manahi,** *who was similarly enthusiastic in sharing details of his father's life.*

**Neil Manahi,** *whose helpful contributions on his uncle's early life and character were invaluable.*

**Hamuera Mitchell,** *who has been instrumental in this book coming into being, and who worked throughout to arrange interviews, locate contacts, and who related many details of Ngāti Whakaue history that were relevant to Manahi's life.*

**Arthur Midwood,** *who was with Manahi during much of the war, and provided often intimate accounts of that period that otherwise would have been unavailable.*

**Norman Bennett,** *whose own research was crucial for the final chapter of this book, and who supplied a great deal of material relating to the work of the Manahi VC Committee.*

**Dr. Monty Soutar,** *who went through the manuscript and made valuable suggestions.*

**Professor Paul Tapsell,** *Otago University, who provided comments and suggestions on Ngāti Whakaue whakapapa and history.*

**Brian Bargh** *of Huia Publishers, who displayed enthusiasm for this project from the outset.*

**Bill Keiha,** *who gave rare eyewitness insights into the foundation of the 28 (Māori) Battalion.*

**Dr Pare Keiha,** *Associate Professor at Auckland University of Technology, who offered personal details on his whānau's role in the battalion, and who has wholeheartedly supported this book from the outset.*

**Fred McRae,** *whose detailed knowledge of his uncle's role in the war, and of whakapapa* *issues surrounding B Company offered a useful context for some of the decisions made involving B Company.*

**Matt Te Pou,** *who helped organise meetings with surviving B Company veterans.*

**Whai Ngata,** *for his generosity in making available material from the Apirana Ngata Collection at the Alexander Turnbull Library, and for his recollections of interviews with men of the Māori Battalion.*

**Darryl Rogers,** *who kindly made available letters written by his father during the war.*

**The Reverend Tom Poata,** *who was so helpful in providing details on Manahi's connection with St Faith's Church.*

**Ike Reti,** *who offered his collection of documentary material on Ōhinemutu's history.*

**Uenuku Fairhall,** *who kindly consented for the words of his haka commemorating Manahi to be reproduced in this book.*

**Bryony Walker,** *who assisted with publishing this book.*

**The staff at the Rotorua RSA,** *who were generous with their resources on Manahi.*

**Dr. Toby Curtis,** *for his support over the last two decades.*

**Cherie Meecham,** *Deputy Director, Rotorua Museum of Art and History.*

**Professor Noel Cox,** *Auckland University of Technology.*

**Dr. Graham Langton,** *Archivist, Archives New Zealand.*

**Richard Ellis,** *Coronial Services Co-ordinator at the Ministry of Justice.*

**Clifford Slade,** *Coronial Services Archivist at the Ministry of Justice.*

**Christopher Brooks,** *from the New Zealand Defence Force Archives.*

**Jody Wyllie,** *Tairawhiti Museum.*

**Fiona Loon,** *Te Puni Kōkiri – Ministry of Māori Development.*

**Dr. Daniel Todman,** *Queen Mary University of London.*

**Gillian Tito,** *Department of Internal Affairs.*

**Eddie Olliffe,** *Business Manager, Waverley Abbey House, England.*

# PROLOGUE

> E papa nga rakau i runga i a koe
> Mau ake te whakaaro ake, ae, ae.
> E haere nga taua i te ao nei,
> Mau e patu. Ae, ae.
> When weapons clash above you,
> You shall have my will to act, ae, ae.
> And if war marches over the earth,
> You shall move to oppose and destroy, ae, ae.
>
> *Whakataukī attributed to Tamatekapua,*
> *retold by Henry Taiporutu Te Mapu-o-te-rangi Mitchell.*[1]

I arrived at the Muruika urupā just before sunrise. It is a small plot lined with a rocky edge that protrudes into Lake Rotorua. On this still, winter morning, it was partly shrouded by a low-hanging sulphurous fog, with the sound of steaming water hissing from nearby geothermal vents – the way I imagined purgatory might look. In the background is the manicured mock-Tudor church of St. Faith's, which leads around to Te Papa-i-Ouru Marae and Tamatekapua[2] – the building that presides over this intimate cemetery, and which is at the cultural heart of the surrounding community of Ōhinemutu.

Muruika is where history is buried. The ground is nourished by the bodies of men from the 28 Maori Battalion and soldiers from other wars – some killed in the war, and others more recent interments, when age finally stopped wearying them. The rigid rows of sombre tombstones – lined up as if on some timeless parade-ground – are a mournful testament to lives that were torn from their whānau and their routines and thrust to the other side of the world, into the heart of the biggest military conflict in history.

Even during the war, and certainly afterwards, the 28 Māori Battalion remained the most famous of all the New Zealand Division's fighting units. It was probably the battalion's distinctive New Zealand identity, its catalogue of triumphs, and the changes it made to the way Pākehā perceived their Māori compatriots, that endeared this group of soldiers in the country's popular memory. As an indication of this, even seven decades on, most New Zealanders still recognise Anania Amohau's rousing song *Maori Battalion March to Victory.*[3]

And even if they do not now know all the lyrics by heart, the final refrain of the chorus 'For God! For King! And for Country! Au–e / Ake, ake, kia kaha e!' – remains familiar to generations who had no direct experience of the Second World War. It is the country's only martial song to have achieved enduring popularity and its performance still summons up the epic achievements of the battalion. These accomplishments are imbued with all those elements that have turned the battalion's feats into a modern saga. They are the triumphs of ordinary men over professional soldiers, the acts of almost unimaginable bravery, the special sort of whanaungatanga developed among men who go to war, the exhilaration of individual initiative, and the fight for a cause that has a profound moral basis. But has the battalion become the sort of institution that the military historian John Keegan identified as 'a cherished ingredient of a fading national myth'?[4] Has the reverence in which the battalion is still held merely become a case of honour for the sake of being honoured? This is a risk, but one that can be avoided provided that the emphasis on the battalion remains on the individuals who filled its ranks. This is where men like Haane Manahi have a role, as champions of the battalion's reputation, and a reminder of the very human dimension of this legendary fighting force.

The role of individuals in war is crucial, yet often overlooked. The temptation for historians can be to examine battles as a composite of statistics, tactics, strategies, equipment, lines on maps, and movements of bodies of troops. But at the centre of every military confrontation are people, all of whom experience the same entanglement of various thoughts and emotions. All wars have this human dimension in common: 'the behaviour of men struggling to reconcile their instinct for self-preservation, their sense of honour and achievement of some aim over which other men are ready to kill them'.[5] However, these extreme impulses – the preparedness to kill people for a cause – tend to last only as long as the extreme circumstances that foster them. When the fighting has subsided, at some point, each soldier is left to his own thoughts. Exhilaration, anxiety, doubt, guilt, sympathy, denial, and pride can all curdle in his mind – sometimes for years afterwards.

Manahi died in 1986, and in the years that followed, the number of his wartime comrades – those that were left to grow old – dwindled to the point where by the time research commenced for this book, they had almost all passed away. As a result, much of the content of this work is an exercise in reconstruction – drawing together documentary evidence, a handful of accounts from survivors of the war, and oral histories from friends and whānau. Inevitably, only a partial rendition of Manahi's life is possible from this pool of material, but it at least affords an insight – however imperfect – into one of the most courageous soldiers New Zealand has produced.

Anyone looking for a detailed analysis of Allied military strategy in the Second World War, or of the history of the 28 Māori Battalion can refer to many worthy books on these topics. In particular, Monty Soutar's superb volume, *Nga Tama Toa: The Price of Citizenship*,[6] which is likely to remain the definitive text on the battalion – especially its C Company – and Wira Gardiner's *Te Mura o te Ahi: The Story of the Maori Battalion*,[7] which was a pioneering study of the Battalion. This work, by contrast, is the account of one man, whose unparalleled heroic achievements added another rich layer of mana to the already formidable reputation of the 28 Māori Battalion. Manahi's life might otherwise never have surfaced above obscurity had it not been for his exploits during the war, and these therefore rightly dominate this book, hopefully as a testament to and reminder of the extraordinary fortitude and commitment of this warrior of Te Arawa and Ngāti Raukawa.

*Paul Moon*
*Auckland, 2010*

## NOTES

1. Whakataukī attributed to Tamatekapua, cited by Henry Taiporutu Te Mapu-o-te-rangi Mitchell, 1944, in W J Phillipps, 'Carved Houses of Te Arawa', in Dominion Museum Records in Ethnology, vol. 1, no. 1, Wellington, 1946, pp. 18–19.
2. This tupuna whare was named after the captain of the *Te Arawa* canoe. It was built in 1878 to ratify the peace between the Te Arawa and Waikato tribes. It was demolished in 1939, but was rebuilt by 1943.
3. F Rennie, *Regular Soldier*, Auckland, Endeavour Press, 1986, p. 26; E Edwards to W Gardiner, 3 July 1985, in W Gardiner, *Te Mura o te Ahi: The Story of the Maori Battalion*, Auckland, 1992, p. 29.
4. J Keegan, *The Face of Battle: A Study of Agincourt, Waterloo, and the Somme*, London, Pimloco, 2004, p. 79.
5. Ibid., p. 297.
6. M Soutar, *Nga Tama Toa: The Price of Citizenship: C Company 28 (Maori) Battalion 1939-1945*, Auckland, David Bateman, 2008.
7. W Gardiner, *Te Mura o te Ahi: The Story of the Maori Battalion*, Auckland, Reed, 1992.

# CHAPTER 1: Whānau and Whakapapa

'Ka whakapakari koe, i patai ai, "ko wai ahau?"' 'You become a man when you ask "who am I?"' This whakataukī[1] alludes to the fact that in traditional Māori society, knowing where you came from – your ancestors and your community's history – was not just some idle exercise in genealogy, it was part of the passage into adulthood. And knowing one's whakapapa meant much more than just being aware of a string of ancestral names that were laid out to be recited and memorised. Whakapapa included places, deities, histories, and was the means by which people understood their role in their community. It also clarified their loyalties, identified their enemies, and emphasised the importance of the collective as the source of the individual. 'Whakapapa is like everything going into a funnel', explained one tohunga, 'each of us is the sum of all our ancestors who have preceded us'.[2] Thus, when Manahi and his siblings were nursed on stories of their predecessors, they were receiving an amalgam of history, mythology, and ancestry, which enabled them to understand who they were, where they came from, and how they fitted into their surrounds. It is not the intention here, though, to render an exhaustive narrative of every one of Manahi's ancestors. Rather, a brief survey of a few of the peaks of his genealogical landscape is helpful in giving an overall sense of its importance to him and all the other members of the hapū and iwi.

The oldest portion of the fabric of Manahi's whakapapa relates to the arrival and formation of Te Arawa in New Zealand. Its basic elements are easily assembled. Te Arawa is a confederation of iwi which share a common descent from the crew of the same migrating waka – the Arawa waka, that landed at Maketū in the Bay of Plenty. From that location, the occupants fanned out inland over several generations to eventually occupy an area described in the whakataukī 'Te Arawa mai i Maketu ki Tongariro' – 'Te Arawa from Maketu to Mt. Tongariro'.[3] Of course, during these centuries of expansion and movement, there was an accompanying history of intermarriage between members of Te Arawa and neighbouring iwi, so much so that the affiliations tightly knitted together over that period, are now almost impossible to disentangle.

The area that Te Arawa occupied was shaped like a tahā – a gourd or calabash: 'The wide interior lands of the central volcanic plateau and the Rotorua Lakes are in the bowl of the pan or the body of the calabash, and the Kaituna River runs down the handle of the pan or the neck of the gourd to the estuary and the sea at Maketu'.[4] The layout of this terrain gave Te Arawa a distinctive geographical attribute: for a major iwi confederation, it had an especially small area of coastline – around fifty kilometres, centred on the Maketū Estuary.[5]

The man who had decided to captain this migration to New Zealand from Hawaiki was Tamatekapua. He even built the waka for the expedition (said to be a double-hulled vessel capable of carrying two hundred people),[6] and named it *Te Arawa*. Just before their planned departure, Tamatekapua's father, Houmaitawhiti, preached to the crew about the importance of living in peace in their new home, and not being swayed by Tū, the god of war[7] (an injunction that ultimately proved too difficult to heed). There is a series of stories about the departure of *Te Arawa*, all of which emphasise aspects of Tamatekapua's cunning and guile. It was these traits, and not Houmaitawhiti's plea for peace, that were esteemed by succeeding generations, and led to the frequently prophetic whakataukī, 'a descendant of Tamatekapua is daring enough for anything'.[8]

One of Tamatekapua's first cousins was Ngātoroirangi, and according to iwi historians, both were the offspring of the two sons of the ariki Atuamatua. Atuamatua's name is associated with the creation myths, and he was said to have prepared the adzes used to separate Ranginui and Papatūānuku. Atuamatua did this on the instructions of Tūmatauenga, who was considered to be Ranginui and Papatūānuku's 'most savage' son.[9] Tamatekapua was the son of Houmaitawhiti, who had been born to Atuamatua's second wife.[10] According to one tradition, Tamatekapua kidnapped Ngātoroirangi from the Tainui waka to act as his navigator.

Tamatekapua chose Maketū as the final landing place of the Arawa waka. In time his grandson, Ihenga was to venture inland and claim the Rotorua region for the descendants of Tamatekapua, especially through his elderly uncle, Kahumatamomoe. His claims, however, did not pass without causing much tension amongst the then current occupiers, the descendants of Ika, also of the Arawa waka. By this time – probably early fifteenth century – Ika's people had retreated to Mokoia, an island of just over one square kilometre rising from the middle of Lake Rotorua. In retribution for losing control over southern geothermal shores they killed Ihenga's only daughter – Karaka. In his grief, Ihenga named the location 'the place where the girl's life was finished': Ō hine mutu. He then left his younger brother, Tamaihutoroa,[11] in charge of Ōhinemutu, and returned to his father's people in the Coromandel, where he eventually died.

Roughly two hundred years later, the area endured a bout of severe seismic activity, resulting in the pā at Ōhinemutu – known as Muruika – sinking into the lake. This happened so suddenly that maybe dozens of its occupants were killed. The adjacent outcrop of rock that remained above the waterline (now the location of St. Faith's Church) became extremely tapu, and it was not until 1884 that Tuhoto, a tohunga from Te Wairoa, lifted this tapu and placed it on a small island just off the shore.[12]

Whakaue. Everyone in the whānau knew the name. He was their hapū's eponymous ancestor, and one of the most notable figures in Manahi's ancestry – on both his mother's and father's sides. A seventh-generation descendant of Tamatekapua,[13] Whakaue was noted to be a daring and highly successful military commander[14] – and political strategist. After the conquest of Mokoia by his father, Uenukukōpako, Whakaue and his wife Rangiuru raised their whānau at Kaiweka on the island,[15] including their sons – Tawakeheimoa, Tūteaiti, Ngāraranui, and Tūtānekai. Tūtānekai was actually Whakaue's stepson (the product of the liaison between Whakaue's wife, Rangiuru, and Tūwharetoa), and as an adult, acquired a reputation as one of the greatest sources of discord in the region.[16] However, it was Tūtānekai's famed relationship with Hinemoa, the daughter of the great chief Umukaria, for which he is best remembered – a union that initially calmed relationships between two very close branches of Te Arawa. Peace however was temporary and it was not until the eighteenth century when a series of battles were fought between Te Ure o Uenukukōpako and Tūhourangi that the lands from Ōwhata (Hinemoa Point) through to Weriweri, including Ōhinemutu, were to come under the exclusive control of Tūtānekai's descendants, Ngāti Whakaue.[17]

**Whakapapa from Tamatekapua to Whakaue**

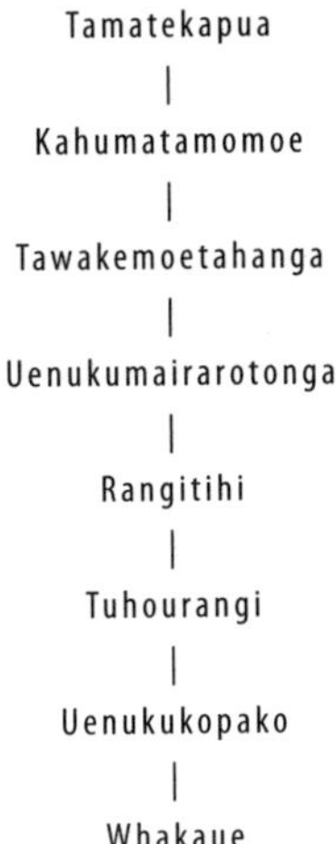

From Te Whatumairangi (the son of Tūtānekai and Hinemoa) came three sons: Ariariterangi, Taiwere and Hurungaoterangi.[18] All proved themselves as able military commanders, with Ariariterangi memorialised for always urging his people to return to battle, even when the odds were piled against them. Several generations later, descendants of each of these three men would unite in the form of Manahi's parents.

Of all the noted ancestors in the inventory of Manahi's whakapapa, Tūnohopū remained the leviathan. His reputation had grown more lustrous over the nine generations before Manahi's birth, and he was regarded as one of the ancestral monuments to the iwi's mana. In particular, he was famous for his individual feats of bravery.[19]

Another important ancestor in Manahi's whakapapa was Pukaki, who was the product of an arranged marriage between his father, Taiwere, of Ngāti Whakaue, and his mother, Tamiuru, of Ngāti Pikiao. His birth was said to herald 'the union of the two lakes' – a reference to Ngāti Whakaue's dominance of Lake Rotorua and Ngāti Pikiao's control over Lake Rotoiti.[20] Pukaki's father, Taiwere, was killed while he was still a child, as were two of his uncles when they tried to avenge his death. What followed were several years of clashes between Ngāti Whakaue (which was based at Parawai Pā) and Tūhourangi of Ōhinemutu. This drawn-out war was eventually ended by Pukaki agreeing to marry Ngapuia, the daughter of the Tūhourangi rangatira, Te Anumatao – a union that enabled Ngāti Whakaue to leave their refuge on Mokoia and return to the mainland.[21] All of Pukaki's daughters were married off to various rangatira in Te Arawa, which enhanced enormously his mana over the region, and later led him to be identified as one of the great unifying forces of Ngāti Whakaue[22] (although his wife eventually left him, enraged over the fact that he had been involved in a cannibal meal, among whom on the menu was reputed to be her father). Pukaki's sons and grandsons were especially noted as warriors of Ngāti Whakaue and upheld the mana of Pukaki on the battlefield.[23] Rau explained the significance of this line of his father's ancestry: 'Manahi's warrior side from Pukaki is attributed to Rangitakuku (Pukaki's son) and then down to his son, Te Whanoa, and then to Te Whanoa's son Te Umanui. Te Whanoa was the younger brother of the famous warrior chief of Pukaki – Te Matapihi o Rehua, or Manaia as he was sometimes named'.[24]

The following Ngāti Whakaue whakapapa shows the relationships between Haane and his ancestors:

# Whakapapa a Haane Manahi

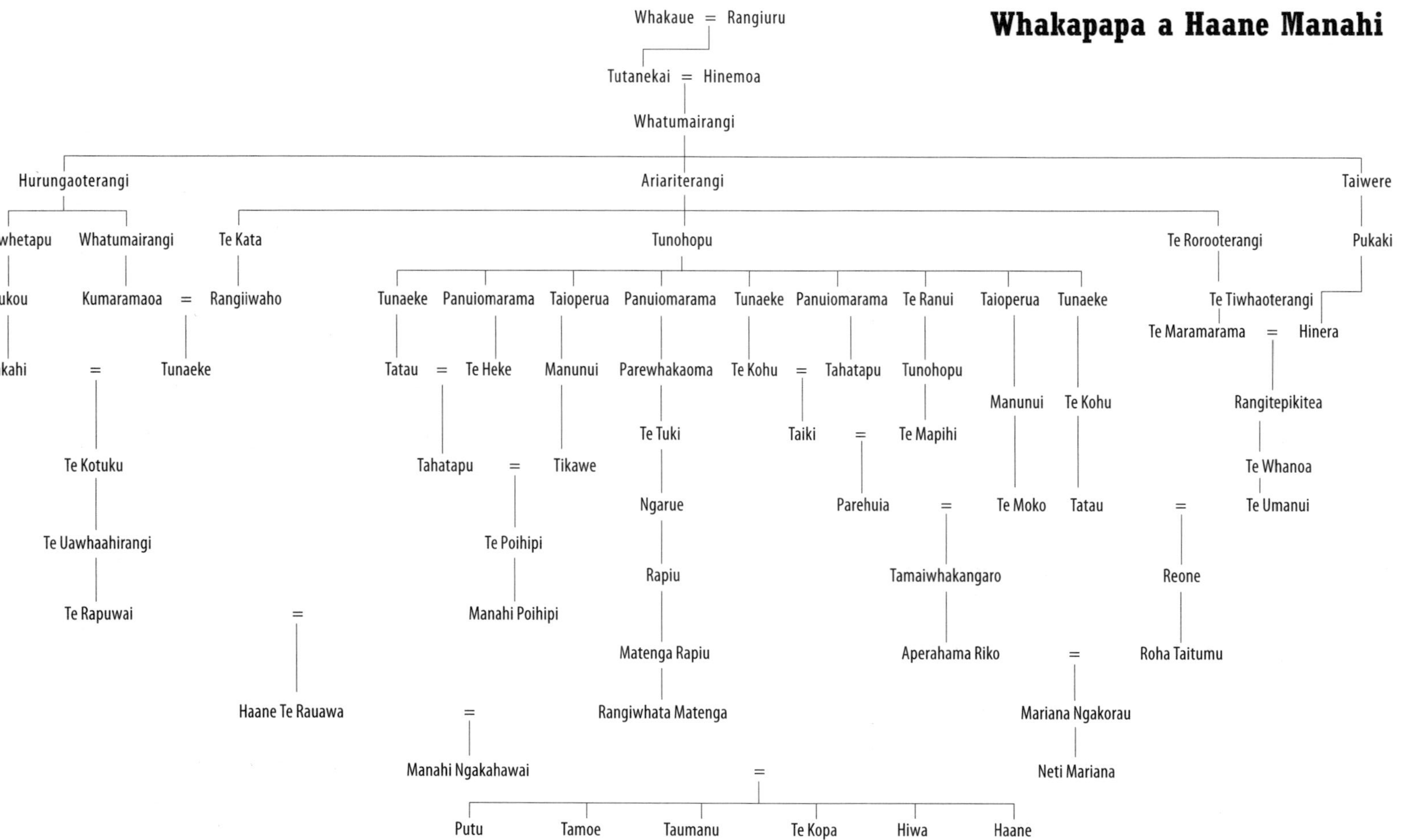

However, for all the hard-earned experience Ngāti Whakaue had accumulated in warfare over numerous generations, nothing could have prepared them for the Ngāpuhi invasion in 1823. What made this inter-tribal conflict distinct from all those that had preceded it was the enemy's use of muskets. That year, the famous (some would say notorious) Ngāpuhi chief Hongi Hika attacked Rotorua as utu for the killing of some Ngāpuhi the previous year (among them was Hongi's nephew) by Tūhourangi. Precise figures do not exist, but potentially hundreds of Te Arawa descended from Uenukukōpako lines were killed and taken prisoner by Hongi, after which a peace was negotiated on Mokoia Island. By September, Ngāpuhi had returned to the Bay of Islands, and Te Arawa was left to lament its losses[25] and ponder the significance that muskets were bringing to battles. Several of Manahi's ancestors would have fought in the battles against Hongi, including Te Umanui on his mother's side, and Rapiu and Te Poihipi on his father's side. And while it might seem to an outsider like ancient history for someone who fought in the Second World War, Manahi was separated by just four generations from his relatives who fought Ngāpuhi in the early 1820s, and just two generations from those of his whanau who fought the last inter-tribal battles towards the end of the New Zealand wars in 1870.

It was from these final few generations that Manahi's name derived. His father was Manahi Ngakahawai, who was the son of Haane Te Rauawa and Rangiwhata Matenga. In turn, Haane Te Rauawa was one of the offspring of Te Rapuwai (a descendant of Rangiiwaho) and Manahi Poihipi (a descendant of Tūnohopū).

Manahi Ngakahawai had married Neti Mariana, the daughter of Mariana Ngakorau, who was the child of Aperehama Riko (like Manahi Poihipi, a descendant of Tūnohopū) and Roha Taitumu (a descendant of Pukaki).

On both sides of the family in the preceding two or three generations, there had been the practice of reversing surnames and first names, with the name Manahi being the first name of his great-grandfather as well as his father, while Manahi's first names (Haane Te Rauawa) were drawn directly from his grandfather. In the Western European tradition, this practice of plucking names from the ancestral family tree had become little more than an act of token honour to an unknown predecessor. But for Māori society at this time, the use of family names was far more significant, as a tohunga from Tūhoe explained: 'the naming can be just as important as the ancestry, and what is important is the reason why the name was given. Because the spirit of that name is also given … a part of people continues in the world through their names'.[26] So the common expectation at the time was that a person would take on some of the traits of the person or people after whom they were named. No details now exist about the specific personality features of the ancestors whose names were selected for Manahi, but it is fairly certain that they were selected with the intent that he would emulate reputed features of their personalities. This view of names gives an added dimension of meaning to the Ngāti Whakaue whakataukī: 'Hei aha noa ake i mate ai au ka tipu aku pakarito' – 'It does not matter if I die, I am survived by my descendants'.

Manahi's father – a short man[27] – worked clearing scrub on farms in the region, and also was involved in road construction. Essentially, he was an itinerant labourer, as were many Māori males in Rotorua (and elsewhere) around the turn of the twentieth century, although later on in life, he served on the local council.[28] Ōhinemutu was where his home was, but Manahi Ngakahawai could be gone for weeks or even a few months at a time, depending on how much work was available, and how far away it was. There was certainly an enthusiasm among the population in general to find employment wherever it was available. One European journalist noted in this period that 'The Maori, wherever he is given a fair chance to win a living from the soil of his ancestors, is manfully doing his best to keep up with his more experienced *pakeha* neighbours', although the lack of landholdings inhibited any real wealth being accumulated by many Māori communities: 'in the Rotorua district, and other parts', the historian James Cowan observed, 'there are Maoris willing and anxious to farm the land, but they have no land to farm'.[29] This forced many of the working-aged men from Ōhinemutu to travel further afield to get employment, and so often left the community with the appearance of a population that was disproportionately high in children, women, and the elderly.

Manahi's mother, Neti, either through inclination or circumstance became a matriarchal figure – a reputation that grew with age. However, that is all that remains known about her life. It is unlikely that she received any formal schooling, as most Māori girls in this period did not attend primary school and tended to remain outside the margins of the education system.[30]

## NOTES

1. This whakataukī pre-dates the European arrival in New Zealand. Supplied to the author by David Rankin, Te Matarahurahu, Ngāpuhi, Auckland, 3 November 2009.
2. Hohepa Kereopa, in P Moon, *Tohunga: Hohepa Kereopa*, Auckland, David Ling Publishing, 2003, pp. 41–2.
3. Waitangi Tribunal, Report of the Waitangi Tribunal on the Kaituna River Claim, Wai-4, Wellington, Department of Justice, 1984, s. 3.2
4. Op. cit.
5. 'within Te Arawa we have grown up with the waka metaphor: Tongariro being the taurapa and Maketu the tauihu', P Tapsell to P Moon, 19 January 2010.
6. E Tapsell, *A History of Rotorua*, Rotorua, Hutcheson, Bowman and Stewart, 1972, p. 7.
7. Ibid., pp. 6–7.
8. Ibid., p. 8.
9. T R Hiroa, *The Coming of the Maori*, Wellington, Whitcombe and Tombs, 1950, p. 439.
10. Waitangi Tribunal, *He Maunga Rongo: Report on the Central North Island Claims: Stage One*, vol. 1, Wai-1200, Wellington, Department of Justice, 2007, p. 16.
11. Most whakapapa of Te Ure O Uenukukōpako show Tamaihutoroa as the younger brother of Ihenga, although a few alternative versions have him as his son.

12. E Tapsell, *A History of Rotorua*, p. 84.
13. The lineage ran through the following people: Tamatekapua, Kahumatamomoe, Tawakemoetahanga, Uenukumairarotonga, Rangitihi, Tūhourangi, Uenukukōpako, Whakaue.
14. W Marsh, in *Rotorua Minute Books*, vol. 1, p. 151, in D M Stafford, *Te Arawa: A History of the Arawa People*, Auckland, Reed, 1986, p. 544.
15. P Tapsell to P Moon, 19 January 2010.
16. D M Stafford, *Te Arawa: A History of the Arawa People*, p. 84. This is a very interesting assertion made on behalf of Rangiwewehi, Pikiao and Tūhourangi peoples in the Native Land Court during the hotly contested hearings for control over Mokoia amongst other prized lands. From Ngāti Whakaue's perspective he was the progeny of a very astute political liaison by Whakaue, who offered his wife Rangiuru to Tūwharetoa in an effort to secure this warlord's alliance and not lose control of Mokoia. At this time Tūhourangi were the occupiers from Ōwhata through to Ōhinemutu, but desired Mokoia because of its strategic importance. Tūtānekai and then later his grandson Hurungaterangi were to avenge the continuing hostilities that Tūhourangi mounted against the descendants of Whakaue. The war was sustained for five generations until the peace made by Pukaki marrying Ngapuia. Ultimately Pikiao and Whakaue ganged up on Tūhourangi and pushed them out of the Rotorua/Rotoiti basin for good in 1800. Also note that Ngāti Whakaue was the name given to the progeny of Tūtānekai and is not applied or used in reference to the others sons of Whakaue. P Tapsell to P Moon, 19 January 2010.
17. P Tapsell to P Moon, 19 January 2010.
18. In accepted genealogical order. P Tapsell to P Moon, 19 January 2010.
19. As an example, see J Cowan, *Legends of the Maori*, vol. 1, Wellington, 1930,H H Tombs, pp. 181ff.
20. For details, see P Tapsell, *Pukaki: A Comet Returns*, Auckland, Reed, 2000, pp. 22–7.
21. Ibid., pp. 30–3.
22. W Winiata, in ibid., p. 129.
23. R Manahi, written material provided to P Moon, 26 February 2010.
24. Op. cit.
25. See P Te Hurinui, 'Nga Moteatea', in *Supplement to Journal of the Polynesian Society*, vol. 64, 1955, p. 108; S P Smith, *Maori Wars of the Nineteenth Century*, Christchurch, Whitcombe and Tombs, 1910, p. 256.
26. H Kereopa, in P Moon, *Tohunga: Hohepa Kereopa*, Auckland, David Ling Publishing, 2003, pp. 94–5.
27. Interview with Rau Manahi, Rotorua, 17 November 2009.
28. Op. cit.
29. J Cowan, *The Maori Yesterday and To-Day*, Wellington, Whitcombe and Tombs, 1930, pp. 13, 17–18.
30. Fewer than one in twenty Māori females received formal primary education at the turn of the century. For details, see L Pihama, *Tīhei Mauri Ora: Honouring Our Voices. Mana Wahine as a Kaupapa Māori Theoretical Framework*, unpublished PhD thesis, University of Auckland, Auckland, 2001, chap. 8.

# CHAPTER 2: Before the War

Haane Te Rauawa Manahi – the taina of his whānau – was born in Ōhinemutu on 28 September 1913 (some sources incorrectly have the date as 25 September).[1] Although the law had made the registration of Māori births compulsory by 1913,[2] Manahi was one of the last of his generation to slip through the net and go through life without any official recognition that he had been born, as was the case with his five older siblings: Putu, Tamoe, Taumanu, Te Kopa, and Hiwa. On 7 June 1914, Haane was christened at the newly-opened St. Faith's Church, by the Reverend Rewi Matataia Wikiriwhi.[3] In attendance were his father and mother, and the godparents, who are listed as Te Wheoro Hamiora (possibly Hamuera)[4] and Tuia Wikiriwhi.[5]

### Whakapapa for Manahi and Siblings

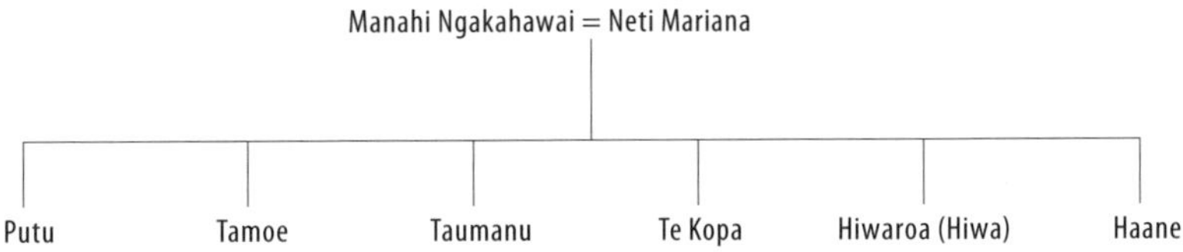


The use of the name 'Manahi' in the whānau as both first and last names is unusual. As Haane's son, Rau, explained, 'It was a sort of mix-up. Manahi was a Christian name, but they thought that it sounded better than anything else, so they swapped it around'.[6]

Haane's first battle had been to fight his way out of his mother's womb, which he did after only eight months' occupation. It was a risky tactic. The Māori infant mortality rate was extraordinarily high in this period, with Maui Pomare estimating that fewer than half of all Māori children made it to their fourth birthday[7] (a rate four times higher than those of their European counterparts),[8] and for a baby born two months' prematurely, the odds of surviving were even slimmer. Disease was the big killer in this period. Just ten weeks before Manahi's birth, there had been a confirmed case of smallpox at Ōhinemutu, and 'stringent precautions' were taken to 'confine the Maoris to the pa … at Ohinemutu'.[9] His siblings were not immune from these dangerous conditions. Te Kopa and

Taumanu died of illness before the age of five, possibly of smallpox, and Putu died aged eighteen, from an unspecified illness.[10] In part because of this high rate of infant mortality, children were given extra attention at the time. As it was uncertain how long a child might survive, they tended to be 'spoiled dirty rotten by the old people', and Manahi was no exception.[11]

To some degree, the environment a person is brought up in has the potential to have a bearing on their character. It can be tempting to isolate an individual from their surrounds and scrutinise their life almost as some sort of biographical test-tube specimen, but the reality is that so much of who a person is can be illuminated by surveying aspects of where they come from, particularly the social and cultural influences that have helped shape the contours of their character. In Manahi's case, the close-knit community of Ōhinemutu – steeped in a history that clung to it like the volcanic fumes that linger over the settlement – was the setting of the formative years of his life, and thus became an inescapable part of his destiny.

Ōhinemutu was one of the oldest Māori settlements in the region,[12] having been continually occupied since at least the sixteenth century, and serving as a base for a community, as well as a military command centre during times of war. However, it appeared to have passed its peak by the late 1840s as a major defensive site in the region. John Johnson, the country's first Colonial Surgeon, noted this in what is one of the earliest European accounts of the village. 'We crossed the stream by a very rickety bridge formed of an old canoe', he wrote in January 1847, 'and soon reached the ancient stockade which surrounds the pā, now neglected and falling into decay, but whose larger palisades were as usual terminated by hideous figures, all with their tongues thrust out in token of defiance, and in a variety of significant attitudes. The entrance, however, a low narrow portal formed in one broad piece of timber, was ornamented as to the detail with considerable taste'. Apart from extensive descriptions of the geothermal features in the vicinity, Johnson gave the first (reasonably) accurate indication of Ōhinemutu's population, which he estimated in 1847 to be around five hundred inhabitants, of whom a disproportionate amount (about two hundred) were fighting men.[13]

With no wars on the horizon, and with the steady advance of European influence beginning to make its presence felt in this region, the days of inter-tribal fighting seemed to have been consigned to the past. Still, though, the community at Ōhinemutu was only a rumoured threat away from reverting to its full defensive posture, as was demonstrated in 1870, when the Rongowhakaata military leader and prophet, Te Kooti Arikirangi Te Turuki, was attacked on 7 February by a branch of Te Arawa that was loyal to the Crown in its pursuit of this rebel. The fighting occurred adjacent to Ōhinemutu, and only six years after another offensive in the vicinity, in which a group of Waikato, Ngāti Raukawa, and Ngāti Haua troops, with the sanction of the King Tawhiao, got close to attacking Ōhinemutu, but failed to launch their planned assault on the pā.[14] So with this recent scare in mind, it is no surprise that the fracas involving Te Kooti in 1870 was all the pretext that was needed for Ōhinemutu to start once again bristling with troops and weapons. By one estimate, there were 280 armed Māori and 30 European volunteers squeezed in the village in anticipation of being called on at any moment to fight against Te Kooti's men.[15] And although Te Kooti managed to escape in the face of a more powerful Te Arawa force, Ōhinemutu was close enough to the fighting to feel its heat. A few decades of relative calm had not sedated its martial spirit, and as the experience of 1870 demonstrated, a call to arms would be responded to at a moment's notice – something that stayed in the blood of its inhabitants for years after the wars of the 1860s and early 1870s had ended. This was no sentimental attachment to some ancient tradition of war as much as a necessary trait to ensure the survival of the community, and for years, and possibly even decades afterwards, a threat of war would have been met with a reflex reaction from the residents of this settlement.

But after the battle against Te Kooti, changes in the development of Rotorua managed to undermine Ōhinemutu's central role in the area in a way that no army had succeeded in doing. In an article that appeared in the *Bay of Plenty Times* in 1882,[16] a journalist outlined the imminent emergence of the town of Rotorua, and how Ōhinemutu would no longer be the 'logical centre of operations for any journey to the thermal regions'. Instead, visitors would be able to stay in a new township – one purpose-built for the expanding tourist industry. This would be Rotorua, but was known 'to the Ohinemutaites as "Rotten Egg Town"'.[17] This was only a faintly humorous reference as Ōhinemutu was about to move from commanding the centre of the area to existing on its periphery.

Overall, the village maintained a slightly squalid reputation into the latter stages of the nineteenth century. The lawyer and politician William Travers conjured up a deprecatory vision of the settlement after spending a few days in the area in 1876: 'the remains of ruined whares, fragments of cast-off clothing, broken bottles, kerosine and sardine tins, old pots and kettles, children in ragged shirts or without any at all, half-starved horses, and all kinds of mongrel dogs and squeaking pigs – the latter, as they root amongst the refuse, avoiding, with marvellous ingenuity, the numberless boiling springs and steam-holes which occur over the whole surface – appear to occupy every inch of available space, the scene being completed by Māori women preparing food, naked men and boys lying in the open baths, and ancient females squatted on the warm stones used for drying the berries of the *tawa*. In fact, it is difficult to describe the state of filth and demoralization into which the Māori population of this ... settlement ... are gradually sliding'.[18] Yet, just four years later, and despite this apparent decrepitude, Ōhinemutu had become the main commercial and communications centre in the region, several Europeans had entered into casual leasehold arrangements with local Māori in order to set up their businesses in this location,[19] and there was an impression that the place was undergoing a burst of improvement.

A depiction of Ōhinemutu around the time that Manahi was born was provided by the historian John Alexander. While he mentioned nothing of the location's former dilapidation, his account does give a contemporary sense of what, for visitors, was still considered an exotic setting: 'Ohinemutu, the capital of Rotorua, is doubtless on the most singular volcanic site a population ever dwelt upon. On a rising ground at the south end of the lake, it is situated on what seems to the unaccustomed eye to be but a crust that forms neither more nor less than the lid of an immense subterranean cauldron of boiling water. Through this lid numerous natural and artificial holes have been punched, and are used by the inhabitants for cooking purposes. In them the water boils furiously, hissing to the very surface, and emitting clouds of vapour, which under some conditions of the atmosphere are almost dense enough to envelope the pa'.[20]

Tourists to Rotorua tended to come specifically for these volcanic attractions, which lay mainly outside this village. However, one journalist, who made a point of wandering around Ōhinemutu in this period, jotted down his observations, which offer – at least from a Pākehā perspective – an insight into the nature of the settlement. 'Ohinemutu is still a place where you can spend many a pleasant hour', he wrote. 'It is delightful merely to wander in and out aimlessly among the narrow streets of the village. Here you will encounter little fellows of three and four and upwards who will clamour loudly to honour you with a haka so that you may reward them with a penny. Such a haka, too – what they lack in skill they make up for in gusto, conscientiously determined to give you your "penn'orth." Perhaps, further along, you will meet one of the old wahines. She smokes her pipe contentedly. She stops when you come up to her, and, giving you a hearty "Tenakoi [sic]," shakes hands quite vigorously, and says a number of things in Maori which you know from her broad smiles must be some friendly message. The wonderfully happy spirit of camaraderie which the Maoris show to everybody alike is their most delightful characteristic, which we are able to appreciate the more keenly because of our natural aloofness'.[21] This is obviously an overly sentimental and even patronising view, but it does provide an outsider's glimpse into Ōhinemutu's character in the early twentieth century.

One of the few surviving indigenous recollections of the village at this time conveys a more intimate sense of the nature of the community that Manahi grew up in. A kuia interviewed in 1981 reminisced how in the early decades of the century, 'the marae … [at Ohinemutu] was full of people, young people, it was a real Maori pa. Everyone lived in whares …. We used to dive for morihana in the Ruapeka, then go over to the lime bath and cook them, jump in and have a bath, and eat them, no problems!' And as for how people lived during that period, 'the floors on their whares [were] covered with coal sacks that were scrubbed, shining, shining, white so white that you could eat off them'.[22] Technology arrived comparatively early to the area, with five electric street lights being erected in Ōhinemutu in 1908, including electric lighting within Tamatekapua,[23] which made it possibly the first marae in the country to have its interior illuminated in this way.

There was a less sanguine side to this village, however, which lay concealed beneath its almost idyllically rustic surface. The state of the settlement was deemed by some more observant Europeans to be less than satisfactory. An editorial in the *Rotorua Times* in November 1910 suggested that 'the conditions of affairs in our Native villages is disgraceful at this present day', with the nearby attraction of Whakarewarewa described as 'a hot-bed of stench and decomposing filth, so much so that two different parties … could not venture to explore the advertised sights and natural wonders in that Native village this week'.[24]

Also, like many Māori settlements at this time, alcohol was proving to be a growing social problem – so much so that in April 1914, Bishop William Sedgwick, who was in Ōhinemutu to open the new St. Faith's Church (the old one had blown down in a storm), presided over a Hui Tapu (a Māori synod) to discuss the threat of alcohol to the local people. At the end of the hui, the synod resolved 'to give every assistance to organised bodies fighting against the drink evil'.[25] And with Ōhinemutu being one of the leading 'wet' areas in the district,[26] every assistance would be needed to contain the destructive effects of alcohol abuse. From the late nineteenth century up until around the mid-1930s, the fight against alcoholism in many predominantly Māori regions in the country was led by women, and this was the case in Rotorua, where the local branch of the Women's Christian Temperance Union had strong Māori leaders (most notably Heni Te Kiri Karamu)[27] who worked in their communities to try to curb the social and health problems caused by alcohol. However, it was often a struggle against almost forbidding odds, with violence and crime resulting from excessive drinking continuing to plague Māori communities in the early twentieth century at a disproportionately higher rate than for the country as a whole.[28]

Yet Ōhinemutu was not merely another residential area in Rotorua with a high Māori population. One of the features that distinguished it from other Māori settlements in the region in this period was the absence of a heavy commercial focus on tourism. Guides were discouraged from working in the village, and at the enlightened recommendation of Henry Taiporutu Mitchell, tourists were allowed entry into the area with no charge, and were given 'absolute freedom in the pa'.[29] One of the results of this open policy was that Ōhinemutu became even more popular with visitors by the 1920s, which in turn obliged the residents to shun any practices and vices that were likely to deter visitors.

Manahi began his schooling at the age of five, near the end of 1918 – a period noted for two events: the arrival of the influenza epidemic, and the end of the First World War. The influenza epidemic struck the Rotorua region towards the end of 1918. It presented one of the biggest threats to the community in the past half century, with Māori seven times more likely than Pākehā to die of the virus.[30] By the end of the year, 2160 Māori had been killed by the influenza epidemic, out of a total national Māori population of 51,000,[31] and its effect was so profound that it left an enduring imprint on many Māori who lived through it. It became a new landmark in people's memories, and individuals for years afterwards could be heard referring to events 'before the flu', or 'after the flu'. Peter Buck, the member of parliament and medical doctor, described the epidemic as being 'the severest setback the [Māori] race has received since the fighting days of Hongi Hika'.[32]

The reasons for Māori suffering from the epidemic so disproportionately give some insight into the nature of life for Māori settlements such as Ōhinemutu just after the First World War. Māori at the time had a greater susceptibility to respiratory diseases, and generally lower standards of housing, clothing, and nourishment than their Pākehā counterparts,[33] which enabled the virus to cut deep into many of these villages. In places like Rotorua, bodies of influenza victims began to pile up, and death again became a prominent feature of Māori communities. Manahi lost cousins and possibly a sibling in October 1918, and although he escaped this mate pākehā (fatal European disease), as locals referred to it, he saw close up the carnage it caused, and he joined the generation of his grandparents, who had similarly become witnesses to widespread and indiscriminate death from a young age. It did not matter if those who contracted the influenza virus were robust and healthy, the disease was just as likely to be fatal to them as to anyone else. Living through this epidemic, the community discovered that it was not so much a case of survival of the fittest as survival of the fortunate.

By the beginning of 1919, the influenza pandemic (as it had become) was receding almost as quickly as it had arrived, but for many Māori, its ravages left them with a heightened sense of fatalism – a perception that life could be cut short at any time. This sentiment was hardly surprising, considering that death rates in some nearby Māori communities (no precise statistics exist for Rotorua) were as high as one in fifteen.[34] And lifestyles during the epidemic had abruptly altered in the short term. It was known, for example, that the disease could spread through human contact, and so hui were abandoned, church services were only infrequently held (and poorly attended), tangi were sometimes replaced by more perfunctory burials, and schools were shut down.

Yet, by February 1919, most aspects of daily life had returned to normal for Rotorua's approximately 1500 Māori,[35] and it was during this month that Manahi returned to school. Every weekday morning, he would walk the few hundred metres from his home to the primary school on Pukeroa Hill (the site of an ancient Ngāti Whakaue pā).[36] The classrooms had been built on the land donated for that purpose by the Ngāti Whakaue rangatira and educationalist Rotohiko Tangonui Haupapa,[37] and although originally designated as a native school, it was open to all children in the vicinity. Even by the standards of the day, however, the school was not well-resourced, and attendance – while a dramatic improvement on previous decades – was still not regular for many pupils. Despite this, though, the school promised (and in most cases delivered) an elementary education, and Manahi attended often enough to complete successfully his primary studies and finish school probably in December 1926, having just turned thirteen.

Outside of school, Manahi was an athletic and boisterous youth. Swimming was a daily summer activity, and he was a keen rugby player at school – 'very good on the wing', his nephew, Neil Manahi, recollected. 'I can remember him going down to the number one ground at Arawa Park. He was on the wing three-quarter. Boy he was fast – a very aggressive man on the field'.[38] But swimming was his passion. 'He had an Australian coach and he broke a few local records in the relays. His team was called the "Flying Squadron"'.[39] However, as with all the locals, Manahi was alert to the dangers of the area where he lived (unlike a Māori youth from Northland who visited Ōhinemutu in 1914, and died after slipping into a hot pool – a tragedy that provided adults in the village with the latest salutary example to give to their children).[40] The place was notorious for accidents. In the 1830s, a missionary working in Ōhinemutu had written how during the first three months that he was there, seven people were scalded to death as a result of falling into hot pools,[41] and to the present day, children are warned by their whānau about the threats that this steamy landscape offers.

By the time Manahi had attended his first class at primary school, however, he had already been receiving another form of education, which went on until his early teenage years. Ōhinemutu was the home of at least two tohunga in the early decades of the twentieth century, and Manahi was one of those few who, almost from the age he started to walk, received instruction from these tohunga, in particular, from Tuoro Pango.[42] 'He was a lovely man', as Neil remembered, 'even lovely to us when we were kids. But he stuck with just one or two families at Ohinemutu – not everybody. So he made connections to Rau's dad [Haane] and my father [Hiwa]. They were both loved by the old fellah'.[43] There was no formal syllabus, and no regular times when 'lessons' were held, but when circumstances brought them together, Tuoro would pass on ancient insights into the physical and metaphysical realms to the young boys. Haane was also close to the tohunga Akapita Te Toa (Tuoro's father), who was the son of Hamuera Pango – the second son of the Ngāti Whakaue tohunga Ngawene Pango.[44] However, as much as the tohunga of Ōhinemutu did their best to ensure that traditional knowledge was transmitted to the next generation, external events increasingly came to have a bearing on the fate of the settlement, and just before Manahi reached the age of one, the descent of Europe into war began to intrude on life in New Zealand.

World War One was New Zealand's first international conflict in which a substantial number of Māori enlisted to fight.[45] The existence of various Māori contingents in the early years of the conflict led to the formation of the New Zealand (Māori) Pioneer Battalion on 1 September 1917 (which in turn became a precursor to the formation of the 28 Māori Battalion just over two decades later). Participation in a foreign war – where immediate interests seemed not to be under threat – was a new concept for most Māori communities, but the enthusiasm to fight for King and country was certainly present among many Māori men – particularly those from Te Arawa. In 1915, the four Māori members of parliament had issued a joint statement noting how the outbreak of war had led to 'the awakening of all races under the sovereignty of King George V'[46] As these MPs listened 'to the tramp of European feet', they were also listening 'to hear the voice of the tribes behind them [but] they could not say anything because the tribes were silent, because this was a thing new to them, which they and the tribes had not even dreamed of. If they happened to be in the marae of both Islands and at meetings at which matters of the moment were discussed, they would certainly have not wasted any time letting the Government know that the thoughts of the Maori race are these or those. Now, when information came that some of the tribes were alert and are asking to be allowed to take part in the war, the Maori Members were enabled to ask the Government to give effect to the wishes of the tribes that they should take part in matters pertaining to the war'.[47]

Te Arawa had a lengthening tradition of loyalty to the Crown, which was reiterated in a speech given to the Duke of Cornwall (later to become King George V) in Rotorua in June 1901. 'In the presence of Your Royal Highness', one rangatira said before the crowd and the Duke, 'we confirm the act of our fathers who gave all to Queen Victoria and her successors. Here ye, O peoples! Today we make a new treaty – new and yet old – inasmuch as we confirm the old to which we but added expressions of continued loyalty from our generation, and pray that our sovereign and our white brethren may give us the strength to live and thrive with them and among them'.[48] Te Arawa were among the most enthusiastic of all Māori communities to support the war, and their volunteers even objected to having to serve with conscripts, on the basis that they felt that their mana was best maintained by staying within their volunteer units.[49]

The deployment of 'native' troops in what was described in 1915 as a war of 'white against white' was initially questioned by the Government, but strategic demands, and the presence of Indians and Africans fighting in Europe,[50] eventually resulted in the Māori contribution being welcomed. Manahi's paternal uncle, Matiu, was one of those who fought overseas, along with several other more distant relatives. Matiu went to war in the first contingent, known as the Hokowhituatu. Neti's three half-brothers – Wi Matenga, Hohepa Te Rake, and Aperahama Riko Te Kiri – also served in the Great War.[51]

However, not all Māori raced to enlist, though, even after conscription was introduced in 1917. The aftertaste of the Crown's comparatively recent land confiscations and wars against Māori was still sufficiently bitter among some iwi as to disincline them to offer their men to fight for the Crown's cause in this war. However, aside from these pockets of objectors, 2227 Māori ended up fighting in the First World War (22.5 percent of total enlistments were from Rotorua iwi),[52] and were welcomed back to the country at its conclusion with great celebration.[53] Major events were held in Auckland, Gisborne and Rotorua for the returning troops, before they had a chance to disperse to their home marae, and although many Europeans failed to appreciate at the time the contribution of these Māori soldiers, New Zealand's military commanders recognised fully the important role Māori had played in the Great War.

The scene in Rotorua was one of euphoria when this latest generation of warriors disembarked from the train. They were greeted by the governor general and the Countess of Liverpool at Ōhinemutu. After the initial festivities, several speeches were offered by local rangatira and kaumātua, most of which were addresses to the governor general to liberate those Waikato Māori who had been imprisoned for refusing military service, and to have the lakes in the region returned to Te Arawa ownership. Evidently, local Māori felt that there was now a responsibility by the Crown to repay the debt that had been created by the sacrifices of the New Zealand (Māori) Pioneer Battalion. The governor general said that he would present these requests to the Prime Minister, and then 'eulogised the Pioneers' before joining in the rest of the celebrations.[54]

Unavoidably, this return home of these troops – heroes in the eyes of local residents[55] – left an impression on most people in Rotorua. The soldiers were described by the Minister of Defence, James Allen, as having 'done their duty to the Empire, fearlessly and well'[56] (New Zealand 'was second only to India in raising a body of "natives"').[57] And for those of Manahi's age, who were too young to understand its significance, people of their parents' generation would later instil in them a sense of pride and reverence for the men who had made the decision to become modern-day warriors and fight in the largest war the world had known. It was as though the old passages to manhood – which involved having a taste of battle – had been revived for the current generation, and that being a soldier, which had been cherished for centuries as a position carrying great mana,[58] was once again an option for Māori. It seemed to matter less that it was really someone else's war than the fact that these young men had the opportunity to fight in it.

In 1920, the Prince of Wales arrived in Rotorua and was welcomed enthusiastically by all the residents of Ōhinemutu, including, presumably, the six-year-old Manahi, who would have been among the group of children that formed part of the welcome programme.[59] The popularity of the village meant that attention was inevitably drawn to its condition, which by the latter half of the 1920s, was again causing some concern. The local residents were aware of this, identifying twenty houses that were in need of replacement, and just as many that required urgent repair. Changes were made, and by 1936, in addition to new buildings having been erected in Ōhinemutu, a modern sewerage system had been installed,[60] ensuring that the village was equipped with the latest essentials that visitors now expected. From that time onward, Ōhinemutu (along with Whakarewarewa) became what was described as a 'model village',[61] with modifications made to put on a more acceptable face to tourists who continued to pour into the area.

After completing primary school, Manahi went to Rotorua District High School,[62] which (again with the help of an endowment from Ngāti Whakaue) became the Rotorua High and Grammar School in 1927. It was essentially a rural school, and as with the local primary school, attendance in its early years was 'markedly lower' than the average for comparable schools in other parts of the country.[63] The school's records do show, however, that Manahi was in the junior school in 1928 (his name was listed as John Rauawa Manahi), and in the senior school in 1930,[64] which was presumably his final year, as he would have been aged seventeen at this time, and it was unusual for students who were not going on to university or teachers' college to remain much longer in secondary school.

In addition to school, sports, and helping the whānau, there was one other aspect of life for Manahi that was shared with many of Ōhinemutu's residents: church. The ornate, almost Māori baroque interior of St Faith's was familiar to Manahi, who was occasionally taken to services there by his mother. Throughout his life, he identified as an Anglican – a loyalty that was slightly accentuated by having been brought up on a denominational fault-line. Anglican and Catholic missionaries had converged in Rotorua since the first half of the nineteenth century, plying their versions of Christianity in competition with each other. In the ensuing decades, neither Church managed to claim the area exclusively as their own – as had been the case in many other Māori communities around the country – and this had become a source of periodic division in Rotorua. A solution, of sorts, was devised by the Ngāti Whakaue rangatira Petera Te Pukuatua, who gathered the tribes in the Tamatekapua meeting house, and divided the assembled group down the middle: 'Standing before them, he decreed that from that moment on, those to this side of his body were Mihingare, or Anglican, and those to the other were Catholic, or Katorika … whole families were affected, many members becoming one, the rest following the faith of the other'.[65] For Manahi, though, his adherence to the Anglican Church became nominal by the time he reached adulthood, and while he rarely attended a service, he showed his commitment in other ways. 'Every Christmas', Neil Manahi recalled, 'a lot of the men from here, including Haane, would get food together for the church, so that it could be distributed to people in the area, and that was their way of getting involved'.[66] The Manahis were known locally at the time as the 'food-gatherers' for the provisions they offered to the church.[67] And as for Manahi's personal faith, his nephew concluded that Haane and his brother, Hiwa, 'were believers', but that they preferred not to flaunt their beliefs. Instead, as he saw it, 'they had that [faith] quietly in themselves'.[68]

In addition to the practical assistance that the men of Ōhinemutu provided to St Faith's Church in the inter-war period, they also helped to maintain and run the other precious building in their community: Tamatekapua. Built in 1870 and opened in 1872, it was named after the great whare that had once existed on Mokoia Island. One of the reasons for its construction was mounting concern among kaumātua that 'old-time carvings of famous Arawa houses were disappearing, uncared for and broken on the scene of their former glory'.[69] Its more immediate purpose, however, was as a 'token ratification of peace between Te Arawa and Waikato tribes, and to induce Tawhiao, the so-called Maori King, to pay the Arawa people a friendly visit'.[70] Religious services, hui, and even the monthly meeting of the Magistrate's Court were held in Tamatekapua, and the building housed a collection of carvings, including those depicting Tūtānekai,

Uenukukōpako, Whakaturia, Tuarotorua and Rangitihi.[71] The effects of gradual decay on the structure made the Tamatekapua meeting house unsafe, and it was pulled down in 1939. Manahi had assisted in its demolition, but would not see its replacement – which was opened in 1943 – until he returned from the war.

For a reader in the twenty-first century, it might appear that Manahi's ancestry, with its inventory of great military leaders and its long experience of warfare, together with his community's comparatively recent experience of battle (the last one on local soil had taken place just forty-three years before Manahi's birth) perhaps destined him for a military career. But those historical and cultural influences were common to several Māori communities in this period, and so it should not be any surprise that Manahi showed no early inclination to become a soldier. Instead, once he completed secondary school, he began work as a farm hand, and then took up carpentry as a more reliable and regular source of employment, working most of the time with his uncle Matiu, although by 1939, he was back as an employee of the Public Works Department.[72] And outside of work his interests were directed at sports and the local women. He continued playing rugby after leaving school, and maintained his love of swimming by heading towards the lake whenever time allowed. However, Manahi grew disinclined to play contact sports – possibly because some regarded him as being a bit clumsy – and so while he was successful in rugby and boxing, his preference was for swimming, hunting, and especially trout-fishing, which was his 'forte'.[73]

But it was his amorous interests that aroused most of the comments about Manahi and maybe a bit of envy from his friends. With his thick, straight, short black hair, slicked down and with a sharp part, his smooth skin and wide hazel eyes ('they would go green when he was angry', Rau observed) and his quiet charm, he became well-known locally for a series of liaisons with the ladies of Te Arawa. Like his parents, though, Manahi was destined to have an arranged marriage, similarly at the behest of the local kaumātua. The woman chosen to be his wife was Rangiawatea Te Kiri, whom his son remembers as 'a very strong woman'.[74] The couple had known each other most of their lives, but as acquaintances rather than anything more serious. However, in 1935, they decided to marry – against the wishes of their parents, and on 17 September 1936, the only child to this union – Te Rauawa (Rau) – was born. The name had a whānau connection, but it was evidently a slightly contentious choice at the time, as Neil explained: 'Rau was named after his grand uncle – Rauawa Ieni Tapsell – who died two hours before he was born. This was Rau's mother's decision to name him, but Haane's family were not happy about it, so they added Haane as Rau's middle name'.[75]

*Carving of Pukaki, c. 1880*

*Reference: PA1-o-329-12 Alexander Turnbull Library*

*Ōhinemutu, c. 1880, with old St. Faith's Church on the right.*
*Reference: G-452-2-2 Alexander Turnbull Library*

*Tamatekapua Meeting House – photo taken in 1916, when Manahi was three years old*
*Reference: APG-0575-1/2-G Alexander Turnbull Library*

*Children at Ōhinemutu thermal pools, c. 1910*

*Reference: PAColl-0380-1-26 Alexander Turnbull Library*

*Apirana Ngata, one of the forces behind the organisation of the 28 Māori Battalion*

*Reference: 1/1-014489-G Alexander Turnbull Library*

*'B Company boys'. Standing from left to right: Darkie Hapi, Bunny Jacob Haimona. Seated from left to right: Haane Manahi, Pine Timihou and Tene Anaru, 1940*

Geoffrey Manahi private collection

*Haane Manahi, 1940*

*Geoffrey Manahi private collection*

*Marty McRae and Haane Manahi in England, 1940.*

*Atareta Stewart (née McRae)*

## Whakapapa for Rauawa Manahi

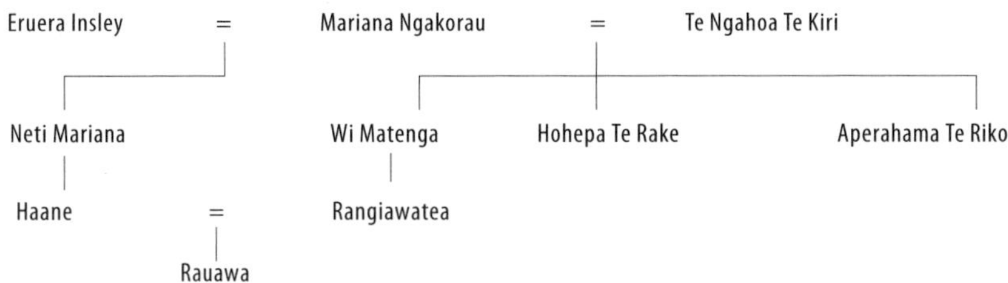


Within a year, Rau was sent to join his cousin, Neil (Hiwa's son) in the Ureweras, where they were brought up by Rangiawatea's whānau – 'Both grandparents wanted us [Rau and Neil] to go to live with my [Rau's] mother's father and his people at Papueru, near Ruatahuna'.[76] From this time, until a few years after the war, Rau had little contact with his father, although there were intermittent visits to Ōhinemutu throughout each year when he would be able to spend time with his parents.

Manahi increasingly seemed to treat his relationship to Rangiawatea more as an obligation. His philandering most likely went on unabated before the war even when he had a young family. When looking back on Manahi's life in the 1930s, his nephew noted that 'there was something very special about him. He was admired by a lot of the chiefs, and that was partly because of his belief in what they taught him. It had a lot to do with his mana, and that he was always helping people. He used to go out fishing and get his bag of fish, but he'd come home with nothing. He'd go around giving it to people, and giving it to his girlfriends. And he was a very popular person … Oh, he was good with the women …. He always had women chasing him'.[77]

Although their son was born in 1936, it was not until 24 January 1940 – just two days before Manahi left to join the army – that he married his partner at St. Faith's Church.[78]. Another possible clue as to the state of his relationship with his wife can be found in an army document from 1944. On it, Rangiawatea was initially named as executor of his will and manager of his estate, but this was crossed out – apparently as a result of a change of heart by Manahi – with a note written on it on 14 February (ironically, Valentine's Day), stating that Manahi 'does not desire to make a will'.[79]

There were liaisons with other women both during and after the war, during which time there was a gradual estrangement between Manahi and his wife. No date can be pinpointed when they separated, and the couple were never formally divorced, but by the 1950s, 'she had just let him go',[80] as Rau put it. By then, it seems to have been the easiest option, but at the start of 1940, all thoughts had been on marriage, especially as dozens of men from Ōhinemutu were shortly off to an uncertain future fighting overseas.

## Notes

1. This is the date listed on his death certificate. Registration no. 1986/36407. It is stated elsewhere as 28 September 1913.
2. G Tito to P Moon, 5 October 2009, Department of Internal Affairs, Ref: 20090193385. Also see Births and Deaths Registration Act, 1913.
3. Baptismal records of St Faith's Church, Ōhinemutu, Rotorua, 1902–1944, p. 64, entry no. 943.
4. Interview with Rau Manahi, Rotorua, 17 November 2009.
5. Born 14 December 1877 in Maketū, died 16 June 1934.
6. Interview with Rau Manahi, Rotorua, 20 August 2009.
7. F S Maclean, Challenge for Health: A History of Public Health in New Zealand, Wellington, 1964, p. 222, in L Bryder, 'New Zealand's Infant Welfare Services and Maori, 1907–60', in *Health and History*, vol. 3, 2001, p. 68.
8. L Bryder, 'New Zealand's Infant Welfare Services and Maori, 1907–60', p. 68.
9. *Evening Post*, 19 July 1913, p. 6.
10. Interview with Rau Manahi, Rotorua, 17 November 2009.
11. Op. cit.
12. D M Stafford, *Te Arawa: A History of the Arawa People*, Auckland, 1986, pp. 33, 42.
13. J Johnson, in N M Taylor (ed.), *Early Travellers in New Zealand*, Oxford, 1959, p. 154.
14. J Cowan, *A History of the Maori Campaigns and the Pioneering Period. Vol. II: The Hauhau Wars, 1864–72*, Wellington, R E Owen Publishing, 1956, p. 161.
15. D M Stafford, *Te Arawa: A History of the Arawa People*, Auckland, 1986, p. 421.
16. *Bay of Plenty Times*, 31 May 1882.
17. Op. cit.
18. W T L Travers, 'Notes on the Lake District of the Province of Auckland', in *Transactions and Proceedings of the Royal Society of New Zealand*, vol. 9, 1876, pp. 5–6.
19. N Te Awekotuku, *The Sociocultural Impact of Tourism on the Te Arawa People of Rotorua, New Zealand*, PhD thesis, University of Waikato, Hamilton, 1981, p. 65.
20. J A Wilson, *The Story of Te Waharoa: A Chapter in Early New Zealand History, Together with Sketches of Ancient Maori Life and History*, Christchurch, Whitcombe and Tombs, 1907, p. 109.
21. New Zealand Railways Magazine, vol. 5, 1 May 1930, p. 54.
22. Cited in N Te Awekotuku, *The Sociocultural Impact of Tourism on the Te Arawa People of Rotorua, New Zealand*, PhD thesis, University of Waikato, Hamilton, 1981, p. 113.
23. D M Stafford, *The New Century in Rotorua: A History of Events from 1900*, Rotorua, Ray Richards and Rotorua District Council, 1988, p. 31.
24. *Rotorua Times*, 4 November 1910.
25. *Evening Post*, 20 April 1914, p. 3
26. *Poverty Bay Herald*, 20 December 1911, p. 5.
27. S Oliver, 'Te Kiri Karamu, Heni, 1840 – 1933', in *Dictionary of New Zealand Biography*, Wellington, 22 June 2007.
28. See S Bull, 'The Land of Murder, Cannibalism, and All Kinds of Atrocious Crimes?' in *British Journal of Criminology*, vol. 44, no. 4, July 2004, pp. 496–519.
29. H T Mitchell, Feb 1916, Rotorua District Council Archives, R/A, T 58.
30. G Rice, *Black November: The 1918 Influenza Epidemic in New Zealand*, Wellington, Canterbury University Press, 1988, p. 102.
31. Op. cit
32. P Buck, in *Appendices to the Journal of the House of Representatives*, 1920, H – 31, p. 13, in op. cit.
33. G Rice, *Black November: The 1918 Influenza Epidemic in New Zealand*, p. 105.
34. Ohinemuri County Statistics, in ibid., p. 193.
35. D M Stafford, *The New Century in Rotorua: A History of Events from 1900*, p. 402.
36. D M Stafford, *Te Arawa: A History of the Arawa People*, Auckland, 1986, p. 66.
37. J Curnow and H Mitchell, 'Rotohiko Tangonui Haupapa, 1836? – 1887', in *Dictionary of New Zealand Biography*, Wellington, 22 June 2007. The name of this three-acre block was Te Wharau a Taharoa Whakarua.
38. Interview with Neil Manahi, Rotorua, 20 August 2009.
39. Op. cit.
40. *Evening Post*, 6 July 1914, p. 7
41. F Gee, 'The First Mission Settlement at Rotorua', in *Rotorua Legend*, vol. 1, no. 3, 1961, p. 20.
42. Interview with Neil Manahi, Rotorua, 20 August 2009; also see P Grace, I Ramsden, J Dennis (eds.), *The Silent Migration: Ngāti Pōneke Young Māori Club 1937–1948*, Wellington, Huia Publishers, 2001, p. 159.
43. Interview with Neil Manahi, Rotorua, 20 August 2009.
44. H W Mitchell to P Moon, 3 February 2010.
45. For details of those who enlisted or were conscripted, see C Pugsley. *Te Hokowhitu a Tu: The Maori Pioneer Battalion in the First World War*, Auckland, Reed, 1995, pp. 85–130.
46. 'Ko Te Kahiti o Niu Tireni [Motuhake]', He Mea Ta i te Mana o te Kawanatanga, Poneke, Turei, Tihema 14, 1915.
47. Op. cit.
48. Cited in V O'Malley and D Armstrong, *The Beating Heart: A Political and Socio-Economic History of Te Arawa*, Wellington, Huia Publishers, 2008, pp. 239–40.
49. V O'Malley and D Armstrong, *The Beating Heart: A Political and Socio-Economic History of Te Arawa*, p. 246.
50. On behalf of the British and French respectively.
51. Material provided by R Manahi, 25 February 2010.
52. V O'Malley and D Armstrong, *The Beating Heart: A Political and Socio-Economic History of Te Arawa*, p. 250.
53. *New Zealand Herald*, 16 April 1920.
54. *Poverty Bay Herald*, 10 April 1919, p. 2.

55. D M Stafford, *The New Century in Rotorua: A History of Events from 1900*, p. 125.
56. J Allen, in C Pugsley, *Te Hokowhitu a Tu: The Maori Pioneer Battalion in the First World War*, pp. 22–4.
57. V O'Malley and D Armstrong, *The Beating Heart: A Political and Socio-Economic History of Te Arawa*, p. 246.
58. See E Best, *The Maori Art of War*, Auckland, 2004; B Haami, in I McGibbon (ed.), *The Oxford Companion to New Zealand Military History*, Auckland, Oxford University Press, 2000, p. 303.
59. D M Stafford, *The New Century in Rotorua: A History of Events from 1900*, p. 125.
60. Ibid., p. 216.
61. V O'Malley and D Armstrong, *The Beating Heart: A Political and Socio-Economic History of Te Arawa*, p. 280.
62. This was Rotorua's first secondary school, and was established in 1914.
63. K J Lyall, *Rotorua High and Grammar School, Rotorua Boys' High School: History and Register of Pupils 1927–1992*, Rotorua, K J Lyall, publisher, 1992, p. 17.
64. Ibid., pp. 52, 90.
65. N Te Awekotuku, *The Sociocultural Impact of Tourism on the Te Arawa People of Rotorua, New Zealand, p. 116.*
66. Interview with Neil Manahi, Rotorua, 20 August 2009.
67. Interview with Rau Manahi, Rotorua, 17 November 2009.
68. Interview with Neil Manahi, Rotorua, 20 August 2009.
69. W J Phillipps, 'Carved Houses of Te Arawa', in *Dominion Museum Records in Ethnology, vol. 1, no. 1, Wellington, 1946, p. 8.*
70. A Hamilton, *The Art Workmanship of the Maori Race in New Zealand: A Series of Illustrations from Specially Taken Photographs, with Descriptive Notes and Essays on the Canoes, Habitations, Weapons, Ornaments and Dress of the Maoris, Together with Lists of the Words in the Maori Language Used in Relation to the Subjects, Dunedin,* Fergusson and Mithcell, 1896, p. 115.
71. J H Kerry-Nicholls, *The King Country, or, Explorations in New Zealand: A Narrative of 600 Miles of Travel Through Maoriland, London, 1884, p. 71.*
72. Record of Promotions, Reductions, Transfers, Casualties, Punishments, Etc., 'Particulars of Will', New Zealand Defence Forces Archives, 14 February 1944.
73. Interview with Rau Manahi, Rotorua, 17 November 2009.
74. Interview with Rau Manahi, Rotorua, 20 August 2009.
75. Interview with Neil Manahi, Rotorua, 20 August 2009.
76. Interview with Rau Manahi, Rotorua, 20 August 2009.
77. Interview with Neil Manahi, Rotorua, 20 August 2009.
78. Marriage record F1, p. NO6, Folio 38
79. Record of Promotions, Reductions, Transfers, Casualties, Punishments, Etc., 'Particulars of Will', New Zealand Defence Forces Archives, 14 February 1944.
80. Interview with Rau Manahi, Rotorua, 17 November 2009.

# CHAPTER 3: Enlistment

Unable to restrain his instinctively aggressive impulses, and gambling on the ongoing British preference for appeasement, on 1 September 1939, Adolf Hitler ordered the German invasion of Poland. However, by now, Britain's patience with the dictator's expansionism had already been stretched to its limits, and on 3 September, Neville Chamberlain, the British Prime Minister, declared that his country (and with it, the long tail of the British Empire) was at war with Germany. On 4 September at 1.55 am, New Zealand duly offered its whole-hearted support,[1] with Prime Minister Michael Joseph Savage later making his famous declaration: 'we range ourselves without fear beside Britain. Where she goes, we go, where she stands, we stand'.[2] Within a few days, the New Zealand Expeditionary Force was formed, and by the middle of October, fifteen thousand volunteers had enlisted.[3]

In keeping with the proudly pro-Crown stance it had exhibited for over half a century, Te Arawa was conspicuous by being one of the first iwi to offer the government its support for the war effort. As Apirana Ngata described it in 1943, 'Te Arawa were the first of the Maoris to offer their manhood to the cause for which England went to war. They have sacrificed their entire eligible youth for the ideologies that underline the best in modern civilisation'.[4]

In Rotorua, a wave of enthusiasm to enlist swept through its Māori communities, and within a month of the outbreak of war in Europe, around 900 Te Arawa men had indicated their eagerness to sign up for the armed forces.[5] And as with Maori participation in the First World War, Ngata was again central in co-ordinating Māori troop involvement, although with the benefit of his earlier experience, much closer attention was paid to the issues of command and structure in the new force.

A full two months before war was declared, and therefore acting with great prescience, Ngata had urged the Minister of Defence to revive the Pioneer Māori Battalion, in case war did break out. His rationale was that a battalion based roughly on tribal lines would be the most effective means of encouraging Māori to volunteer.[6] Even before the government had given its authorisation for the formation of the New Zealand Expeditionary Force, Ngata sought and quickly received support for the concept of a Māori battalion from two of the Māori MPs who were members of the Labour Government: Paraire Karaka Paikea (Northern Māori), and Eruera Tihema Te Aika Tirikatene (Southern Māori).

Given this mainly behind-the-scenes preparation, when the announcement was made by the government on 4 September that New Zealand was at war with Germany, the concept of a specifically Māori battalion had already sunk deep roots into the minds of many politicians. Predictably, there were objections at what some MPs perceived to be a separatist initiative,[7] but their views were those of a small minority, and any lingering government reticence over the idea of a Māori battalion was dissolved when a request arrived on the Defence Minister's desk from Pare Keiha[8] – who had chaired a major hui on the matter[9] – which gave a commitment that Māori would 'serve with his Pakeha brothers whenever needed', and that the experience of the First World War proved the value of a specifically Māori unit. As a show of the extent of Māori commitment to the war effort, Keiha offered wharenui in the East Coast district for the accommodation and training of troops,[10] but he remained insistent that Māori be appointed as officers for the Battalion's companies.[11] Some politicians were initially opposed to Māori entering the war because the entire Māori population stood at only 90,000,[12] but the growing threat posed by the enemy soon overrode these concerns.

By the end of September, the government had consented to the formation of a Māori rifle battalion, and made its announcement on 4 October. The one fly in the ointment, however, was the government's dogged insistence that Pākehā officers be appointed to key positions in the battalion. With all the enormous goodwill shown by Māori, particularly Ngāti Porou and Te Arawa, for involvement in the common cause, this demand was simply unpalatable. Te Arawa in particular were 'incensed',[13] and convened a hui, under the guidance of the rangatira Hemana Pokiha, to make known their displeasure at this official snub of Māori equality with Pākehā. A faint concession was wrung out of the government as a result of this protest, with Captain Rangiataahua Kiniwe Royal put in command of B Company, and Captain Tiwi Love despatched to Headquarters Company. It would be left to events in the course of the war for the 'natural' echelon of Māori military leadership to filter its way up the ranks.

The 28 Māori Battalion was part of a much larger structure that constituted New Zealand's army contribution to the war, which came under the title of the New Zealand Division. The Division was divided into three infantry brigades, supported by a number of logistic units. Each of these brigades originally had three infantry battalions, which were numbered 18 to 26, and every one of these battalions was commanded by a lieutenant-colonel. The Māori Battalion was, in effect, a floating battalion, which at various times during the course of the war was put at the disposal of each of the three infantry brigades.

### Structure of the New Zealand Division at the Beginning of the Second World War[14]

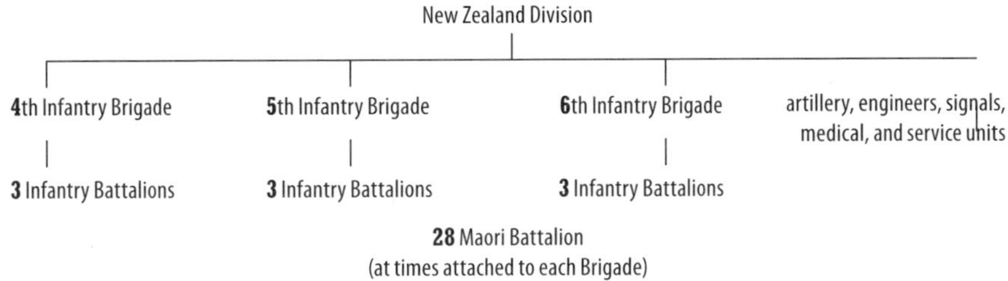


The structure of the Māori Battalion differed from all the other New Zealand infantry battalions in the war, and not only because it was ethnically based. It was divided up into five companies, four of which were rifle companies, consisting of about 125 men in each and headed by a major or a captain, and a headquarters company of about 200 men. The headquarters company was pan-tribal, but the four rifle companies were divided loosely along tribal lines. A Company was made up of Ngāpuhi and Ngāti Whātua, B Company (Manahi's) was Te Arawa and Mataatua, C Company drew its men from the East Coast region, and D Company covered the remaining regions of the North Island and all of the South Island.

### Structure of the 28 Maori Battalion[15]

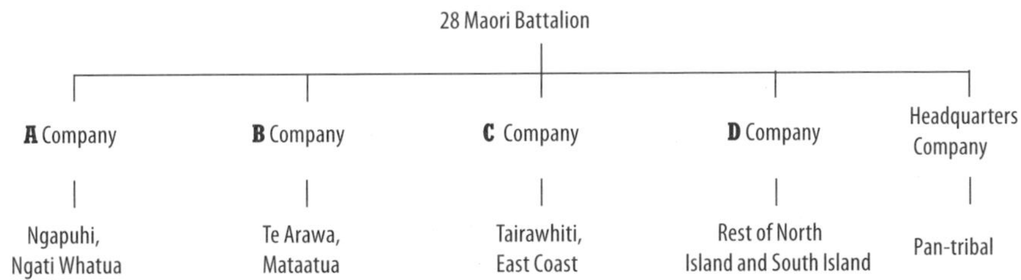


Due to a massive effort undertaken primarily by Ngata over just a few days to organise the logistics of the Māori Battalion, on 9 October registration opened for Māori volunteers. It was open to men between the ages of twenty-one and thirty-five, and required as a prerequisite for entry a standard medical examination. Manahi was among the first group of Māori to enlist, and his army medical records at this time give a useful insight into his physical state. He was examined on 23

November 1939 in Rotorua, when he was 26 years old. His height was given as 5 feet 10½ inches (179 centimetres), and his weight as 14 stone (89 kilograms). His chest measurement was 40 inches (101 centimetres), and his physical development was described by the army medic as 'very good'. Manahi's eyesight was good (a 6/6 measurement) as was his hearing, tests revealed he was free of disease, and for added good measure, it was noted in the record of the Medical Board that he 'plays football'. Manahi was therefore deemed 'Fit for Active Service in any part of the World', although the medic examining him did not consider him 'Fit for Garrison Duty in Tropics'. Possibly the only explanation for this reservation was a hastily written comment about the condition of Manahi's heart, which although not serious enough to preclude him from active service, was still of some concern.[16] It seems that this sole note of caution was based on Manahi's pulse rate, which when sitting was 108 beats per minute – well above the average for a healthy adult male of around 72 beats per minute. The problem, according to his son, was that Manahi had an enlarged heart.[17] Following his successful medical examination, Manahi was enlisted at the rank of private, and given his regimental number, 39099. On 3 February 1940, he underwent a final round of medical tests (including an x-ray), in which no abnormalities were detected, and he was given a Grade 1 physical rating by the army.[18]

While tuberculosis and venereal disease were the two main reasons for volunteers being rejected by the army, one of Manahi's brothers was turned down because the whānau believed that as he had three children, and as Manahi was obliged to leave his son, Rauawa, behind, there was a need for at least one male of that generation in the whanau to remain at home. As Neil Manahi later explained, 'My father travelled all round New Zealand to try to get in to the army, and he went under different names, but he got kicked out and kicked out and told to look after the family, but he was so proud of his brother'.[19] It was also part of Ngata's plan for the battalion that initially, single males would be the preferred group from whom volunteers would be drawn.[20] In addition, he personally reserved the right to veto the enlistment of any man 'whom he thought should remain at home because of age, family responsibilities, or their usefulness in production on the home front'.[21]

Whānau and whakapapa links were to come to the fore even in the heat of battle. For those troops from close-knit communities like Ōhinemutu, whakapapa could sometimes influence who could take to the battlefield in a skirmish. Lance-Corporal Martin McRae (also from Ōhinemutu) when serving as Regimental Sergeant Major, would keep back certain men from combat at particular times because of their family connections back home.[22] And as the war progressed and the casualties mounted, Māori commanders grew even more aware of how their men fitted into the mosaic of family and community connections back home and kept an eye on many soldiers with a view to the welfare of these communities once the war was over.

The issue of Māori soldiers training and serving under Pākehā commanders was more than just a stubborn bone of contention held by a few Māori politicians or borne out of some obscure cultural angst. There were very real concerns about the responsiveness of Māori troops to commanders whose background was often considerably different. This was illustrated in one episode when a Pākehā commanding officer at the military camp at Trentham informed Ngata that the Māori candidates were not performing as well as was expected in areas such as geometry, map-reading, and plotting coordinates. Ngata turned to the officer and said, 'I tell you what, take them into the bush at Rimutaka and see if you can lose them there'. The commander was up for the challenge, and organised four platoons – two Māori and two Pākehā – to make their way in the bush to an agreed point, with just twenty-four hours to achieve the objective. When the time had elapsed, only the two Māori platoons had achieved the target, with the Pākehā troops taking longer than the allotted time to complete the task. Ngata's point was made.[23]

In the case of B Company, while it was under the overall command of Major George Dittmer, who was the Battalion's first commanding officer, its junior officers were Māori. These included Captain (later Major) Rangiataahua Kiniwe Royal, Second Lieutenant Whetu Werohia, Lieutenant (later Lieutenant Colonel) Charles Moihi Te Arawaka Bennett, Lieutenant Henry Te Rupe Vercoe, Lieutenant Horton Oliphant Te Apatu Stewart, and Second Lieutenant Tuhawaiki Manahi[24] (a distant relative on Haane's Ngati Pikiao side).

The motives for men enlisting in the battalion varied considerably. The feeling of adventure and the possibility of escaping the ordinary routines of life was definitely appealing, while the element of peer pressure cannot be discounted either. To stand against the tide of friends and relatives surging to join the army would have been difficult for any individual who had some objection to volunteering, not that there was any evidence of that among the men of Te Arawa.[25]

Some of these volunteers perhaps sensed that they needed this sort of opportunity to make their mana felt, in the way that some of their forefathers had in the First World War, and in other wars before that. The evocation of the mythology and glamour of warfare was still pronounced among this generation. 'All their long history had been steeped in the religion of war', one soldier from the battalion later described it, 'and the training of the Maori child from his infancy to manhood was aimed at the perfection of the warrior-class, while to die in the pursuit of the war god Tumatauenga was a sacred duty and a manly death'.[26] This might be a slightly melodramatic interpretation, but it nevertheless contains at least an impression of the role that culture played in the thinking of some volunteers. Ngata echoed this sentiment in more moderate tones: 'These young men of Te Arawa tribe showed in desperate circumstances the value of the tribal spirit founded in tradition and the pride of past achievement'.[27]

There was also a wider political expectation within the iwi that its young men would again rise to the challenge of fighting for the Crown. The extent of Te Arawa's commitment to the cause of this war was considerable and unqualified. The iwi was pleased for its enlisted men to travel 'beyond the shores of the great ocean of Kiwa'. 'Let others hesitate in this our extreme hour of peril and need', the kaumātua lectured, 'but the spirit of the Arawa ... demands that they again be allowed to cross the seas to stand shoulder to shoulder with their white brothers, sharing with them equality of sacrifice in defending the same ideals they fought for twenty years ago'.[28] The motif of achieving racial unity through fighting for a common cause became a popular one during the war. In March 1943, Prime Minister Peter Fraser (himself once a conscientious objector), suggested that as a result of their shared participation in the war, Māori and Pākehā were now bound together by 'bonds that can never be severed'.[29] The King's cousin, the Earl of Listowel, addressed Te Arawa the same year, and emphasised how the iwi's willingness to support the Crown would have a profound effect on life after the war. 'I believe', he told the audience, 'you are emerging from the valley of shadows into the sunlight of a new and brighter era'.[30]

However, it was not all wide-eyed enthusiasm in the community when enlistments began. The parents of Manahi's generation knew the sobering facts of the First World War (over four hundred Māori soldiers were killed in the 'War to End All Wars', and at least twice as many returned with debilitating injuries),[31] and privately held apprehensions about their children becoming involved in a similar type of conflict.[32] There was honour in fighting – and the details of certain battles would sometimes be noisily discussed, and victories were boasted of – but then there were also the quiet comments, muttered under the breath, about the risks involved, and the costs to the whānau of young men going off to fight. Relationships with wives and girlfriends had to be put on hold, and those with children, like Manahi, would miss several years of seeing their offspring grow up. Living conditions for a fighting army were tough, the money troops received was negligible, and the longer you were away, the greater the chance that you would return home as a corpse, or be left entombed in a place few had heard of and fewer would ever visit. But it was not this parents' generation that was enlisting from 1939. The young men from Rotorua and numerous other locations who signed up to fight in the Second World War were compelled to do so by another set of considerations. Certainly, the sort of adventure that was on offer drew its own pilgrims, and sharing this adventure with your mates became an irresistible impulse for many. And could being in the army really be any worse than spending every daylight hour of every day, in all weather, clearing scrub in some remote block of land?

There was also an element of pride for soldiers and their families. 'My boy's off to fight' was a boast a father could make to his mates in the pub (although the same phrase was equally an anxious confession a mother would make to her friends),[33] and for the young men themselves, once they had been fitted for their uniforms and done some basic training, could bask in that special sort of prestige reserved exclusively for soldiers.

In the case of B Company, many of the troops were the descendants of soldiers who had fought against each other during the Land Wars of the 1860s. Eighty years on, these arcane divisions were still known about, but as they had sifted through three or four generations, that had transformed from being a source of animosity to one of humour. 'We laughed about it, but we didn't take it seriously', Arthur Midwood, a fellow B Company soldier, recalled, 'and when we went off to England, we were all just one group'.[34] The divergent strands of their history were now braided by a common cause.

For Māori volunteers, though, there was an extra dimension involved in volunteering to fight. Ngata was later emphatic that there be some dividend in return for the contribution that Māori were making to the war. 'In this war', he wrote in 1943, 'he [Māori] asked to take his full share in the front line, and in this he has been fully indulged. Has he proved to be an asset to his country? If so, he asks to be dealt with as such. An asset discovered in the crucible of war should have a value in the coming peace. The men of the New Zealand Division have seen it below the brown skins of their Maori comrades. Have the civilians of New Zealand, men and women, fully realised the implication of the joint participation of Pakeha and Maori in this last and greatest demonstration of the highest citizenship?'[35] Ngata's belief was that through participating in the war, Māori had paid the price to be equal citizens in the country.

Manahi and his comrades from Rotorua arrived at the army training camp at Palmerston North on 26 January 1940, having attested (that is, formally enlisted) on 23 November 1939.[36] This group of volunteers was accompanied by rangatira, kaumātua, and other whānau, as well as a number of men who had not yet gone through the enlistment process but at the last moment had decided to join the battalion. The atmosphere on the train trip was a festive one, and on arrival at the station in Palmerston North, out poured men, women, and even a few children from the carriages, all wearing brightly-coloured clothes (many in their Sunday best), with some of the men carrying banjos, accordions and ukuleles. The punctilious Major Dittmer, on seeing this mêlée, was said to have gone 'a little pale'.[37]

An account of the training regime, written just sixteen years later, gives a near-contemporary perspective of some of the character of this first encounter between the army and Māori volunteers: 'Training began immediately the preliminaries of marching in, the issuing of clothing, and the organisation of platoons were completed. The raw material of the Battalion was very malleable and very inexperienced; even the long train journey was to a large number something of an event, but they [the Maori volunteers] brought with them a philosophical outlook and a carefree cheerfulness. Events were to show that this typical Polynesian disposition seldom failed the Maori soldier. One advantage the Maoris had over the Pakeha trainees was that, living in close proximity to their fellows in their own communities and being used to sharing amenities, they did not have to become accustomed to camp life'. However, despite this easy adjustment to the environment of the camp, there were some areas where the volunteers had to make extra effort in their training: 'The battalion command was faced with a multitude of problems arising from the fact that the Maori is predominantly agrarian, and that consequently all specialists have to be trained – medical orderlies, mechanics, clerks, drivers, radio technicians, signallers, and other tradesmen necessary in a modern battalion'.[38] Yet, the Māori recruits excelled in the field of weapon handling, and 'the mechanical skills and repetitious nature of stripping and assembling weapons was an area in which the Maori had few peers'.[39]

For the volunteers themselves, there was still a high-spirited mood about this undertaking, and the battalion soon developed nicknames for each of its companies. Those in A Company were called Nga Kiri Kapia – the Gum Diggers – because of the association of Northland with the kauri gum industry, B Company acquired the name Nga Rukukapa – the Penny Divers – as a reference to a popular tourist attraction in Rotorua, C Company were kown as Nga Kaupoi – the Cowboys – because of the prevalence of horses as a mode of transport on the East Coast, while D Company – the remainder of the tribal areas that contributed to the Battalion, were called the Foreign Legion.[40]

To the Pākehā officers, the experience of a concentrated body of Māori troops was an unfamiliar one, but these volunteers quickly earned the respect of their commanders. Lance Corporal Frank Rennie, an instructor at the camp, later explained that 'having this experience with the Maoris provided a new dimension in soldiering for me. Their boundless and infectious enthusiasm and their tremendous pride in their reputation as warriors was something I had to see to believe. I saw it again and again. Many times I was personally grateful for it'.[41]

The differences between Māori and Pākehā undergoing basic training were sometimes slight, but at the same time suggestive of the size of the cultural gap that existed in the country. As one example, at the camp in Palmerston North, 'the Medical Officer was faced with long queues parading with sore feet – happy-go-lucky recruits who had tried to make Maori feet fit into Pakeha boots. A wider-than-usual last was necessary for men who seldom wore boots in youth and, to get the width, boots several sizes too big were issued by the perplexed Quartermaster'.[42] As far as Te Arawa was concerned, the problem with the feet was one mainly for C Company. 'The fellahs from here, they were a bit more civilised', Rau recalled, 'it was those cowboys from the Coast that had the big feet'.[43]

Palmerston North was new territory for these young men, and naturally, they were keen to explore the town. However, not all the locals were favourably disposed towards this influx of Māori recruits, and early on, the local council even considered banning them altogether from the town. Dittmer dealt with this potentially unpleasant situation by addressing these trainees firmly, and issued the challenge to them that 'before we go, we are going to make Palmerston North sorry to see us go'.[44] The change in behaviour among the battalion and in the attitudes of the local residents was almost immediate, and there was a warm-hearted civic function held to farewell the troops in May.[45]

Overall, the 700 recruits, of which Manahi was one, formed 'a happy group', as one officer noted. 'Wherever you turned, there were chaps smiling. I suppose it was because they were there; they were part of the Battalion'.[46] Occasionally, however, tribal chauvinism spilt over into open hostility. In one instance, in a bar in Palmerston North, a group of Te Arawa men, led by John Hall, lashed out after being constantly taunted by trainees from another Company for being penny divers.[47] A brawl ensued, and Manahi stepped in to help break it up. Once tempers had calmed a bit, Manahi identified the instigator of the fight and told him 'you go home if you want to be like that', and the man did leave, telling his whānau on his return home that he had dropped out of the army.[48] By the end of the nearly three-month training period at Palmerston North, though, the lesson had sunk in that the one topic to be avoided by everyone was talk of tribal history.

The battalion was given two weeks' leave in April, just before their scheduled departure. This was an opportunity for the men to return to their homes for a final time. Manahi and others from B Company made their way back to Rotorua, and once there, he spent most of his time with his wife, and Rau, who was now aged three-and-a-half years. It was not all time with relatives, though. The anticipation of their imminent passage to uncertain destinations and circumstances played on the minds of a lot of these men, and led, in Manahi's case, to small gatherings of these soldiers in Rotorua. As much as they were inclined to spend their final days with their loved ones, they were also being drawn to each other. The gravity of impending conflict – and the dependence they would place on each other – was growing increasingly strong.

Like most of the young men in Rotorua who had been enlisted, Manahi sometimes made a point of casually walking around the town in uniform. There was no requirement to do so, but it did give them the sort of attention they had never received before. Young boys were in awe of these soldiers, old men were suddenly taking them more seriously, and of course, women were impressed. Manahi had been married less than a year, yet he still liked to attract the attention of the local ladies.

Then came the final few days. The proud walks around the streets of Rotorua ceased, the socialising with other Company members in the area wound down, and the soldiers retreated to their homes to be with their whānau. The mood in Ōhinemutu sunk into sombreness. As the hours ticked away to the scheduled departure, the potential that this could be the last time that they saw each other settled into everyone's minds, but remained mainly unspoken.

Finally, it was time for good-byes. Hugs, kisses, hongi, firm handshakes among the men, eyes welling with tears, and fathers lifting up their children who were too young to understand the reason for this unusual show of emotion. The train would not wait, and so lips stiffened, tears were wiped away, and the men of B Company boarded their carriages, with the only solace now being the companionship of their comrades. This was the point when the fun of being in the army was displaced by solemnity, and when the ties that bound these men to each other really started to be felt.

From the slightly bedraggled and disordered band of recruits they had been in late January, on the morning of 1 May, B Company woke up in Palmerston North for the last time as well-trained soldiers. Boots were given an extra polish, all the kits were packed, beds made, and by mid-morning the 28 Māori Battalion were putting on their coats for the chilly Manawatu weather. With their lemon-squeezer hats and rifles mounted, they marched towards the railway station and past a big crowd of local residents who had gathered to see them off, along with hundreds of whānau who had travelled to Palmerston North to witness this historic departure.[49] Manahi's parents did not make the journey to the training camp for this farewell as they had already seen him off at Ōhinemutu. The train carrying the battalion left Palmerston North just after midday, and arrived in Wellington four hours later. Its windows were shuttered and its doors guarded, and as it reached Aotea Quay, crowds of friends, relatives and other onlookers were kept at a distance as the men disembarked after their journey.

Although Manahi kept no diary, and therefore left no direct trace of his life during the early years of the war, detailed information on his company, and even more so on his battalion, enable his movements and the circumstances he encountered to be pieced together with some accuracy. After weeks spent training in Palmerston North, followed by a fortnight's leave, the pace of events suddenly quickened. The train pulled into Wellington late in the afternoon, and the troops disembarked and marched straight on board the luxury Cunard White Star liner *Aquitania*. The Māori Battalion was joined by other New Zealand troops, and by early evening, almost 3000 men from the New Zealand Division were on board. The ship had served as a troop carrier, transport and hospital vessel during the First World War, and in 1940 was still one of the fastest ships of its class.

The arrangement for the troops to sail in the *Aquitania* were officially supposed to be secret, but any undertaking on this scale was bound inevitably to become common knowledge, which was why thousands of people crowded outside the wharf's gates (which were manned by troops with fixed bayonets) to farewell the soldiers. And having waited all night, just as the ship was about to depart, the gates were opened by the port authorities and the crowd surged forward to get a final glimpse of their friends and relatives as the vessel steamed out of Wellington Harbour at 6.00 the following morning.[50] One group that had been allowed inside the otherwise sealed military cordon on the wharf was an ensemble of young Ngāti Pōneke women, who sung farewell songs to the men on the ship. As the ship's propellers finally began to churn the waters and move the vessel out of the harbour, men of the Māori Battalion on board gave a throaty and heartfelt rendition of 'Po Atarau' ('Now is the Hour'). It was one of the most poignant episodes in the battalion's early history as tears flowed among those in the crowd and those on the ship.[51]

B Company (like the other companies of the battalion) were good-humoured as they left New Zealand, always joking and teasing each other, and generally enjoying the camaraderie fuelled by the excitement of imminent adventure – the sobering effects of the war were still unknown to them. Since enlisting, the time these young men spent together, first in training, then when they departed for England, was like a reunion. Most of them could identify shared relatives 'somewhere along the line',[52] and as they talked and swapped stories, each soldier opened up their own repository of anecdotes which were attached in various ways to the limbs of their whakapapa.

However, there was a subterranean current in this strengthening rapport. All the banter and all the budding familiarity was part of the ritual of building trust. They may not yet have consciously appreciated it, but their mates – both new and reacquainted – would be the only people they would be able to rely on in the life-and-death circumstances that lay ahead.

## NOTES

1. F L W Wood, *The New Zealand People at War: Political and External Affairs*, Historical Publications Branch, Department of Internal Affairs, Wellington, 1958, p. 9.
2. M J Savage in R Rabel, "Where She [Britain] Goes, We Go': But With Eyes Wide Open', in *New Zealand Defence Quarterly*, vol. 27, 1999, pp. 26–7.
3. Op. cit.
4. A Ngata, *The Price of Citizenship: Ngarimu V.C.*, Wellington, Whitcombe and Tombs, 1943, p. 17.
5. D M Stafford, *The New Century in Rotorua: A History of Events from 1900*, pp. 226–7.
6. R Walker, *He Tipua: The Life and Times of Sir Apirana Ngata*, Auckland, Penguin Publishing, 2001, p. 339.
7. J F Cody, *28 (Maori) Battalion*, Wellington, War History Branch, Department of Internal Affairs, 1956, p. 1.
8. Keiha's sister, Heni Materoa, and their relation, Henare Ruru, also lobbied strongly for the formation of the Battalion. P Keiha to P Moon, Auckland, 9 November 2009, personal correspondence. Also see A Ngata, *The Price of Citizenship: Ngarimu V.C.*, p. 18.
9. Interview with Bill Keiha, Whakatāne, 15 November 2009.
10. J Ferris to A Ngata, 14 September 1939, MS -Papers-6919-0347, Alexander Turnbull Library, in M Soutar, *Nga Tama Toa: The Price of Citizenship*, p. 34.
11. Interview with Bill Keiha, Whakatāne, 15 November 2009.
12. Interview with Norman Bennett, 28 January 2010. Also see J V T Baker, *The War Economy*, Wellington, War History Branch, Department of Internat Affairs, 1965, p. 443.
13. R Walker, *He Tipua: The Life and Times of Sir Apirana Ngata*, p. 345.
14. M Soutar, *Nga Tama Toa: The Price of Citizenship: C Company 28 (Maori) Battalion 1939–1945*, p. 44.
15. Op. cit.
16. New Zealand Military Forces, 'Record of Medical Board for Haani Manahi', 23 November 1939, Rotorua, War Form N.Z. – 355.
17. Interview with Rau Manahi, Rotorua, 17 November 2009.
18. New Zealand Military Forces, 'X-Ray Chest Record for Haani Manahi', 3 February 1940, War Form N.Z. – 735.
19. Interview with Neil Manahi, Rotorua, 20 August 2009.
20. When registration started on 9 October 1939, it was initially open only to single men aged between 21 and 35.
21. R Walker, *He Tipua: The Life and Times of Sir Apirana Ngata*, p. 347.
22. H Mitchell to P Moon, 1 February 2010.
23. R Walker, *He Tipua: The Life and Times of Sir Apirana Ngata*, p. 348.
24. Details obtained from Cenotaph Database, Auckland War Memorial Museum.
25. Although there was still some hesitation in 1939 from a few other iwi about participation in the war.
26. Cited in 'Maori and the Second World War', Ministry for Culture and Heritage, Wellington, 31 August 2009.
27. A Ngata, *The Price of Citizenship: Ngarimu V.C.*, pp. 16–17.
28. Cited in D M Stafford, *The New Century in Rotorua*, pp. 226–7.
29. P Fraser, in *New Zealand Herald*, 25 March 1943, in V O'Malley and D Armstrong, *The Beating Heart: A Political and Socio-Economic History of Te Arawa*, p. 299.
30. Earl of Listowel, in *New Zealand Herald*, 23 July 1943, in V O'Malley and D Armstrong, *The Beating Heart: A Political and Socio-Economic History of Te Arawa*, p. 301.
31. 'The Maori Roll of Honour', in C Pugsley, *Te Horowhitu A Tu: The Maori Pioneer Battalion in the First World War*, Auckland, 1995, pp. 131–40.
32. Manahi's brother was advised by kaumātua not to enlist because he had several children, and the whānau could not afford to lose him. Interview with Neil Manahi, Rotorua, 20 August 2009.
33. At least one Māori mother used the phrase 'Farewell my son. Take care of yourself and always remember your Father in Heaven'. Such departing wishes were more melancholic than jubilant. Cited in J F Cody, *28 (Maori) Battalion*, p. 1.
34. Interview with Arthur Midwood, Rotorua, 7 September 2009.
35. A Ngata, *The Price of Citizenship: Ngarimu V.C.*, p. 18.
36. New Zealand Military Forces, 'Victory Contingent', History-sheet, Haane Manahi , 39099, War Form N.Z. 307.
37. J F Cody, *28 (Maori) Battalion*, p. 5.
38. Ibid., p. 7.
39. W Gardiner, *Te Mura o te Ahi: The Story of the Maori Battalion*, p. 31.
40. W Gardiner, *Te Mura o te Ahi: The Story of the Maori Battalion*, p. 31.
41. F Rennie, *Regular Soldier*, Auckland, 1986, p. 28.
42. J F Cody, *28 (Maori) Battalion*, p. 7.
43. Interview with Rau Manahi, Rotorua, 17 November 2009.
44. G Dittmer, in W Gardiner, *Te Mura o te Ahi: The Story of the Maori Battalion*, p. 32.
45. W Gardiner, *Te Mura o te Ahi: The Story of the Maori Battalion*, p. 32.
46. R Logan, in M Soutar, *Nga Tama Toa: The Price of Citizenship*, p. 58.
47. M Soutar, *Nga Tama Toa: The Price of Citizenship*, p. 61.
48. Interview with Rau Manahi, Rotorua, 17 November 2009.
49. W Gardiner, *Te Mura o te Ahi: The Story of the Maori Battalion*, p. 33; J F Cody, *28 (Maori) Battalion*, p. 11.
50. J F Cody, *28 (Maori) Battalion*, pp. 11–12.
51. M Soutar, *Nga Tama Toa: The Price of Citizenship*, pp. 78–9.
52. Interview with Arthur Midwood, Rotorua, 7 September 2009.

*Martin McRae (left rear), Haane Manahi (right rear), Les Hall (left front) and Darkie Hall (right front)*
Atareta Stewart (née McRae)

**Erratum:** In the index and photograph above, Darkie Hall should read **John** Hall.

*Johnny Ingram (killed at Takrouna) with his mother, Ngāhaka Rangiriri, and father, James Ingram*
*Rita Ngatai*

*Joe and Ted Douglas, who were both killed at Takrouna*
*Isobel Berryman (née Douglas)*

a.

b.

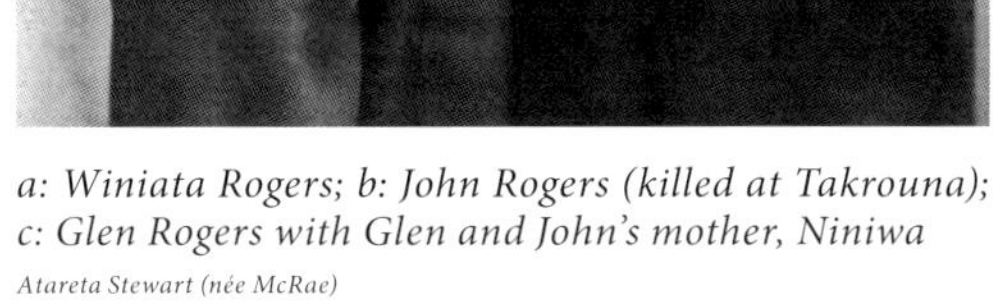

c.

*a: Winiata Rogers; b: John Rogers (killed at Takrouna);*
*c: Glen Rogers with Glen and John's mother, Niniwa*

*Atareta Stewart (née McRae)*

# CHAPTER 4: Britain and Beyond

The *Aquitania* was first to enter Cook Strait, followed by the *Empress of Japan* and the *Empress of Britain* – the other troop ships which made up the convoy heading to Australia, escorted by the British light cruiser HMS *Leander*.[1] As far as the men on board knew, there was only a vague inkling of their final destination. There was talk of going to Egypt or England, and in the absence of any official information (military secrecy was now strictly maintained), all sorts of rumours and speculation populated the troops' thoughts and conversations.

First, though, the men on *Aquitania* had to contend with serious sea-sickness that affected just about everyone on board as the ship entered a storm in the Tasman Sea.[2] By the time they neared Australia, however, many of the soldiers on board had found their sea legs and the incidents of sea-sickness abated. For Manahi, the conditions on the ship would have initially been a pleasant surprise. There had been no time for a comprehensive refit of the vessel for military purposes, and so the troops enjoyed luxury accommodation and matching menus. Their days were filled with training sessions and lectures on aspects of warfare, which as the *Aquitania* steamed towards its eventual destination became much more than just some obtuse academic exercise. All the exercise, weapons training and classes were preparation for impending fighting, and everyone treated them as such.

On 5 May, the *Aquitania's* convoy was joined off Sydney by the *Queen Mary* and the *Empress of Canada*, all of which sailed on to the first port of call since leaving Wellington: Fremantle in Perth, Western Australia. After ten days on the seas, the men of the Māori Battalion were keen to go onshore, but the size of *Aquitania* forced it to anchor almost four kilometres offshore. The troops on the ship were growing increasingly frustrated at being confined on the vessel, to the point where one of the commanders, Brigadier James Hargest,[3] arranged for the port authorities to provide some boats to ferry the men ashore. The men of the Māori Battalion were warmly welcomed by the Australians, but their stay was less than a day. On 12 May, the *Aquitania* along with the other ships in the convoy set sail again, with the next stop announced as Colombo, in what was then Ceylon (later Sri Lanka). It was three days after leaving Australia that the men on board were informed that they would be going to South Africa, and then somewhere else after that.

Predictably, this dramatic change in route gave rise to a new bout of rumours. Were the waters around Ceylon mined? Were there German vessels dangerously close to the convoy? The sense of not knowing what lay in the immediate future was heightened by rationing suddenly being introduced on the *Aquitania*, as a consequence of the ship having to follow a much longer route.[4] And the fresh news that the Italians had just entered the war on the side of the Germans only furthered the impression that the war was escalating and becoming more directly threatening. As the *Aquitania* cut through the waters of the Indian Ocean there was a gradual realisation among its cargo of troops that they were going from travelling to the war to being part of it – something that evasive action by the convoy to avoid mines set in the approach to Cape Town confirmed.

On 26 May, Cape Town, on the south-western edge of South Africa, was sighted, and the soldiers – no longer able to conceal their boredom at the days spent at sea – were eager to explore this new location. Well, most were. There was some ambivalence among men of the Māori Battalion. They had been advised of the degree of racism that they might encounter in the country, and were told by Major George Bertrand that 'their reception would probably be cool, and that if they were turned out of shops or had any other indignity thrust upon them they were not to make a fuss. It was the custom of the country'.[5]

Manahi was among those of the battalion who were taken by bus from the port to the centre of the city,[6] where they had around an hour before they were due to return to the ship. There was little of the anticipated hostility, and as Major George Clifton recorded, 'after lunch they [the Maoris] went round the shops for a couple of hours, and then returned by bus to Simonstown – none missing, none drunk. Their behaviour and bearing created a great and lasting impression which, I feel sure, will remove the objection to Maoris being included in our Rugby teams for South Africa. I understand the 28 Battalion is the first native regiment ever allowed in Capetown [sic]. They were a credit to their people and a marked example for the remainder of our troops'.[7] Indeed, so welcoming was the reception some of the Māori troops received that they decided to disobey orders and stay in town until the next morning.

With the ships in the convoy replenished with fuel and provisions, on 31 May, they departed for the next leg of the journey, although the soldiers on board had no idea where. As the *Aquitania* headed into the South Atlantic Ocean, more rumours abounded. England was the most popular choice for the voyage's final destination, although Egypt was a strong contender, as it was known that that was where the New Zealand First Echelon was training.[8]

After a brief stop at Freetown in Sierra Leone on 7 June – where all men remained on board – the convoy headed north, and a week later, was joined by a naval escort, including the battle cruiser HMS *Hood*, together with an aircraft carrier and six destroyers. If any indication was needed that the dangers were escalating as the fleet neared Europe, this was it. On 14 June, news came through on the ship's radio that Paris had fallen to the Nazis, who were now only separated from Britain by the English Channel. Two days later, the convoy reached the Scottish coast, and the *Aquitania* entered the Firth of Clyde off Gourock, bringing to an end a journey of 27,000 kilometres.[9]

The fall of France had sunk Britain into its darkest hours. The United States would not enter the war for another eighteen months, and lined up against Britain was a Nazi-dominated Europe. What now looked to everyone to be imminent was a German invasion of England on its west coast.[10] Hitler and his generals had devised a plan – known as Operation Sea Lion – to defeat the Royal Air Force and then launch a mass landing of German troops in Britain, all along the coast from Dorset to Kent. Nazi intelligence-gathering in Britain was at its zenith at this time, and the arrival of the Māori Battalion in Scotland was observed, and even became the subject of German propaganda. The Māori troops were called cannibals and headhunters by the Germans, and were said to be keen about their involvement in the war only because the British Government was allegedly paying them to make patriotic statements.[11] For the British public, the first they learned about the arrival of 'the Maoris' was on a newsreel film that was used, predictably, to cast the battalion's presence in a more favourable light. In the affected accent of the newsreader, accompanied with scenes of Māori troops disembarking, the British heard that 'The Maori Battalion arrive in the United Kingdom, keen to protect its shores from the Nazi threat – another step on the great adventure that has caused many of them to leave their tribal homes 17,000 miles away. They bring with them their language, songs, and cultural expressions of war – an easy marriage with the British traditions of army discipline'.[12]

On arriving in Scotland, the battalion heard a statement by the King, read out by the General Officer Commanding of the Scottish Command. Its final portion stated 'it has fallen to your lot to take your place beside us. You will find us in the forefront of the battle. To all I give a warm welcome, knowing the stern purpose that brings you from your distant homes'.[13] For Manahi and his colleagues, the reality of the war was 'suddenly closer',[14] and the atmosphere in the train carriages that were transporting the battalion from Scotland to England was 'like a morgue'.[15] The train journey lasted twenty hours, and was followed by an eight kilometre march from the station to their camp at Ewshot (misspelt Ewshott in some sources), adjacent to the town of Aldershot. This was the command area for the south of England, and was strategically located midway between London and Portsmouth.

Manahi liked England.[16] As with just about all the battalion, this was his first trip outside of New Zealand, and prior to enlisting, it was the first time he had even left the Bay of Plenty region.[17] However, unlike many of the other men in the battalion, Manahi did not write letters home to his wife telling her of all that he had seen and done, and neither does it appear that she wrote to him. 'That's just the way they were', their son Rau explained, 'they just didn't contact each other while the old man was away'.[18] However, gradually, as the men became more accustomed to moving, and as the novelty of the experience began to wane, homesickness started to be felt. As one small but poignant example, a relative of Lieutenant Stewart later recalled 'Dad once saying – when it was all quiet at night he could hear men around him saying "goodnight Mum"'.[19] Trained soldiers they may have been, but detachment from the whānau was at times difficult to bear for some of these men.

Ewshot was the base for the battalion for the next three weeks, during which time the Second Echelon was reconstituted as a small division.[20] The division was put under the command of General Bernard Freyberg, and included a mixed brigade, comprising the Māori Battalion and a composite battalion formed from the reinforcements of the 5 Brigade battalions.[21] Before commencing several weeks of training, the troops were granted four days' leave to visit London. It was undoubtedly an impressive sight for Manahi and his colleagues, but the excitement of exploring this enormous city was tempered by the signs everywhere that an invasion was looming. Barbed-wire barricades had appeared seemingly on every street, road signs were being removed, some intersections were mined, sandbags were appearing in some windows, and preparations were in place for the underground to be used as a massive air-raid shelter.[22]

In the second week of July, the battalion, along with the rest of the mixed brigade, was relocated to a camp at Dogmersfield, about eight kilometres away from Ewshot, where even more intensive training commenced. The emphasis was on the troops being able to deploy quickly should a German invasion materialise. By September, Hitler was flinging the full force of the Luftwaffe in a bombing campaign against British cities, particularly London. This coincided with the time when the Māori Battalion was judged ready for front-line duty,[23] and when preparations were being made to send it to Egypt.

However, plans to despatch the battalion to Egypt were put on hold as the threat of a German invasion began to build even further. On 5 September, the battalion was on the move, not to Egypt, though, but to Kent, where they arrived the following morning. By the end of October, the weather would start to close in, making an amphibian invasion almost impossible for the Germans, so if there was to be any Nazi offensive, it would happen in the next few weeks. Above their heads, the men of the battalion could hear and sometimes see the aerial combat that came to be known as the Battle of Britain, and by early October, with the weather deteriorating, and an easing off of Luftwaffe attacks, there was a sensation that the threat of an invasion had at least been forestalled until April 1941 at the earliest.

By the second week of October, Manahi and the other men from B Company had moved from their tents to billets in Doddington, a small rural village in the Syndale Valley in Kent.[24] Better, warmer accommodation, coupled with a respite in the threat of an invasion, boosted the men's morale. The battalion's padre, the Reverend Kahi Harawira, wrote to Ngata at this time about the state of the troops, commenting that 'the family [the battalion] is fine. Our shortcomings are minor – pinching fowls, noisy when intoxicated. However, they do not harm each other or anyone else for that matter .... An Englishman had many complimentary things to say about your family when they had come back from the dances. The best thing he said to me was, "We never knew how ill-mannered our boys were till we met your Maori boys. They are perfect gentlemen".'[25]

Apart from socialising, the troops underwent further drills, and got involved in sports – forming their own rugby and hockey teams – and by the end of October, the fear of a German offensive had reduced considerably. On 4 November, B Company was once more on the move, leaving Kent and returning to Aldershot, where they were scheduled to remain for the winter. The battalion was separated at this time, with Manahi's company sent to Waverley Abbey House in Farnham, Surrey.[26] In the freezing damp weather, the men spent every second day on long, often shivering route marches, interspersed with weapons training, field firing, and the occasional visits of local dignitaries.

In keeping with the need for secrecy, on 29 November, an announcement was delivered to the battalion that they would soon be despatched to 'a warmer climate'.[27] This was as specific as the army could be, but given the cold conditions that the troops had been enduring for almost two months, the news was greeted with optimism. The old favourite – Egypt – again was mentioned as the probable destination, and with this belief firmly planted in the minds of most of the men, there was a growing sense of certainty that the purpose of all their travel and training over the eleven months was about to be fulfilled, and that the chance to confront the enemy head-on was just weeks away.

Christmas Day was celebrated in England, with members of the battalion augmenting their rations with local farm animals that were surreptitiously captured, killed and cooked. After Christmas, all equipment and clothing was packed, and the rooms in Waverley Abbey House cleaned thoroughly, before leaving on 3 January by train to the Canada Docks in Liverpool, where their convoy awaited to transport them to Egypt. The troop transporter that the battalion boarded was the *Athlone Castle* – which although much smaller than the *Aquitania*, was still a luxury liner.[28]

While Manahi had been training with his men in the south of England, the strategic situation in North Africa was in a state of flux. During September 1940, the Italian General, Marshal Rudolfo Graziani had invaded Egypt from his base in Italian-held Libya. This opportunistic thrust shunted back the diminutive British force in Egypt, but in December, General Archibald Wavell led an Allied counter-attack that not only pushed back the Italians 800 kilometres west – to the Libyan port city of Benghazi – but more importantly, captured 130,000 Italian troops in the process, seriously weakening the Axis force in the region, and making Egypt much more secure for the Allies until such time as either the Italians or the Germans managed to get enough troops back into Libya to compensate for this loss. The British then withdrew back to Egypt, leaving an Australian garrison to hold the strategically important port of Tobruk, about 100 kilometres from the border with Egypt.[29]

So by the time of the Māori Battalion's departure to Egypt, the Allied hold on that country was at its strongest since the start of the war. The entire New Zealand contingent to Egypt was therefore being viewed by Allied High Command as being surplus to requirements. However, under Dittmer's command, his Māori troops had been shaped into 'a compact, well-trained unit that had been tactically disposed to meet an enemy',[30] and so the battalion was a useful asset to have in this region, especially given the volatility of recent events.

All the while, Dittmer maintained an almost religious devotion to ensuring his men were fighting fit, regardless of where they were to finally be sent to. Even while the *Athlone Castle* remained berthed in Liverpool, waiting for the convoy of which it was a part to assemble, more training was undertaken. The battalion's commanding officers appreciated the risk to the troops' fitness levels if they remained idle during transit, and so implemented a daily exercise programme that consisted mainly of running back and forth along the length of the ship's deck.

The *Athlone Castle* left Liverpool on 7 January 1941, just three hours before a German bombing raid on the docks.[31] The first, brief leg of its journey was to the deserted seaside resort of Colwyn Bay in North Wales, just two hundred kilometres from Liverpool. Here, the *Athlone Castle* anchored for three days as it was joined by other vessels. The next destination for the now enlarged convoy was just off the coastal town of Bangor in Belfast Lough, where the final group of vessels joined the fleet. By 12 January, there were 21 ships in the convoy, protected by a naval and airforce escort. However, within three days, with the convoy now beyond the reach of long-range German aircraft, only two destroyers remained with the troop ships as they headed out into the Atlantic Ocean.[32]

The most direct route to Egypt was to head south towards the coast of Portugal, then past Gibraltar and into the Mediterranean Sea. However, with the prevalence of enemy ships, aircraft, and mines, this course was far too dangerous. With the lives of many thousands of soldiers at stake, the comparatively safer though substantially longer passage was charted as the preferred alternative. So for Manahi and his comrades, it was a return to familiar places: Sierra Leone, Cape Town, and then to the Indian Ocean. On the way south from Belfast, many of the men on board suffered from influenza, which spread quickly in the relative confinement of the ship. But as the temperatures warmed, the effects of the virus diminished, and the rate of its infection slowed dramatically.[33] By the time the *Athlone Castle* and its fellow vessels approached the equator, though, it was the temperatures that became the biggest threat. As the ships entered the port at Sierra Leone for supplies on 25 January 1941 (a four-day stopover), the temperature in the shade was recorded by one officer as a sweltering 49 degrees Celsius.[34]

Once around the Cape of Good Hope though, the convoy turned north, and into a region of the world that was new for the members of the battalion. The ships travelled a further nine thousand kilometres to Twefik Harbour at the entrance to the Suez Canal, where they dropped anchor on 3 March. This was immeasurably more of a culture shock than anything the battalion had experienced in Britain. As the historian Joseph Cody observed, 'the Maoris were not prepared for the sights that were their introduction to Egypt when they stepped ashore … indescribably filthy children and adults dressed in what looked like dirty white nightshirts and brimless red hats … and fighting like mad dogs when a coin was thrown among them'.[35]

The troops were directed to a train and were transported through the desert to Helwan, on the southern outskirts of Cairo, and on the edge of hundreds of square kilometres of sand. The position of all the New Zealand soldiers was precarious: 'Our propaganda wisely did everything possible to conceal our real weakness, even proclaiming that we had half a million troops in the Middle East. No doubt it was fortunate for the ill-prepared though resolute New Zealanders – and the other troops in Egypt – that there were then no Germans in North Africa to take advantage of the situation …. And so, providentially, the 2 NZEF was allowed ample time to train, equip and organise'.[36] For the first week that the troops were in Egypt, the men 'settled in and adapted themselves to living in the desert—or on the fringe of a desert. About the fifth day a wind began to raise the dust. Dust got into, over, and around everything. To make the tents more or less dust-proof, the skirtings were held down with sandbags, and guy ropes were tied to pieces of wood or rock buried in the ground'.[37]

One of the officers in charge of training jotted down the daily routine for the men, which emphasised the need for them to 'toughen up' and acclimatise to desert conditions: 'Reveille – 5 minutes after all on parade in gym. kit. 20 minutes' P.T. followed by about 1½–2 mile gallop over the desert. Shower – and spit and polish, not to mention rifle cleaning, no mean task – dirt and sand. Breakfast. Platoon, company and then battalion parades and inspection. 10–12 mile route march – foot inspections, methylated spirits. Lunch. Work until "Mad dogs and Englishmen" proved true, then siesta period introduced. Rifle exercises, etc., and elementary gun drill. Evening meal'.[38] However arduous it might sound, it was vital training, and put Manahi and his comrades in good stead for the sort of conflict they were expected to be involved in within possibly just a matter of weeks. And the thought of coming face to face with the enemy was all the incentive any of the troops needed to commit themselves fully to the training regime.

On 18 March, two weeks after arriving in Egypt, the battalion was again on the move, packed into train carriages for the 200-kilometre trip to the transit camp at Amiriya – which was situated just under ten kilometres from the Mediterranean coast. And for once, the rumours circulating among the ranks were true – the next destination would be Greece (Freyberg had arrived there eleven days earlier), and finally a chance to fight the enemy. But in case there was any unwarranted exuberance at this prospect, the General had issued a special order to the troops which was read out to them shortly after they had arrived in Egypt. Most of Freyberg's statement was in the form of a warning: 'We shall be meeting our real enemy, the Germans, who have set out with the avowed object of smashing the British Empire. It is clear therefore that wherever we fight them we shall be fighting … in defence of our own homes'. To this was added a précis of the nature of the enemy and the essence of fighting in a modern battle: 'The German soldier is a brave fighter so do not underestimate the difficulties that face us …. Do not be caught unprepared. In war conditions will always be difficult, especially in the encounter battle; time will always be against you, there will always be noise and confusion, orders may arrive late, nerves will be strained, you will be attacked from the air …. But you have been trained physically to endure long marches and fatigue and you must steel yourselves to overcome the ordeal of the … battlefield'.[39]

By the date of their departure, although the destination was still officially secret, 'anyone who was interested knew perfectly well' that the Battalion was off to Greece. Even traders at the port in Egypt were seeking to sell Greek currency to the 'Kiwis' because they knew that preparations were in place for the New Zealand soldiers to be sent there.[40]

# NOTES

1. See J J Colledge, B Warlow, *Ships of the Royal Navy: the Complete Record of All Fighting Ships of the Royal Navy from the 15th Century to the Present*, London, Chatham, 2006.
2. W Gardiner, *Te Mura o te Ahi: The Story of the Maori Battalion*, p. 34.
3. Hargest was killed by shell fire in August 1944 after being part of the Normandy invasion.
4. Up to twelve extra sailing days were added by this change of course.
5. J F Cody, *28 (Maori) Battalion*, p. 14.
6. Interview with Rau Manahi, Rotorua, 17 November 2009.
7. G Clifton, in J F Cody, *28 (Maori) Battalion*, p. 15.
8. J F Cody, *28 (Maori) Battalion*, p. 15.
9. Ibid., p. 17.
10. Indeed, this was what Hitler was planning. See W Carr, *A History of Germany: 1815 - 1945*, London, Edward Arnold, 1969, p. 413.
11. *Gisborne Herald*, 25 October 1940.
12. British Paramount News, 'Anzacs will help man the fortress', London, 16 June 1940.
13. George VI, in J F Cody, *28 (Maori) Battalion*, p. 18.
14. M Soutar, *Nga Tama Toa: The Price of Citizenship*, p. 87.
15. P Tureia, cited in op. cit.
16. Interview with Rau Manahi, Rotorua, 17 November 2009.
17. Op. cit.
18. Op. cit.
19. Quote cited on 28 (Māori) Battalion website, posted by next-of-kin, 6 October 2009.
20. This change came into effect on 29 June 1940.
21. J F Cody, *28 (Maori) Battalion*, p. 20.
22. Interview with Roy Harrison (London resident during 1940), Auckland, 16 October 2009.
23. W Gardiner, *Te Mura o te Ahi: The Story of the Maori Battalion*, p. 41.
24. Other companies went to Eastling (A Company), Wichling (C Company), a local hospital (D Company), Stalisfield (Headquarters Company).
25. K Harawira to A Ngata, 23 September 1940, in M Soutar, *Nga Tama Toa: The Price of Citizenship*, p. 95.
26. This is misspelt as 'Averly' by Cody, see J F Cody, *28 (Maori) Battalion*, p. 29.
27. J F Cody, *28 (Maori) Battalion*, p. 30.
28. The *Athlone Castle* was 725 foot long.
29. D Thomson, *Europe Since Napoleon*, London, Penguin, 1969, pp. 731–2.
30. J F Cody, *28 (Maori) Battalion*, p. 33.
31. G L Burke, 8 January 1941, in W. Gardiner, *Te Mura o te Ahi: The Story of the Maori Battalion*, p. 42.
32. J F Cody, *28 (Maori) Battalion*, p. 34.
33. W Gardiner, *Te Mura o te Ahi: The Story of the Maori Battalion*, p. 43.
34. G L Burke, 27 February 1941, in W. Gardiner, *Te Mura o te Ahi: The Story of the Maori Battalion*, p. 43.
35. J F Cody, *28 (Maori) Battalion*, p. 37.
36. R Kay, *Official History of New Zealand in the Second World War 1939–45: 27 (Machine Gun) Battalion*, Wellington, War History Branch, Department of Internal Affairs, 1958, p. 12.
37. Op. cit.
38. C C Johansen, in ibid., p. 14.
39. B Freyberg, in J F Cody, *28 (Maori) Battalion*, pp. 39–40.
40. G Clifton, *The Happy Hunted*, London, Cassell, 1962, p. 62.

# CHAPTER 5: Greece and Crete

During the war, detailed official information about military operations was frequently smothered by the demands of secrecy. This lack of knowledge of the plans of the military hierarchy was imperfectly compensated for by details passed on from soldier to soldier. New arrivals in an area might be hastily briefed by their commanding officer, but would sometimes find out more informally from other troops over a mug of tea or during a meal. This was what had happened in the third week of March 1941, with the men of B Company speculating on their next destination. 'Oh yes, we all knew it would by Greece', Midwood recalled, 'but then, you could never be certain, because the Army was always changing things'.[1]

As the evening of 25 March 1941 settled on Egypt, the Māori Battalion walked up the gangways leading on to another passenger ship now serving as a troop carrier – the *Cameronia*.[2] It was not until the following morning, when the ship was approaching Greece, that the men on board were formally advised of their destination, by which stage no one was really surprised.[3] The port of Piraeus – just ten kilometres from the Greek capital, Athens – was where the *Cameronia* was bound. It entered the port at midday on 27 March, but due to a lack of available transport, the soldiers of the battalion had no option but to march to their staging camp at Hymettus, ten kilometres east of Athens.

This part of Greece – the southern portion of the country – was about five hundred kilometres away from the fighting in the north, and it was to that conflict zone that the battalion travelled by train on 29 March. They arrived at Katerini on 31 March, where their initial task was to protect the left side of the entrance to the Olympus Pass, while the 23 Battalion took up its position on the right side. As the historian Angus Ross observed, this was finally where the German soldiers would become more than just an abstraction: 'This time the men were conscious of entering upon their first real operational role. Hearts beat a little faster as their owners realised they would almost certainly face the enemy in the positions they were about to occupy'.[4] The northern area of Greece had unexpectedly become strategically important to the Allies at the beginning of the month. As would be expected, the political and military developments behind this change are intricate, but its main elements fall into a convenient sequence, and were buttressed by predictable motivations.

In part because of Benito Mussolini's defeat in Libya in December 1940, the Italian dictator had become impatient to restore his reputation, and was 'overjoyed' when Greece came into sight as a prospective target for a fresh wave of Italian aggression, especially as Mussolini considered Greece 'such a miniscule opponent',[5] which would almost guarantee Italy the victory its leader craved for. Mussolini had already attacked Greece in October 1940 and again in March 1941, but these were ham-fisted efforts that saw Italian troops limp back to their base in neighbouring Albania. However, by April 1941, circumstances had left Greece in a far more vulnerable state. The previous month, Bulgaria had been occupied by the Germans, while Romania was already under Nazi control. Then, on 6 April, Hitler launched an attack on Greece and Yugoslavia, which led to the Nazi conquest of most of Yugoslavia within a fortnight, and the movement of Nazi troops from occupied Yugoslavia south into northern Greece. The direction at which these dominoes were falling made it plain that Greece was bound to be the next country to be subject to an Axis occupation.

So the New Zealanders had fortuitously been sent to Greece at just the right time to assist with the defence of that country. The British War Cabinet had decided that it was preferable to have the New Zealand troops, along with other Allied brigades and divisions, positioned in Greece to confront German expansion in the southern Balkans, rather than deploy them in North Africa to chase the remnants of Mussolini's defeated forces in Libya. However, this was a reactive strategy, and its deficiencies soon became apparent.

The Māori Battalion was put under the command of the New Zealand Division's 5th Brigade, and on 1 April, B Company took up its position on the Olympus Pass, about a kilometre ahead of the other companies in the battalion. Now the final preparations for battle began to be put in place. Communications were set up, pits were dug, barbed wire was put in place, ammunition transported, mortar platoons established in position, stretcher-bearers prepared, and evacuation routes determined.[6] However, one of the most hazardous tasks fell to Lieutenant Charles Bennett – who would later become commander of B Company – to conduct reconnaissance missions to ascertain the position and scale of the enemy force.

The timing was against the Allies, though. Not all of their divisions and accompanying air support were ready when the German offensive began, and the presence of New Zealand Division was used not so much as a defensive option, but merely as a means of delaying the Axis advance so that the remainder of the Allied troop support had a chance to be deployed in that theatre of conflict. Just how underprepared the Allied forces in Greece were was revealed when the Germans resorted to their now familiar tactic of blitzkrieg. On the evening of 6 April, the port at Pireaus, where the New Zealanders had only recently disembarked, was bombed by the Luftwaffe, inflicting widespread damage on ships and the port's facilities. The same day, German troops invaded Greece through Bulgaria, followed by another flank which advanced through Yugoslavia. Hitler threw 27 experienced combat divisions and 800 aircraft at the invasion, which was poised to easily overpower the Allied divisions in Greece.

By 9 April, Salonika had fallen to the Axis troops, and the direction of their advance was towards the Olympus Pass, while another German flank, stretching out from Yugoslavia, threatened to end up encircling all the Allied forces in the north of Greece. Having overrun Salonika, German Panzer and infantry units were again moving forward on 12 April, by which time it was abundantly clear that the 5th Brigade had no chance of defending the Olympus Pass, and so instead of the New Zealand troops holding their position, they were ordered to delay the Germans for as long as practicable, and then withdraw. This was when the Māori Battalion got its first taste of war, first as German shelling of the area began to get closer, then three days later, when enemy vehicles came into sight, and German patrols made forays into the area held by the New Zealanders.[7] On 16 April, heavy fog descended on the gorge, and platoons from the battalion sustained two casualties from enemy shells. From their positions in the gorge, B and C Companies fired in the rough direction they estimated the Germans to be in, and although they had no way of knowing, they succeeded in halting the enemy advance. Towards nightfall, a group of German troops tried to cross through B Company, but were repulsed. However, this offered nothing more than a reprieve, as the order to retreat was finally carried out.[8]

The weather was deteriorating rapidly by this stage, with winds ripping through the gorge, and rain lashing its slopes. The retreat could not be orderly under such circumstances, and with an enemy quickly penetrating the region, the situation was confused, and exacerbated by a lack of transport for the men. Manahi was somewhere in this lot, having fired and been fired at, he was now making his way along the slippery slopes of the gorge, out of the range of German infantry and hopefully artillery. B Company was the last to retreat, by which time they were making their way in total darkness under almost impossible conditions, as the Regimental Sergeant-Major wrote: 'The trip out was unmitigated Hell. Intensely dark .... Visibility almost nil. No stars for direction, compasses useless owing to windings of track. Grade was terrific, I should say 1 in 3 or 4. Speed was no more than 1 to 2 miles per hour'.[9]

Manahi was among the last of the battalion to join up with the other companies, and no sooner had he reached his colleagues when the order was given to the battalion to advance to a position on a nearby hill that overlooked a possible route the Germans might take at the rear of the Olympus Pass. More fighting was avoided at this point only because the Axis troops were getting bogged down in the muddy tracks, which had ground their advance almost to a halt.

With the news arriving on 22 April that the Greek Army in the north of the country had capitulated, the order to evacuate as soon as possible was given to the New Zealand troops. Realistically, there was no alternative, as it would have been hopeless trying to fend off the overwhelming advantage in troops, equipment, and air support that the Germans had. The New Zealanders went from Larisa to Volos, and then hugged the coast until they arrived at Lamia. The roads were packed with transport and troops, and at times, the retreat slowed to a standstill as the columns negotiated difficult roads and the inevitable jams caused by such congestion.

From Lamia, the troops of the battalion moved to Aghia Triada, and from there, to Molos. Once at Molos, the men began to dig themselves in, and succeeded in avoiding any casualties as a few German planes bombed from overhead. The next day, the soldiers travelled to Aghios Konstantinos, and although there were enemy planes in the sky for most of the day, they did not attack the battalion, possibly because its men were well dispersed, and many of them had sought refuge from the sun under the numerous olive trees around the village. Some other members of the battalion in nearby locations did endure German bombing, however, and a few were killed. It was obviously still far too dangerous to risk travelling further at daytime, so only when the sun set did the battalion don their gear and start the final leg of the evacuation – an eight-hour, 240-kilometre journey to Marathon, which was where they were due to embark from nearby beaches.

As morning approached on 24 April, and with the German forces rapidly moving towards on the Greek capital to secure their claim to the country, the battalion, along with other soldiers from the defeated Allied force, slipped through the outskirts of the city and headed towards Porto Rafti, where they began to board the infantry landing ship HMS *Glengyle*[10] at around nine o'clock in the evening. The vessel was soon crammed with fatigued soldiers who were still unable to relax as enemy planes were known to be in the vicinity, and German tanks were advancing with greater ease towards the coast. The mood on the ship was understandably anxious as the battalion's men headed for their next destination 300 kilometres south: Crete.

After the exhausting retreat through Greece, there was time on the ship for the men of the battalion to take stock of what had happened. Ten of their comrades had been killed in the fighting, and ninety-four had been taken prisoner, of whom eleven were wounded.[11] And it had been for a campaign that was hopeless from the outset, doomed by a lack of numbers to take on the better armed and experienced German divisions. The lack of any strategic planning was also exposed in the Greece campaign, which had been little more than a reflex response to German threat.

Manahi was among the 600 men of the battalion packed on to the *Glengyle*, but any discomfort at being squeezed into the vessel was easily mitigated by the relief at having escaped what would otherwise have been annihilation at the hands of the German Army. As the *Glengyle* powered away from Greece as fast as its engines enabled it to, the tail of the Luftwaffe lashed out, in the form of Messerschmitt 109s and Junker 87 Bs (commonly known as the Stukas) strafing and bombing the ship, which was responded to with the men on deck opening fire with all the weapons at their disposal. This, along with the strength of the ship's anti-aircraft armament,[12] was sufficient to eventually deter the enemy attackers.[13] Having left under the cover of darkness (around 4.30 in the morning), by the time there was enough light for an aerial attack, the ship was almost out of range of the Luftwaffe anyway, and so the assaults it faced were short-lived and unsuccessful.[14] As Crete neared, the tension on board abated, but the mood among the troops was still subdued. This was in the immediate wake of many of their comrades being killed, wounded, or captured by the enemy. Manahi, like most of the rest of the soldiers on the ship, talked only about what was ahead of them in Crete, and did not discuss Greece at all. 'If someone talked about something that had happened in Greece – it might be about nothing really important – well, we all went silent as soon as we remembered the boys who had been killed … and Haane was like that. He didn't like to talk too much about anything to do with fighting. He'd rather talk about other things'.[15]

Manahi was now heading towards Suda Bay, a sheltered harbour on the north-west coast of Crete. There, the battalion was due to spend two or three days, joining forces with other Allied troops before heading en masse to Egypt. It was clear to all the men of the battalion that the German advance through Greece had been rampant, and so while there was some relief at having escaped from the mainland, the island that they were en route to was still vulnerable, and most of the men probably sensed that it was at most only a question of a month or so until Crete also fell under German control.

By around 9.00 on the morning of 25 April (Anzac Day) Crete came into view for the men on the *Glengyle*, but any sense of reprieve that the battalion felt at being out of danger suddenly evaporated when, as they approached the harbour, they saw the slumped carcass of the British heavy cruiser HMS *York*, which had been attacked by Italian motor assault boats the previous month. At 2.00 that afternoon, the convoy of ships from Greece, including the *Glengyle*, entered the harbour and dropped anchor.

Crete was crucial for Allied strategy in the eastern Mediterranean. As long as the British held it, the Germans could not consider the area totally secure, which had implications for the German-controlled oilfields at Ploesti[16] (that could be reached by Allied bombers if the British foothold in Crete was strengthened). And if the island was taken by the enemy, the safety of the Suez Canal (which was still in British control but which could be reached by German bombers if the Axis forces established themselves in Crete) would be in jeopardy. Crete is a substantial island, though, with an area of 8,336 square kilometres. So there was at least the possibility that with sufficient forces, the Allies could hold it in the face of an enemy attack, and maybe even use it for a future counter-attack against German interests in the region.

There were also deficiencies with the island, however, from a tactical perspective. Suda Bay was Crete's only major harbour, and the few facilities it had for larger ships were generally inadequate. On the southern coast of the island, which was where a modern port was most needed for supplies of troop movements, all that existed were a series of small fishing villages, which would have been as much a hindrance as a help for the logistics of large-scale deployments of men. And separating these two coasts of Crete was a mountain range, the spine of which arched along an east-west line, and which contained only a few rough tracks linking the north of the island to the south.[17]

Given Crete's strategic importance, however, Allied High Command determined that it should be defended, and so turned the retreat from mainland Greece as an opportunity to strengthen the hold on the island. In the final week of April, General Bernard Freyberg (who held a Victoria Cross, and had been the first soldier on the beach at Gallipoli in World War One) was put in command of all Allied forces on Crete – what became known as Creforce – and was charged with defending it. But as an indication of the makeshift character of Allied planning in this theatre of the war, Freyberg was only informed that his troops were to take part in the defence of Crete on 30 April.[18] From the start, he was not hopeful of the prospect of defending the island without adequate naval and air support, and a much larger body of troops, all of which were promised, but at an unspecified future date. At best, Freyberg believed his troops could withstand an airborne attack, but not indefinitely.[19]

With its unsuitable geography, and the slightly panicked nature of the arrival of thousands of Allied troops, it is little wonder that from the moment of landing, the movement of men and equipment in this hurried transit was a shambles. Because the harbour in Suda Bay was not sufficiently deep, ferries were sent to unload the troops from the *Glengyle* and take them ashore. Manahi and his friends disembarked into a scene of 'total confusion'.[20] The dock was choked with men, equipment, a few trucks trying to squeeze their way through, commanding officers attempting to bring order to the scene, and local port workers doing their best to organise things, often with the opposite effect: 'We didn't know what was happening, and there were no orders for us', so we got off the boat, but after that, we just waited while everything was sorted out'.[21]

The men of the Māori Battalion looked as unkempt as any of the other troops landing that day, but with one crucial exception. The soldiers of the battalion still had most of their heavier weapons with them. Despite orders to dump all weapons but their rifles, the New Zealanders had kept their Bren gun and three-inch mortar that they had somehow managed to smuggle on board the *Glengyle*. As the writer of official history of the Crete Campaign observed in light of forthcoming events, 'the scepticism of those who refused to part with their hard-kept weapons had been bitterly justified'.[22]

The immediate task was to get the battalion out of the chaos of the port, and to their first destination – on the outskirts of the town of Platanias. It was not until after dark that they started their march out of Suda Bay, and that night, they slept on the side of the road, bearing the chilly temperatures with no blankets.[23] The next morning, the battalion had to shift its location slightly as it had been misdirected the previous day.[24] It was to act as the reserve for 5 (New Zealand) Brigade in its defence of the strategically vital airfield at Maleme.

By 30 April, Manahi was among those troops who were already in position and preparing defences with whatever told they could lay their hands on, even digging trenches with their bayonets and helmets at times. With initial preparations completed, the war was momentarily put to the back of the minds of the battalion's troops. They frequented local cafés, and helped themselves to the oranges that were ripening just at that time.[25]

During this surreal interval of peace, the Wehrmacht's commanders were finalising their plans to snatch Crete from the Allies. From the German perspective, Crete was the final stage of their campaign to conquer Greece, and they were committed to applying the same overwhelming force to secure the island. The 9th Fliegerkorps – the Luftwaffe's autonomous airborne unit – would lead the assault. It comprised fighter, bomber, and transport aircraft, as well as a complete airborne division, which would be supported by a mountain division that would make a landing by sea (supported by the German Navy).[26] All this was only possible, however, if the Germans succeeded in gaining mastery of the air over Crete, and for that to happen, the airfield at Maleme had to be neutralised.

On 3 May, as preparations for the German assault were being completed, the Māori Battalion was again being shifted, this time to a position between Platanias and the nearby river of the same name. This was part of the contribution to the defence of the Maleme airfield, which was about eight kilometres to the west of Platanias. If the Germans managed to capture the airfield, the battalion's orders were to both prevent the enemy advancing eastwards, and defend the coast to the north from a German seaborne landing. Manahi's company was stationed with C Company overlooking the river, defending enemy approaches from the west and south.[27] Once they had dug themselves in, planted mines, and erected barbed wire,[28] the men from B and C Companies familiarised themselves with the surrounding terrain – often clambering over goat tracks – and practiced tactics to defeat various forms of anticipated attack from by the enemy,[29] which everyone now knew was on its way.

The German assault on Crete commenced with force on the evening of 13 May 1941, when Maleme 'got its first serious battering' by the Luftwaffe,[30] and the following day, the bombardment intensified as more German aircraft joined in on the attack. The paltry RAF presence on the island was promptly dispatched with by the enemy, and within just four days, the Luftwaffe had achieved complete mastery of the airspace over Crete[31] – exactly what it required as a prelude for a ground invasion.

The operational instruction for 5 Brigade, to which the Māori Battalion had been assigned, required that 'in the event of the enemy making an airborne or seaborne attack on any part of the area, to counter-attack and destroy him immediately', and that 'the whole essence of the bde's work is a spirited defence'.[32] Throughout the days leading up to 20 May, the battalion could hear the enemy planes bombing Suda Bay, but this was a sufficient distance away not to be an immediate threat, and apart from occasional machine-gunning from German planes, the battalion's training and preparations for the enemy's imminent land assault continued.

On 16 May, Dittmer gathered the battalion's officers together for a conference, and it was then they discovered the sort of force they were expected to be up against. Within the next three days, the colonel predicted, 500 German bombers would strafe the area, after which 25,000 airborne troops, augmented by a landing force of another 10,000 soldiers, would invade Crete.[33] Within hours, B Company's officers, Captain Rangiataahua Kiniwe Royal, Lieutenants Henry Te Rupe Vercoe and Horton Oliphant Stewart, and Second Lieutenant Ruhi Pene, had briefed their men on what lay ahead of them. The scale of the enemy force must have been daunting when these troops first heard of it, but they had no choice but to prepare to repel the enemy, whatever its size.

Manahi and those around him were each handed 100 rounds of ammunition, and were ordered to remain in positions all day. Although the next few days passed without event, fourteen kilometres to the east, the men could hear the pounding of the relentless German bombing of Suda Bay, and see the smoke from burning ships churning in the sky, while just eight kilometres in the other direction, they could see dozens of enemy planes dive-bombing the Maleme airfield, destroying just about everything in the immediate vicinity. Then, as that target started to be obliterated, Messerschmitts flew back and forth at tree-top height, following the line of the road from Maleme to Canae, shooting or bombing at anything that looked like a useful target.[34]

On the morning of 20 May, Manahi was returning to his position in a shallow trench that lay about 1.5 kilometres from the coast. The bombardment of the nearby airfield had commenced again, just after sunrise, but this time it was noticeably heavier. Perhaps this was the final aerial assault before the German troop ships landed? Manahi had just finished breakfast when he looked up, as did all the men around him, and saw gliders discharging dozens, then hundreds, then thousands of enemy paratroopers. One of the battalion members described the scene: 'The lumbering dark-bellied formations of German planes released their deadly cargo as they flew westward to Maleme ... the air was filled with billowing parachutes .... Canisters were hanging from some of the parachutes, while airborne troops swayed in most of the others. The foliage of the young grape bushes forming a green belt to the very edge of the airfield suddenly became dotted with colours. Almost like instant mushrooms cast from the heavens'.[35] For another Māori soldier, crouching behind a small protrusion of rock, it was an almost surreal experience: 'It was a beautiful sight, and because it was something new, something unique to any warfare, we were dumbfounded and we looked at the planes in amazement more than anything else'.[36]

There was heavy fighting around the airfield, but the Māori Battalion were separated from the initial area of engagement by 21, 22, and 23 Battalions. The first batch of German paratroopers were out of range of the Māori Battalion, but were occasionally close enough that they could see each other. As the fighting intensified at the Maleme airfield during the early afternoon, Brigadier Hargest – Commander of the 5th Brigade – decided to keep the Māori Battalion as a reserve in case the battle spread beyond the area of the airfield,[37] but as the afternoon wore on, it became evident to him that this reserve force would have to be called into action as the defensive lines began to be broken by the increasing numbers of Germans that were being landed in the vicinity.

Late that afternoon, the enemy looked like it was on the verge of seizing the airfield. An urgent call for assistance came from 22 Battalion, which had all four of its infantry companies and its headquarters involved in the thick of the battle. Dittmer was instructed to send one of the companies of the Māori Battalion for support, and chose B Company, most probably because it was the furthest away from the fighting, and was therefore of least defensive value in its present location. B Company was given the order to stand by for deployment, and a route was determined that would curve inland before arriving at the airfield from the south. However, Captain Royal, who had just returned to service after being in hospital for the previous two days, was unfamiliar with this course, and so decided to lead the company along the main road, and confront directly any Germans they found along the way.

At 7.00 that evening, B Company left its position overlooking Platanias, and marched to Maleme, a journey of about thirteen kilometres. Along the way, the company encountered a few German paratroopers, whom they 'cleaned up without much trouble'.[38] Then, just before reaching its destination, two paratroopers jumped out right in front of Midwood and Manahi. On seeing this group of Māori soldiers, the Germans called out 'we surrender'. Midwood described what happened next: '[of] course, I got down on my knee with my rifle. They [the Germans] were still standing with their hands up. And within a matter of seconds these two dropped to the ground. At the same time, they opened fire and I copped it in the chest. Then what happened, Haane [Manahi] … lobbed a grenade over … Pine Timihou and one or two others charged in and started bayoneting wounded and all'.[39] In an instant, the fury of fighting took hold of the men. Manahi and his comrades, with bayonets mounted, charged at the enemy, shooting then stabbing. Twenty-four Germans were killed in this encounter, as were another eight further along the road to the airfield. It was almost certainly the first time bayonets were used by New Zealand troops in the Second World War,[40] and for the troops employing this weapon, it took a bit of getting used to at first, as a battalion member recollected: 'Many times, when the bayonet went in, they would have to fire a round to create the looseness to get it out. In most cases, they just put their foot on the body of the opponent and jerked their rifles'.[41]

The rest of the Allied forces in this part of Crete were having less fortune in fending off the Germans, and shortly after making contact with 22 Battalion, which was losing its grip on the airfield, B Company withdrew back to Platanias. There was a short period where the Māori Battalion now waited for fresh orders. As far as the Commander-in-Chief of the German forces in Crete, General Student, was concerned, the capture of the Maleme airfield was the point where the battle for Crete was won.[42] However, the Allies were not about to concede a defeat, and the Māori Battalion was selected (together with the 20 Battalion) to form part of the counter-attack. Both battalions advanced west to the airfield in the early hours of the morning of 22 May, and the closer they got, the stronger the German resistance they encountered. The delays caused by tackling enemy machine-gun posts meant that by the time they reached the airfield, the battalions would be fighting in daylight. Fighting intensified around sunrise, but after an exhausting six hours of skirmishes, in which the men of the Māori Battalion distinguished themselves, the impossibility of re-taking the airfield became evident to their commanders, and the troops were ordered to pull back.

From a distance, the encounters between Māori and Germans differed slightly from engagements involving other Allied troops. A sergeant in 20 Battalion described one such episode of fighting: 'Sounds of German attack. Heavy fire steadily approaching. Much tracer. Then blood-curdling tracer from the Maoris as they went over to counter attack. Immediate decrease in German fire. Confusion, pandemonium and war cries for a few minutes then silence'.[43] The reason for the silence from the Germans was explained by Sergeant Edward Morgan, originally from Whakarewarewa: 'the bastards are still running like Hell'.[44]

Despite these occasional flourishes, overall, there the battalion endured considerable losses. Another hundred Māori troops were killed, injured, or went missing as a result of the failed assault on the Maleme airfield,[45] adding to the casualties that the battalion suffered in Greece. Having failed to capture the airfield, the portent of defeat loomed large for the Allied troops on Crete. Although there were a series of rearguard actions which were designed mainly to slow down the enemy advance, the continual flow of German troops into the island meant that at some point in the near future, the Allied soldiers would be forced off Crete. The number of Māori wounded was now so great, and the transport shortage so acute, that Dittmer was left with no option but to organise the battalion to retreat, leaving behind those who were injured, with the almost vain hope that they would somehow find their own back to the battalion. Manahi was among those who were wounded in close combat with the Germans on 23 May 1941 (he was classified as a battle casualty),[46] but still managed to remain with his company and was able to fight (even though military authorities initially considered his injury so serious that his next of kin was notified).[47] Manahi had taken a shot in his upper body and suffered from severe blood loss. According to his son, the wound was so serious that one of Manahi's B Company friends from Ōhinemutu – Martin McRae – believed that Manahi was close to dying. 'Martin McRae grabbed all the old man's loot', Rau explained with a grin. They thought he was going to die, so they took all the stuff the old man had taken from the Germans'.[48]

The Māori Battalion was ordered to be the rearguard in the withdrawal of the 23 Battalion – something that infuriated Dittmer because of the danger it placed his men in: 'I went extremely rude about being left in such a manner but had little time to go into the reason for it. I knew that enemy would see other units going over high ground to East and then 28 Bn would catch it'.[49] However, this withdrawal was not a retreat from Crete, but part of the preparation for a counter-offensive. As the companies of the battalion prepared to respond to the

German advance, Dittmer was called to a brigade conference at which Brigadiers Kippenberger and Inglis were 'anxious to use the Maoris in a night attack and recover the ground. It was clear to all of us that if this was not feasible, Crete was lost'. However, it looked like an almost impossible operation for the battalion to undertake: 'darkness, olive trees, vineyards, no good start-line, only 400 men in the battalion'. Dittmer was understandably hesitant, as was a senior staff officer for the division, Colonel Gentry, who pointed out that 'the Maoris were our last fresh battalion, and if used now, we would not be able to hold a line tomorrow'.[50] It was clear that exiting the island was the only sensible tactic open to Creforce.

By 26 May, the Germans were advancing swiftly eastwards through Crete, and the new defensive line that the New Zealand battalions had set was already beginning to tear as the Germans strafed the New Zealand troops with aircraft fire, and used mortars and machine-guns to attack the New Zealand positions. There was little chance of permanently holding this line, especially given the dwindling logistical support the Allied troops were receiving, and the exhaustion of so many of the soldiers. Moreover, the nerves of the battalion's men were getting 'ragged' as a result of the relentless low-flying attacks from German planes, and from a lack of sleep and meagre rations.[51]

The following day descended into confusion for the Allied forces in Crete. Communications had broken down in some cases, and some of the men of the battalion had just about run out of food. They had been ordered to go to Suda Bay, and from there, to head due south to Sfakia, a distance of about thirty kilometres. However, some of the orders failed to trickle down through the chain of command, while what seemed like wave after wave of German attacks forced the battalion off the roads and paths during the daytime. A and B Companies, with the assistance of British commandoes (making up a total of about 130 men)[52] made up the rearguard of the retreating Creforce, but when the German assaults on their flanks intensified, the commanding officer ordered the men to fall back to a position behind the ridge that they had been defending. From there, the men moved south, taking unmapped tracks and routes that offered the best cover from enemy aircraft.

Most of the fighting on 27 May took place in an area known as 42nd Street, which was a sunken road, inland between Canea and Suda Bay. Heavier-than-average casualties were inflicted on B Company in particular as the fighting shifted from firing from a distance to close combat, often involving bayonet charges. And despite the losses that B Company sustained, the Germans came off this encounter far worse. Around 100 were bayoneted – a figure that was once thought to be exaggerated until a report of the action was released that revealed a count of over 100 German corpses with signs of bayonet wounds.[53]

Nobody was under any illusion by this stage, though, that any reversal in the war in Crete was possible. German ascendency was mounting, and slender victories along the path of withdrawal did nothing to alter this fact. If anything, the situation looked grave for Manahi's company. From the north, the enemy was moving with greater strength, speed, and confidence, and to the south, the escape route was impeded by the White Mountains.[54] This area was part of the mountain range that ran across the island, and comprised 'thirteen huge gorges ... ravines, forested crags and high-level plains ... and everywhere, there are rocks, so that then underfoot is as rugged as any you will find'.[55] The immediate task facing Manahi was to get from Stilos south to Askifou – a distance of around fifteen kilometres in a straight line, but through the sort of terrain described as 'an obstacle so formidable as almost to rank as a second enemy'.[56] Vehicles could only get the men so far, and for two days and nights, they struggled through this forbidding environment, discarding any of their equipment that was not absolutely vital in order to ease slightly their passage. Even as the men struggled through, they could hear the Germans 'getting a bit closer', and their gunfire 'getting louder and louder', and at one stage, they were told the enemy was 'just half an hour away',[57] which was all the incentive needed to keep pushing on to what the troops hoped would be sanctuary on the southern side of the island.

For all the soldiers enduring this crossing, the experience was exhausting, but for Manahi, who was injured, it was even more gruelling. He began to slip behind the main body of men and join the lengthening tail of stragglers which was shuffling and limping their way through the passes of this forbidding mountain range. Brigadier Hargest described the scene at the close of the first day of the ascent: 'Never will I forget it. As the sun fell the men struggled upwards lame and sleepy even after their rest but the road surfaces were galling them. Near Vrises there is a huge incline, steep and ending in a pass—near it was a rocky eminence which had been prepared for demolition by the RE. Just after we passed some fool ordered its explosion and up went the road in *front* of our tired troops and the Aust'.[58] The road was blown up by mistake, as it was timed to be exploded after the Allied troops had passed through. This made crossing this portion of the range even harder.

Once through the range, the next destination on the trail of the retreat was Sfakia. By the time the battalion reached this point, the southern coast of Crete was in sight, but on the morning of 29 May, more distressing news was received from the battalion's commanding officer. Dittmer was obliged to advise his men (against his protests to high command) that not all of them would be able to embark on the vessels waiting to ferry them away from the island. Six officers and 144 ranks would have to remain behind. The rest of the battalion marched on, and by the time they had crossed the White Mountains, they were entering the final phase of the withdrawal. By that evening, the remnants of the battalion had arrived at the embarkation area, awaiting the final order that would enable them to leave Crete. At 2.25 in the afternoon of 30 May, that order came that the first section of the Māori Battalion (colloquially known as the 'goers') which included Manahi,[59] would be moved to the embarkation beach at sunset. The remaining group, initially called the 'stayers', but soon grimly renamed the 'Suicide Company', were to stay on the island until the following day.

Manahi left Crete in the early hours of 31 May 1941. He was part of the convoy that departed under cover of darkness. The danger from the German force in Crete was not quite over, however. The troop ships were being escorted by four destroyers,[60] and as day broke, German bombers began to pepper the sky, searching for their prey, and forcing the vessels to take evasive action, as Dittmer later described: 'It was a real thrill during these attacks to see how the destroyers could be manoeuvred at full speed to dodge the sticks of bombs and delightful to watch the enthusiastic actions of the ship's anti aircraft gunners while they strafed the enemy bombers'.[61] Maybe Dittmer wrote this in a state of euphoria, because for Manahi and his comrades, it was a terrifying experience. Midwood, who had been badly wounded, recounted how they felt 'like sitting ducks', and that they were able to see the enemy planes get closer while not being able to do anything to stop them. 'We felt like easy targets really',[62] was his more realistic conclusion of the mood of the troops as the breath of German aggression exhaled over the seas south of Crete.

The Māori Battalion had suffered substantial casualties on Crete in their second major encounter with the Germans, and what turned out to be their second hasty retreat in the face of a better-equipped enemy. The only consolation the officers could draw from the experience in the previous two months was that most of their men had survived, and that they were now fully battle-hardened. For the troops themselves, Manahi, Midwood and a few others slowly got over their wounds, although they would not be fully healed by the time they arrived at their next destination – the safety of Alexandria in Egypt, 600 kilometres south-east of Crete.

But while there was sanctuary ahead, and the comfort of returning to a familiar area, the thoughts of many of the men were with those of the battalion who were left to catch the next convoy out of Crete, and the increased danger they would face from the encroaching German forces. All they could hope and pray for was that their comrades would have a speedy exit and would quickly be out of the reach of the Luftwaffe.

# NOTES

1. Interview with Arthur Midwood, Rotorua, 7 September 2009.
2. The *Cameronia* was 552 feet in length.
3. W Gardiner, *Te Mura o te Ahi: The Story of the Maori Battalion*, p. 48.
4. A Ross, *Official History of New Zealand in the Second World War 1939–45: 23 Battalion*, Wellington, War History Branch, Department of Internal Affairs, 1959, p. 29.
5. D Mack Smith, *Mussolini*, London, Weidenfeld and Nicholson, 1983, p. 268.
6. J F Cody, *28 (Maori) Battalion*, pp. 46–7.
7. M Soutar, *Nga Tama Toa: The Price of Citizenship*, p. 122.
8. Ibid., pp. 123–4.
9. Cited in J F Cody, *28 (Maori) Battalion*, p. 65.
10. The vessel was 570 feet in length.
11. W Gardiner, *Te Mura o te Ahi: The Story of the Maori Battalion*, p. 56.
12. J F Cody, *28 (Maori) Battalion*, p. 78.
13. Although the *Glengyle* had to make another trip to Greece to pick up more soldiers.
14. As the ship moved closer to Crete, it came under the protection of the RAF.
15. Interview with Arthur Midwood, Rotorua, 7 September 2009.
16. C W Koburger, *Wine-Dark Blood Red Sea: Naval Warfare in the Aegean, 1941–1946*, Westport, Greenwod Publishing,1999, pp. 14–5.
17. Ibid., p. 15.
18. D M Davin, *Official History of New Zealand in the Second World War 1939–45: Crete*, Wellington, War History Branch, Department of Internal Affairs 1953, p. 27.
19. Ibid., pp.35–6.
20. W Gardiner, *Te Mura o te Ahi: The Story of the Maori Battalion*, p. 58.
21. Interview with Arthur Midwood, Rotorua, 30 November 2009.
22. D M Davin, *Official History of New Zealand in the Second World War 1939–45: Crete*, p. 28.
23. W Gardiner, *Te Mura o te Ahi: The Story of the Maori Battalion*, p. 58; D M Davin, *Official History of New Zealand in the Second World War 1939–45: Crete*, p. 23.
24. J F Cody, *28 (Maori) Battalion*, p. 79.
25. Op. cit.
26. C W Koburger, *Wine-Dark Blood Red Sea: Naval Warfare in the Aegean, 1941-1946*, p. 15.
27. W Gardiner, *Te Mura o te Ahi: The Story of the Maori Battalion*, p. 58.
28. D M Davin, *Official History of New Zealand in the Second World War 1939–45: Crete*, p. 62.
29. F Baker, 1941, MA 52/4d, Archives New Zealand, in M. Soutar, *Nga Tama Toa: The Price of Citizenship*, p. 134.
30. D M Davin, *Official History of New Zealand in the Second World War 1939–45: Crete*, p. 63.
31. C W Koburger, *Wine-Dark Blood Red Sea: Naval Warfare in the Aegean, 1941-1946*, p. 15.
32. 5 Brigade Operation Instruction No. 4, May 1940, in D M Davin, *Official History of New Zealand in the Second World War 1939–45: Crete*, p. 66.
33. J F Cody, *28 (Maori) Battalion*, p. 89.
34. H G Dyer, *Ma Te Reinga*, p. 39.
35. J Mohi, 'Forty Years On', in H Lambert (ed.) *The Maori Battalion Remembers*, Auckland, 28 Maori Battalion Association, 1984, p. 59.
36. Cited in T Stevens (Director and Producer), *Maori Battalion March to Victory*, Television New Zealand documentary, 1990.
37. D M Davin, *Official History of New Zealand in the Second World War 1939–45: Crete*, p. 67.
38. J F Cody, *28 (Maori) Battalion*, p. 93.
39. A Midwood, 15 December 2004, in M Soutar, *Nga Tama Toa: The Price of Citizenship*, p. 137.
40. J F Cody, *28 (Maori) Battalion*, p. 93.
41. Cited in T Stevens (Director and Producer), *Maori Battalion March to Victory*, Television New Zealand documentary, 1990.
42. Case no. 24, Trial of Karl [sic] Student, British Military Court, Luneberg, Germany, 6 – 10 May 1946, A. Outline of the Proceedings, in *Law Reports of Trials of War Criminals. Selected and Prepared by the United Nations War Crimes Commission*, vol. IV, London, 1948, p. 118.
43. J G Sullivan, in J F Cody, *28 (Maori) Battalion*, p. 106.
44. E Morgan, in J F Cody, *28 (Maori) Battalion*, p. 106.
45. W Gardiner, *Te Mura o te Ahi: The Story of the Maori Battalion*, p. 67.
46. J F Cody, *Official History of New Zealand in the Second World War 1939–45: 21 Battalion*, Wellington, 1953, p. 260; New Zealand Military Forces, History Sheet, Haane Manahi, 39099, Form N. Z. 307.
47. New Zealand Military Forces, History Sheet, Haane Manahi, 39099, Form N. Z. 307.
48. Interview with Rau Manahi, 19 January 2010.
49. G Dittmer, in D M Davin, *Official History of New Zealand in the Second World War 1939–45: Crete*, p. 252.
50. Cited in H Kippenberger, *Infantry Brigadier*, Oxford, Oxford University Press, 1949, p. 69.
51. J F Cody, *28 (Maori) Battalion*, p. 115.
52. D M Davin, *Official History of New Zealand in the Second World War 1939–45: Crete*, p. 393.
53. J McLeod, *Myth and Reality: The New Zealand Soldier in World War Two*, Auckland, Reed Methuen, 1986, p. 101; W Gardiner, *Te Mura o te Ahi: The Story of the Maori Battalion*, p. 73.
54. T Simpson, *Operation Mercury: The Battle for Crete, 1941*, London, Pen and Sword Military, 1981, p. 262, in W Gardiner, *Te Mura o te Ahi: The Story of the Maori Battalion*, p. 74
55. L Wilson, *Crete: The White Mountains*, London, Cicerone Press, 2002, p. 11.
56. D M Davin, *Official History of New Zealand in the Second World War 1939–45: Crete*, p. 402.
57. Interview with Arthur Midwood, Rotorua, 30 November 2009.
58. J Hargest, in D M Davin, *Official History of New Zealand in the Second World War 1939–45: Crete*, p. 406.
59. Manahi was included in this group on the basis that he was married with a child, which gave him priority.
60. The destroyers were *Nizam, Kelvin, Khandahar,* and *Napier. Khandahar* broke down, and *Kelvin* was damaged by a German bomber.
61. G Dittmer, in J F Cody, *28 (Maori) Battalion*, p. 130.
62. Interview with Arthur Midwood, Rotorua, 7 September 2009.

# CHAPTER 6: North Africa

The evacuation of Crete would prove to be a mixed blessing for the Māori Battalion, and the rest of the New Zealand troops who were on their way to Egypt. There was no question that their escape from the island was preferable to capture and imprisonment by the enemy, but with the flushing out of the final remnants of the Allied force from Crete by the start of June, only a relatively small German occupying force would be needed on the island, with the surplus divisions freed up to be diverted by the German High Command to North Africa, where some of these soldiers would again encounter the Māori Battalion. And while the New Zealanders and with other Allied divisions in Greece and Crete had been fighting the Germans, the Axis divisions in North Africa had taken advantage of this distraction to move eastwards from the Libyan coastal city of El Agheila, forcing the Allies back into Egypt, and leaving only the coastal stronghold of Tobruk (the Libyan town about 120 kilometres from the Egyptian border) in Allied hands.

There was also a new force that the Allies were to encounter in this theatre of the war – the German Lieutenant-General Erwin Rommel.[1] Already, he had earned a reputation among soldiers on both sides for the brilliance of his innovative approach to desert warfare, his capacity to engineer tactical surprises on the enemy, his intuitive sense for the ebb and flow of battles, and the extraordinary devotion he inspired in his troops. In the German Afrika Korps led by Rommel, the men of the Māori Battalion would encounter an enemy that was even more vigorous than that which had pursued them through mainland Greece and Crete, and in an environment which the Germans by now had become fully acclimatised to.

As Alexandria loomed on the horizon, Major Dyer spoke to the men of the Battalion, who were still exhausted and frayed by the previous months' fighting, 'Let's tidy ourselves as best we can, smarten ourselves up and march off the ship like the good soldiers we are.' One of the men wrote, 'There was little we could do, but we worked with a will and did what we could. The results weren't spectacular either. When the ship was finally tied up and the gangway down, we marched off and formed up in company groups, then with Major Dyer leading and Rangi Royal following, we marched off to the trucks waiting to take us to Amiriya camp',[2] on the outskirts of Alexandria.

The desert conjures up images seas of sand, glistening under a scorching sun, an arid landscape of brown set against an endless stretch of cloudless blue sky, but within a few hours of the battalion walking down the gangway from their troop ship on 1 June, they were surprised by the almost freezing temperatures. It could take a week or two for some men to adjust to the cycle of extremely hot days succeeded by shiveringly cold nights. 'Oh yes, it was cold alright', Midwood remembered. 'We thought the desert would be hot, but at night, it got very cold, and we would be shivering under our blankets sometimes'.[3]

Thrust into North Africa, where the lines of battle advanced and retreated unexpectedly and often with great speed, Manahi and his comrades underwent frequent training on aspects such as navigation in the desert, tactical approaches to desert warfare, and received lectures on the strategic situation affecting the armies in this region. What was evident to the troops from the start was that the demands of fighting in this new terrain, against an enemy which was already used to the surrounds, were going to be both difficult and dangerous.

When it came to orders regarding equipment, many of the men in the Māori Battalion were notoriously defiant, not out of any surliness but because one's own weapons were necessary for survival (hence the decision by the men of B Company to keep their machine guns and mortars in Crete after being ordered to abandon them) and because captured enemy weapons and other military paraphernalia had become a prized currency. It was probably after one of the mopping up efforts in Crete, in which wounded German troops were killed by men of B Company, that Manahi, who was almost certainly involved in this, collected some baubles from the corpses of the slain enemy troops. He also managed to smuggle these with him into Egypt, either with a view to eventually taking them back to New Zealand as trophies, or to sell or trade in Egypt should the need arise. However, when one of Manahi's friends decided to cash in on these items, it almost caused an altercation, as Rau recounted: 'They got all this loot from the Germans in Crete but when they ended up in Cairo, Martin McRae (also from Ohinemutu) sold it all, and the old man was bloody well going to kill him. They were about to get into a fight but this other fellah stopped him, though he was just as bad, and that was Charlie Shelford' (later a Distinguished Conduct Medal recipient).[4]

After the physical and emotional stress of Crete in particular, the men of the Māori Battalion needed some time to recuperate – a fact that the army readily appreciated. The inventory of losses for the battalion after just nine weeks' fighting made for dismal reading. Of the 730 men who had landed at Greece, 84 were now dead, and 161 were prisoners of the enemy, and another 108 had made it to Egypt but were wounded.[5] Morale was still high, but the shock of intense fighting and the loss of friends and whānau were not experiences that could simply be brushed off by going to a new location. As the battalion historian Monty Soutar put it, 'each man had to find his own way to cope with the ghosts of Crete'.[6]

The enforced break from fighting was beneficial to the men, but they were never free from the routines of army life. Within two days of arriving in Egypt, they were issued with new uniforms, were given a series of medical inspections, and went through the now very familiar muster parades. In the spare moments, many of the soldiers wrote letters home, but not Manahi.[7] It is possible that he was already beginning to experience an emotional estrangement from his wife, and decided that there were better things he could occupy his free time with.

With the men fitted out for the desert, on 3 June, they embarked on the 200-kilometre trip inland from Alexandria to Helwan, which was followed by a dusty truck drive a few kilometres south to the camp at Garawi. Although it looked like a desolate setting, it was just 20 kilometres from Cairo, and so when a week's 'survivors' leave was given, the majority of the men in the Battalion, including Manahi, went to the Egyptian capital to sample what it had to offer them.

For Manahi, the particular attraction was in the city's red-light districts, where he sought out the company of women of more relaxed virtues. One woman in particular became enamoured with him – the famous courtesan known as Tiger Lil. Manahi developed a reputation for his fondness for women in Egypt, and for his liaisons with Tiger Lil. As Rau explained, 'I remember back in the late 1940s, whenever they used to have a bit of a booze-up back at the old place, with the boys from Ohinemutu, and I used to listen to the stories about Tiger Lil. Whenever B-Company were around, she would say, "Where is Jacques?" That's what she called the old man. He was her favourite'.[8]

The seven days' leave went by quickly, and as their money ran out – for some sooner than others – the men of the battalion returned to base. There was more training in the days that followed, but on Sunday 15 June, a special church service was held, led by the battalion's chaplain, the Reverend Kahi Takimoana Harawira. Harawira used this opportunity to focus the men's minds on some of the more sombre issues they had recently had to contend with, especially the death of comrades, and the killing of enemy troops. Harawira offered thanks for the deliverance of these men from the fighting they had recently been a part of, and spoke in memory of those who had not survived it. The service concluded with a mournful rendition of 'Piko nei te Matenga' ('In solemn grief we bow our heads'), prompting many in the congregation of hardened soldiers to shed tears. The loss of friends, and the strain of homesickness were emotions that were normally bottled up in the minds of the men, but this service allowed a rare release of feelings. Harawira concluded with a karakia, after which a hākari was held to lift the tapu of the service.

With this cultural indulgence satisfied, the commanding officers of the battalion set to work that afternoon reorganising the companies, filling in any gaps with a recent arrival of fresh volunteers, and commencing yet another round of training. Although the terrain in this part of Egypt was much easier than that which the battalion had strugged with, especially in Crete, the temperatures in Cairo in June (the hottest month of the year) averaged 35 degrees Celsius during the day, and sometimes peaking in the mid-40s, while at night, it could drop down to under 15 degrees. The heat made marching hard-going, but it was necessary if the troops were to be a match for Rommel's men.

Apart from regular marching and other physical training, there was not much else to occupy the men. Midwood recalled how 'most of the time, we just filled in time some way or other. You couldn't do much. Out in the desert, there was no mischief, so you just talked, rested, or you played games. We would make a ball out of any bits and pieces we could find and kick it around and run with it. But in that heat, you couldn't really even do that'.[9] With the inevitable boredom that grew as the weeks passed, discipline in the battalion's ranks occasionally showed signs of sagging. This led to an order being published on 1 July, which observed that 'too many men are wandering around the lines', and that 'in future such personnel will be collected and sent on a long route march if they are absent from training parades without reasonable excuse'.[10]

This was sufficient to get the troops back to full commitment, and despite the energy-sapping heat, they continued with training, including compass skills, which was vital in a terrain where there were often too few landmarks to provide a sense of orientation. There were no tracks or trails, maybe only the occasional crumbling ruin, no signposts, and in some parts of the desert, nothing but billowing mounds of sand, which could change form within a day if whipped up by the fierce arid winds that sometimes made visibility (let alone getting a bearing) and any movement at all practically impossible.

Other challenges the troops faced included 'Wog guts',[11] which was a generic term applied to a range of types of food poisoning or diarrhoea, heat fatigue, the incessant presence of flies, and the ever-present sand. The sand – where it was deep – made any efforts at trench-digging futile as the walls would slide back in as soon as they were dug out. Yet, where the sand deposits were shallower, the men had the exhausting task of cutting unto land that felt almost as hard as rock. And the sand got everywhere: in clothing, food and water, machinery, and weapons. This was to be Manahi's environment for the remainder of the time he fought in the war.

Yet, as much as the terrain was 'a land of bare stones and drifting sand, of escarpments and defiles, of low ridges and shallow depressions',[12] once troops became accustomed to its nuances, they could use it to their advantage.[13] And there were probably no men among all the New Zealand soldiers who knew how to handle difficult terrain as well as those from Ōhinemutu, who had been brought up in a hazardous landscape, and so had developed an intuition about the character of territories that was to prove especially useful in the desert in North Africa.

Another feature of fighting in this theatre was the expanse of land that had to be covered from base camp to the front line. In Crete, the front line and base camp often came perilously close to being the same thing. In North Africa, however, the men would be transported by trucks, at night (which made the already poorly-defined routes all the more hazardous) to where they would prepare to fight as soon as the sun rose. Manahi now had to adjust to a new routine. Daytime was occasionally occupied by fighting, but otherwise, by as little movement as possible, as the men on both sides of the front kept still in their trenches, using their groundsheets to screen out the scorching sun. As night set in, they would dig to make their fighting pits (or slit trenches) a bit deeper. Given the unsuitable geology of the region, these pits were typically only deep enough to allow one man to lie horizontally and shelter from shell blasts and enemy fire.[14] As soon as it was dark, the troops would also have a meal (the other main meal of the day was just before sunrise), and try to catch up with some rest as the temperatures cooled (and the flies retreated).[15]

There were occasionally distractions to this routine, however. The Olympic Games scheduled for 1940 had been cancelled because of the war, but in July 1941, it was decided that a competition would be held among the men of various battalions in and around Cairo, as a sort of substitute. The swimming contest was held at Helwan on 8 July, where Manahi won the 50-yard race.[16] 'All the boys who won those races were from Rotorua, they were all good swimmers', is how Rau proudly remembers the winners at this tournament.[17]

On 16 August, Manahi was again on the move. He was being deployed, along with the rest of the battalion, to El Tahag – which lay about thirty kilometres west of Ismailia.[18] This was 'a huge camp, composed mainly of marquee-type tents with a lesser number of bell tents and a few wooden buildings of Army style',[19] where the battalion was to be kept until the next part of Allied strategy in the desert was finalised. The Germans were to the west of Egypt, so there was little doubt that in the following month or so, that was where the next destination was for the battalion. In the meanwhile, there were further rounds of training, in which the new additions to the companies were merged with the 'old hands' who had been hardened by many months of training and fighting. There was a generous roster of leave organised for the men at this time, partly for maintaining morale, but also possibly because the commanders knew that there would be few options for any sort of leisure once at the front line, facing the enemy.

On 3 September – the second anniversary of the start of the war – Manahi boarded the train carrying the battalion to El Alamein, which was a small coastal town just over 100 kilometres west of Alexandria. As soon as they disembarked, they were led to a fleet of trucks that transported them thirty kilometres south to a position known as Kaponga Box, where the Petrol Company was in the process of constructing defences.[20] The setting was described as 'a semi-circle of low, steep-sided ridges in an area where the navigable desert ... where mechanical transport could move freely, [and which] was, between north and south, only forty miles wide'.[21] Manahi was involved in the construction of a section of road extending sixteen kilometres from Kaponga Box towards El Alamein. However, the rate of the battalion's work astonished the 5th Field Company engineers, who witnessed the Māori troops building the road at four times the speed suggested in their Field Service Pocket Books.[22] Martin McRae had been put in charge of the construction and engineering works, utilising his experience as an engineer and surveyor's assistant.[23]

With their work at Kaponga Box completed, ahead of schedule, on 5 October, the battalion was again on the move, once more heading west (and closer to the enemy). Over two nights, they travelled in trucks across terrain with no tracks, let alone roads, and arrived at a location known as Baggush Box – a stony, sandy area of uninhabited desert adjacent to the Mediterranean[24] – around 150 kilometres west of El Alamein.

It was not until late November 1941 that Manahi saw conflict again. Since leaving Crete, he had spent close to six months being deployed in various parts of Egypt, training, digging trenches, and joining his friends in the nearest town whenever they had leave. The first signs that there would soon be a resumption of fighting came on 8 November, when the battalion's bayonets were collected for sharpening, and the next day, the troops were issued with battle dress. All this was ostensibly in aid of an exercise involving a number of battalions working together. However, this time it would not be merely another exercise, but the start of a campaign to drive the enemy out of North Africa – one which would be fought for the next eighteen months.[25] Of course, none of the troops could have known, as winter began to be felt in the desert, that they were about to be plunged into this arduous war of attrition. After all, as far as the Māori Battalion's experience went, battles were fervidly-fought but short-lived events, followed by months of inactivity. One-and-a-half years of relatively frequent fighting would probably have been inconceivable to most of the men at this time.

On 11 November, the 5th Brigade, of which the Māori Battalion was a part, was again moving west, arriving near Siwa later that day – a location just forty kilometres from the Libyan border. This was where the High Command had decided to assemble the entire New Zealand force – all 20,000 troops. It was the first time that all the New Zealanders had been together, and over the next few days, they made new acquaintances and shared experiences as the anticipation for a major advance built among this mass of soldiers.

The move into Libya was to be made by an enormous convoy of vehicles. On 15 November, the engines of almost 3000 trucks spluttered into life, filling the air with fumes and smoke as they moved the thousands of soldiers closer to the border. As they reached the western edges of Egypt, the troops made their way through an easily-severed barbed-wire defence, and on 18 November, crossed about 25 kilometres into Libya, in the direction of Tobruk.

For Manahi and his fellow soldiers, this was the first time they had advanced into enemy terrain (as opposed to being chased out of Allied-held territory), and the effect on morale was considerable,[26] which was just as well, as other troops were already engaged in clashes with the enemy that had begun further to the north a few days earlier. The Māori Battalion's role in this huge push against the enemy in east Libya was to seize Sollum, which was part of the strategy of cutting off Axis traffic along the coast road leading to Bardia.[27] The battalion moved onto a plateau around three kilometres west of Sollum. C and D Companies spearheaded the attack, lunging at the lightly-defended Italian barracks just before sunrise. The raid was a success, with more than 250 Italian prisoners taken,[28] but 20 of the battalion had been killed in the fighting, and a further 34 wounded.[29] Manahi was not involved in this episode of fighting, but was sent with the rest of B Company to occupy Fort Musaid, which after numerous attacks was little more than a collection of crumbling walls and piles of rubble. It was important, though, because its elevated location made it a good defensive position as the Allies advanced in this area, and because it formed a vital link between the rest of the battalion, which was now on the coast, and 23 Battalion, which had occupied Fort Capuzzo to the west.

The Germans, with their logistics lines stretched too thinly in the region, and having had their Italian allies defeated in some of the key local positions, had no option but to retreat. Rommel ordered his Afrika Corps back to Tobruk.[30] However, the Desert Fox, as he was known, used this tactical withdrawal as an opportunity to strike back at the Allies. A column of the 21 Panzer Division charged towards Musaid (with other columns of the Division heading towards the coast and Capuzzo). In the evening of 26 November, Musaid was subject to heavy German shelling, but as Manahi and the other men occupying the fort had built adequate trenches, they suffered no casualties from this barrage.[31] The Germans then began a further phase of advance, along the eastern flank of Musaid. A short but intense period of fighting followed, in which B Company managed to fend off the German advance, and kill 76 Germans in the process.[32] During the fighting, a German light tank managed to kill two members of B Company before it got caught in one of the trenches. While its crew was struggling desperately to dislodge their vehicle, Manahi, Martin McRae and others attacked them: 'the boys went mad and went after it' was one officer's observation.[33] Having killed the crew, three soldiers from Rotorua jumped in the vehicle and, after fumbling around for a few moments, Manahi managed to drive the tank, while McRae worked out how to fire its gun. Heading in the direction of some stray German artillery units, Manahi and his 'crew' cut off a 75 mm gun carrier, and once they had captured it, gave it to B Company of 23 Battalion. They then succeeded in capturing an enemy armoured car before jumping out of the tank.[34]

In the aftermath of the battle, Manahi was among those from B Company who ventured out to obtain whatever they could from their fallen foe. Hall had been killed in the fighting, and so there was a sense of needing to assert utu to avenge his death in some way. Weapons and ammunition were taken, and so too were other 'souvenirs', such as medals, watches, and whatever other items could be carried away.[35]

Manahi and the other B Company troops remained at Musaid until 30 November when they were relieved by the arrival of 23 Battalion. The Company was then able to leave its post and return to the rest of their Māori Battalion comrades. At 3 am on 11 December, the battalion once more started heading west, with their immediate objective being Point 209 – one of several strategic points that made up part of the 5th Brigade's advance to Gazala (about sixty kilometres west of Tobruk), where Rommel had established a new defensive line. Taking Point 209 would be a difficult task for the battalion, though. Its surrounds were mined, and it was defended with anti-tank guns, machine guns and mortars. B Company led the attack on the site, with Manahi getting his first experience of raiding an enemy stronghold (and helping to take 200 Italian prisoners in the process). Sixteen kilometres further west was the next planned target to assault: Point 182. However, instead of meeting fierce resistance, which all had anticipated, the battalion found the site deserted. The Italians had fled in such a hurry that they had left much of their equipment behind, something that further enriched Manahi and the other 'ratters' as these souvenir hunters were known.[36]

The final location to take before their planned arrival in Gazala was Point 181. After just over an hour of brisk fighting, the battalion overran this position as well (Manahi had been part of the group that charged the defences head-on),[37] taking

382 prisoners from the Italian Parvia Division, and suffering only three fatalities and 27 wounded.[38]

The bravery of Manahi's friend Charlie Shelford in the attack on Point 181 was acknowledged by his commanding officers. As his platoon was under heavy machine-gun fire, Shelford volunteered to silence those enemy troops manning the guns, despite being seriously wounded by grenade splinters. In the process, he managed to capture four Italian officers and 36 other ranks. For this act of considerable bravery, he was recommended for a DCM (Distinguished Conduct Medal) which he was promptly awarded.[39]

The strain of a month of continuous fighting was beginning to show on the men of the Māori Battalion. Despite their high levels of physical fitness and their enthusiasm to keep pressing ahead, the long hours travelling through the desert, combined with extended stretches of combat, had exhausted many of the troops. Yet, as Freyberg noted in a letter to the New Zealand Minister of Defence, 'morale is exceedingly high. The men feel that the fighting of the Division was the turning point in the battle, which in my opinion is now over'.[40] With less optimism but perhaps more realism, though, the General looked ahead and concluded that 'there can be no doubt that 1942 will be a difficult year'.[41]

By the close of 1941, after five successive victorious engagements in under a month, the enemy forces had been pushed out of the region, while the troops of the battalion were developing an understanding of the nuances of desert warfare, and of some of the aspects of their opponent's nature. Even at this relatively early stage in the desert campaign, for example, Manahi and his friends had noticed a difference in the levels of fortitude between Italian and German troops. 'The Germans were good fighters, oh yes', confirmed Midwood. But as for the Italians, 'Well…', he said, and then left the answer as a pause – too polite to give voice to what was commonly known in general about Italian bravery in the war.[42] There was also immense pride within the battalion in its role in what was known as Operation Crusader – the major Allied offensive that had relieved the German and Italian siege of Tobruk, and led to the capture of the Cyrenaica region in the east of Libya. It was to Tobruk that Manahi headed on Christmas Eve for what the troops were in need of the most: 'a change'.[43] However, Christmas Day was almost like any other day for the men, apart for a Christmas service that was conducted by Padre Harawira. Then, having successfully completed its role in Operation Crusader, the battalion headed back to Egypt in a fierce sandstorm, and reached the base camp at Baggush on 29 December.

There is no way of knowing what emotions Manahi experienced during the Libyan campaign. The expression of feelings was usually tightly contained, but there are occasional glimpses of the emotional strain that the fighting and the loss of colleagues inflicted generally on the men of the battalion. Ten days before returning to Baggush, a special service was held by Harawira to give thanks for those who had survived the battles and to remember those who had not. A young private, Eruera Te Kahu Iver Whakarau, wrote a letter home in which he described this rare show of sentiment: 'Friday 19th. Our first church service was held. I think that was the saddest day I ever experienced in my life. Saw the hardiest of men shed tears during the sermon, in fact I couldn't hold back myself. Happened to be wearing a pair of goggles so I just pulled them up over my eyes so that no one would see me'.[44] Death was the constant companion of the battalion, and if any emphasis of this was needed, ten months later, Whakarau himself would be killed in the Western Desert. All that men like Manahi could do was to focus on tasks immediately at hand, and enjoy themselves whenever the opportunity arose. 'You never knew what would happen tomorrow', was the guiding observation of Manahi and his friends.[45]

New Year's Eve celebrations for the battalion gave a chance for the troops to 'let off some steam'. There were bonfires (despite black-out orders) and guns were fired in the sky as part of the mood of jubilation[46] and relief that swept over the men. The menu was also cause for great satisfaction. Instead of the monotony of the usual rations, there were kumara, pork, eels, and muttonbirds cooked for the troops. But this was a short interlude of revelry in what everyone knew was a phase of conflict that was far from over. In the first week of 1942, Manahi and the rest of the battalion were sent eastwards, to Kabrit. There, they spent the next two months going through the usual routines of training, although with all the experience many of these men had acquired in numerous battles, a return to the repetitive route marches and muster parades was becoming tedious.[47]

It was during this period of training in early 1942 that the Māori Battalion was passed from the command of the 5th to the 4th Brigade, which was part of the High Command's juggling of its forces in response to Rommel's capricious strategy that had made Allied planning that much more difficult. The proximity of Cairo was again proving a temptation to the battalion's men, but as their money dwindled, increasingly they preferred to remain at base rather than wander around Egypt's dirty and now familiar capital. It was in early February that speculation about the next destination for the battalion began to firm up (although even as late as 10 January, Freyberg was still uncertain where and to what use the New Zealand Division was next going to be put).[48] Syria was the rumoured location among the troops, and it was spoken of with increasing favour, not because they knew much about the country, but because they were 'heartily fed up with having their tents blown down by the winter gales and eating their meals in sandstorms ... wherever

Syria was, it could not be any worse than where they were'.[49]

However, the strategic decisions were the consideration of High Command. All the soldiers could do was wait. Then, on 28 February, there was finally some movement. Manahi boarded one of the battalion vehicles as part of what was known as A Convoy, and was sent with seventeen other vehicles loaded with troops to Kantara, 160 kilometres northeast of Cairo. Kantara was the location of the cemetery where 1562 Commonwealth troops from the First World War were buried, and was serving as a major hospital centre by 1941.

From Kantara, it was a further 250-kilometre bone-rattling drive across the Sinai Desert to Gaza, and then slower progress as the convoy wound its way though Palestine and north to Syria, finally arriving in Bekaa, just a few kilometres east of the settlement of Baalbek, in what is now Lebanon. The stationing of the Second New Zealand Division in Syria was part of strategy to prevent a possible German invasion of North Africa coming from Turkey. Egypt, and especially the Suez Canal, was vital to Allied interests in the region, and so it had to be protected from the strengthening Axis presence to the north.

Getting to Bekaa was a tiring journey that took the best part of three days to complete. But if the troops thought it would be a reprieve from the poor conditions they had tolerated in Egypt, they were mistaken. Night-time temperatures could drop as low as zero degrees Celsius, and they were struck by gales, heavy rain, and then snow. It was the last blizzard of the winter season, but must have made many of the men long for the warmer temperatures of Egypt. Once this bout of bad weather passed, though, the battalion was assigned to preparing defences in case a German offensive from the north transpired. By the final week of April, most of the work in readying this defensive line was complete, which was a relief as temperatures were getting into the low forties.

There was a short, sharp change to the battalion's command a few weeks later, however, that was simultaneously the cause for regret and joy. The regret came from the departure of the battalion's commanding officer, Dyer, who asked to be relieved of his command on 13 May, having led his men since the start of the war. The reason for Dyer leaving was his failure to comply fully with instructions he received to hand in any weapons the battalion had captured from the enemy. Dyer was replaced by Major Eruera (Edward) Te Whiti o Rongomai (Tiwi) Love, the first Māori to command the Māori Battalion, although his triumph would be short-lived. Two months later, Love was killed in combat[50] – another one of those reminders to the troops of how precarious the hold on life was during the war.

As it turned out, all the defensive construction that the battalion was involved in during its time in Syria was for no purpose. Rommel had been smarting ever since the Axis forces had been pushed back from Tobruk, and since his retreat, he had been piecing together the elements of a major counter-offensive. At the end of January, he had captured Benghazi, and was on the verge of a major advance east into Allied-held territory. On 26 May, with lightning speed Rommel pounced on the British strongholds in Libya. Hundreds of German tanks rumbled towards the Allied lines, supported by 88-millimetre anti-aircraft guns which Rommel turned to fire on Allied tanks, while Italian infantry units outflanked the Allied forces at Gazala. From there, the Germans and Italians rushed to Tobruk and took the town on 21 June, along with 33,000 Allied prisoners. There was no question that Egypt – and control of the Suez Canal – was next in the sights of Rommel, who was now a freshly-appointed Field-Marshal.

As the enemy force hurled itself towards Tobruk, Allied commanders realised the scale of the danger that now faced Egypt, and the Second New Zealand Division was hurriedly ordered to return to Mersa Matruh – just 200 kilometres to the east of Fort Musaid, where the Italians had been overrun in November the previous year, and which Manahi's company had subsequently occupied.

Against Freyberg's wishes, the Second New Zealand Division was ordered to hold Mersa Matruh, but when the Māori Battalion arrived there on 19 June, they were met with a flurry of orders and counter-orders, which led them to being shifted within and outside the town on several occasions over the next five days.[51] Finally, a new order came through which looked as though the commanders had clarified the situation. The battalion (apart from D Company, which was to be rested) was sent to Bir Abu Batta – an escarpment about five kilometres from Minqar Qaim. The terrain there made building even slit trenches almost impossible. Some of the troops were forced to pile up rocks and sand in a desperate effort to create some protection for themselves.

By 26 June, an advance column of Germans was just ten kilometres away and approaching swiftly. The battalion was protected by mines laid around their defensive positions, but knew that this would only delay rather than halt any enemy onslaught. Just after midnight, the men of the battalion – wide awake with apprehension at facing a German attack – could see a column of enemy vehicles moving eastward along the coast road. It was evident that in their fixed position, they would be an obvious target of the German forces. The enemy was then lured by the New Zealanders, with a small mobile column being sent out to shell the Germans and force them to deploy south to attack the New Zealand position.

During the early afternoon of 27 June, enemy formations had approached the area where the battalion (and the rest of the 4th Brigade) were stationed and made minor attacks, mainly to test the response. These short exchanges lasted until sunset, and then ceased when darkness seemed to bring an end to the German assaults. Freyberg wrote with undue optimism to the Minister of Defence on 27 June, stating that 'We have been holding a position [Minqar Qaim] and have been attacked from north, south, and east. All attacks have been repulsed. The troops have been excellent and morale is high'.[52]

However, the enemy plan was not to launch a sudden assault, but to first surround the entire Second New Zealand Division – a potential prize of prisoners that seemed easily within the reach of the German troops. Manahi, along with thousands of other New Zealand troops, was encircled by the Germans. Freyberg summarised the events of that day and the breakout that the New Zealanders made: 'We were attacked on the north, south, and east by the 21st Panzer Division and elements of an infantry division and were shelled throughout the day. Supported by our armoured division we repulsed the enemy tank attack, and the enemy infantry attacks were also repulsed. The enemy suffered heavy casualties. By evening, however, when the code-word was received to retire to the Alamein position, there were enemy concentrations all round .... A most successful night attack was carried out by the 4th Brigade, who broke through the encircling forces at the point of the bayonet. Bright moonlight made the move of the large body of transport hazardous and the column had to run the gauntlet of enemy tanks, causing disorganisation and casualties. An estimate of the casualties for the fighting to date is 150 killed and 450 wounded. The withdrawal was successfully executed and the Division is now reorganised'.[53] The Alamein position was 150 kilometres further east, and despite facing considerable defensive fire at times, the Māori Battalion managed finally to get out of the reach of the enemy, albeit temporarily. There, they were part of what Freyberg described as 'a mobile striking force with an offensive role against the enemy flank'.[54] The reputation of the soldiers of the Māori Battalion had by now made them prized among commanders such as Freyberg because of their initiative and resourcefulness, and their capacity to move quickly during battle.

Such had been the speed and devastating effectiveness of the German advance that Allied High Command were contemplating withdrawing from Egypt altogether, and had not Rommel's supply lines been stretched almost to breaking point, he could well have forced them to retreat, possibly even to Syria.[55] However, as the Germans paused to allow their logistical support to pump resources back into their front line, the Allied commanders settled on a plan to defend El Alamein. Manahi was one of those deployed to what was known as the Alamein Line, where he was deployed digging trenches and preparing defences. A general indication of the circumstances he was in at this time was later revealed by Kippenberger. 'Summer was at its height and the flies at their worst', he wrote. 'Strengths were so low and there was little rest for anyone. We were depressed and cynical. The men's faces were gaunter and more strained each week and there were many cases of jaundice'. This was possibly one of the hardest periods in the war so far for Manahi and his comrades.[56] It was certainly a more intimate assessment of the condition of the troops than Freyberg's depiction of that period, which was his almost stock phrase: 'Our troops are in good condition and keen for decisive action'.[57] Even the normally sanguine Cody conceded that by the end of July, 'the New Zealand Division was in no shape to attack'.[58]

July slipped into August, and the heat and the flies seemed to get worse. Moreover, the lack of any fighting further drained the morale of the men. There was a simmering sense of purposelessness about their presence in a theatre of war where all the battling against the enemy was apparently being done by others. How did Manahi handle this period? No direct record survives, but according to his son, Rau, he managed such situations by becoming quiet and just focussing on whatever it was he was doing at that moment – 'even if something bothered him, he didn't show it. He was just like that, he didn't want others to know if there was a problem. He'd prefer to sort things out for himself'.[59] For many of the men, though (including possibly Manahi as well), frustration over their circumstances was growing within them, and at some point, would need to be vented.

Then, on 24 August, an order came down for a raid to be conducted against a German position, in anticipation of a major assault Rommel was obviously planning.[60] For two weeks, there had been no prisoners taken by the Allied Eight Army, and its newly-appointed General, Bernard Montgomery, wanted this changed. Kippenberger was instructed to organise the raid, which he did, appointing A and B Companies of the Māori Battalion for the task (chosen because they were 'the freshest').[61] At last, after several static weeks, Manahi was again going into battle. With artillery support, the two companies were to advance on a salient in the El Mreir depression. Planning was meticulous, and Kippenberger stressed to the selected troops that he wanted 'prisoners and not scalps'.[62]

The date set for the assault was 26 August, and the advance was due to start in the early evening. During that day, Kippenberger noted that the men of A and B Companies 'were delightful, laughing and talking with one another, working busily at oiling and cleaning and polishing their weapons, and all giving me the most cheerful grins'.[63] It seems that another opportunity to exact utu on the enemy for the deaths the battalion had suffered was all that was needed to pump morale back into the veins of the troops.

Half an hour before the assault was due to commence, Kippenberger went to see the troops off and left a written account of this meeting. It is another of those episodes which allows a brief insight into both the state of mind and the physical preparedness of this group of men, of which Manahi was one: 'Both companies, Ngapuhi under Porter and Arawa under Pene, were ready, waiting together …. I walked about among them and was amazed and amused by the number of weapons they were carrying. Every other man had an automatic, mostly captured Spandaus or Bredas, they were loaded with grenades, many had pistols, very few had rifle and bayonet only …. The Maori padre spoke to them, most eloquently and impressively. Then he said a prayer, very moving in the utter silence. Baker asked me to speak. I did so briefly. I said how many guns would be in support – there were grunts of satisfaction – that I was confident they would do well'. Kippenberger then wished the companies well and returned to Battalion Headquarters 'to wait and watch'.[64]

As the attack got under way, B Company penetrated deep into the enemy position and began to take prisoners (all Italian) as they captured more ground. Although the assault was viewed very satisfactorily at the time, the term 'massacre' was later applied to the battalion's actions during this engagement on the basis that possibly up to 500 Germans were killed in this encounter, while only 41 prisoners were taken.[65] However, the chaos of the fighting, and the extreme ferocity of the combat and the artillery being fired into the location easily account for this apparently disproportionate ratio of deaths to captives, and the suggestion of any massacre was easily disproved.

Manahi would have been exhausted by this episode of fighting, but all leave had been cancelled and everyone was on high alert as the time approached for what would be Rommel's final offensive against the Allies in North Africa. On the afternoon of 27 August, it looked like the German assault had begun, with the New Zealand troops enduring 'the heaviest bombardment … [they] had stood under for some time'. Two thousand shells rained down on the area in which the battalion were positioned in just one hour.[66] Communication lines were cut, and the men of the battalion waited anxiously in their defences for the inevitable enemy infantry assault. Manahi was huddled in his lonely slit trench, uncertain of the fate of any of his comrades, and hoped that none of the shells would land directly where he lay. The hold on life in the trenches was fickle. Midwood later related an episode during one such bombardment when three men from the battalion were squeezed into a trench. An enemy shell exploded, fatally wounding two on either side, but leaving Midwood unscathed.[67]

Two days later, the tide seemed to be turning in favour of the battalion. Allied planes were seen overhead, engaging in dogfights with the Luftwaffe, while under the rotating-company policy, D Company returned to the front line, giving Manahi and the rest of B Company a respite from the fighting.

By 9 September, the Māori Battalion had been relieved, and withdrew to Burg el Arab, which was about 40 kilometres from Alexandria and just over a kilometre from the beach. Here the men enjoyed ten days of rest, free from the immediate threat of the enemy, as one of the B Company members (Second Lieutenant Kuru Waaka) wrote in his diary. 'To laze around doing nothing; to walk around without fear of getting blown sky high by shells; to sleep above ground in a comfortable bed; to sit at a table and eat every kind of delicious food; to drink beer by the any amount you like; to know there's not a German within fifty miles of one; all these things seem to make life almost a dream'.[68] This, then, was the setting Manahi found himself in, and doubtless he enjoyed the relaxed, peaceful environment, the swimming, and the opportunity to take a leave pass to go to Alexandria and Cairo.

The ten days spent at Burg el Arab were little more than an intermission. Rommel was building up and deploying his forces – as was Montgomery – for a major confrontation. The first stage of this which affected Manahi occurred on 24 September, when he and the rest of B Company were transported 65 kilometres south. There, the men underwent training in night- and day-time fighting, and were involved in divisional manoeuvres. In mid-October, the battalion returned to Burg el Arab, where the normal routine of morning marching and afternoon swimming resumed. The message got around that 23 October was to be the date of a major offensive. No details of the operation were given, but the amassing of men and equipment indicated that it was going to be much more than just another set of skirmishes. The Allied bombardment of enemy positions in the vicinity began on the evening of the 23rd, with a thousand artillery pieces involved in the operation. Montgomery's plan was for the New Zealand Division to hold the Miteirya Ridge,[69] although for some unknown reason, the Māori Battalion was left out of the initial deployment.[70]

By the following day, the Axis forces had been shunted back, and although the war in the desert was far from over, this was a decisive turning point in the conflict. At sunset on 26 October, the men of the Māori Battalion assembled to relieve 21 Battalion on the Miteirya Ridge. As they were forming, German dive-bombers strafed them, inflicting several casualties, and over the next day, there were more men killed and wounded as the enemy continued to attack the battalion's positions by shelling and small arms fire. However, the Axis forces were eventually forced back, thus allowing the Allied commanders to be able to withdraw the New Zealand Division from the Miteirya Ridge and allow it to regroup for the next stage of the offensive.[71]

There were no immediate orders for the battalion after its withdrawal on 27 October, and some of the men looked forward to another stretch – perhaps of a few weeks – without fighting as the commanders got on with reorganising aspects of the offensive.[72] However, the following day, the battalion was ordered to prepare for an attack it was going to be a part of that evening. The battalion was to be put under the command of the British 151 Infantry Brigade[73] for what was called Operation Supercharge.

Major Charles Bennett (aged just 29 at the time) was put in charge of the battalion from that morning, and would lead Manahi and the other ranks until April the following year, with Major Keiha acting as second in command during that time. From sunset on 1 November until midnight, the sections of the Brigade moved into their assigned areas, and by 1.00 am on 2 November, they were all in position, with Manahi and the rest of B Company instructed to mop up in the wake of the assault. This would involve clearing out any remaining pockets of enemy resistance, and taking prisoners where possible (although a week earlier, Montgomery had issued a personal message to the troops which required them 'to fight and to kill' – no mention was made of taking captives).[74]

However, in keeping with the old military adage that no plan of battle survives contact with the enemy,[75] once the assault had begun, the stiffness of opposition broke up some of the battalion's line, and so instead of dealing with stray German or Italian troops, B Company found itself 'opposed by a wall of enemy firing at us with all they had', as Bennett wrote, 'we had to fight almost every inch of the way'. The response of Manahi and those around him was almost instinctive, as their commanding officer reported: 'We all broke into the haka 'Ka mate! Ka mate!' and charged straight in with the bayonet'.[76] Bennett described this action as 'the most spirited attack that I myself had taken part in'.[77] Men on both sides were dropping in the hail of gunfire, resulting in what Montgomery called 'a real killing match',[78] with Māori Battalion troops shooting, lobbing grenades, and stabbing their way through the enemy positions. With darkness blanketing the region, the fighting died back and there was a calm that descended over the battlefield during the night. Manahi again found himself lying in a shallow trench that he had dug for himself, and waiting for what was anticipated to be Rommel's major counterstrike that would burst out from the enemy positions the following morning. The men of B Company were especially vulnerable, as part of a section of troops which were 'like a little finger poked out into the enemy positions and likely to be nipped off with ease'.[79] And to make the situation even more dangerous, there were no anti-tank defences ahead of the battalion, so they were easy prey for an enemy tank attack. All the afternoon of 2 November, Manahi lay, motionless, in his slit trench. There were thousands of men in the vicinity, but communication between them was reduced to a minimum. It was one of those situations that tested the nerve of every soldier, as they had hours to contemplate an attack that was almost certainly due be launched at sunrise the next day.

The feared Axis counter-offensive never eventuated, however. Rommel had his hands full with other tactical concerns, and during 2 November, ordered his forces to withdraw westwards, in the hope of opening up a new front to fend off the Allied 8th Army. There was still heavy shelling in some sectors on 3 November, but Allied High Command knew that the Germans were now retreating, which signalled the start of one of the longest pursuits of the war. By 12 November, the last remnants of Rommel's army had been forced out of Egypt, and despite occasional shows of obstinacy, the enemy was finally evicted from Libya, with Manahi and the rest of the battalion entering Tripoli on 23 January 1943 (they would have entered the Libyan capital a day earlier but were forestalled by a rearguard unit from 15 Panzer Division).[80]

After the entry into Tripoli – which symbolised the end of this phase of the pursuit of the enemy – the battalion had a chance to rest, without the anticipation of being called to fight at a moment's notice. This was something that the men had been unable to do in the previous two and a half months, during which time the Allies had chased Rommel's forces westward across 2200 kilometres of North African desert, picking out pockets of enemy resistance and enduring strafing from German aircraft as they were trucked and marched towards Tripoli.

That sense of relief – that the bulk of the fighting was now behind them – was broken on the morning of 1 March, when an urgent order was issued to the battalion to pack up and check their ammunition. Another descent into battle was facing the troops. Rommel may have been in retreat, but it was not a free-fall withdrawal. Hoping to bring the Allied advance to a halt, the German Field Marshal set up a new front, known as the Mareth Line.

Rommel had been rebuilding his tank divisions and had allotted the Italian divisions to defend the Mareth Line in order to delay the advance of the Allied forces and prevent their Armies from joining up. His plan then was to attack and push back the Allied forces out of Libya as the first stage in a much larger counter-offensive.[81] As an imminent Axis attack came into view as a possibility, the New Zealand Division was assigned the task of rushing to one of the anticipated flash-points in any ensuing offensive. Just before midnight on 1 March, Manahi and the rest of the battalion found themselves again on transport vehicles, this time on a 300-kilometre journey to the Medenine area, where they slept until sunrise, when they were instructed to deploy in a defensive position. Manahi's company was in a reserve position, behind the other three companies, but was expecting to be in the thick of fighting by the end of the day.

For the next two days, though, there were no signs of the enemy, but the troops prepared trenches in order that they would be protected as much as possible from what was expected to be a barrage from the 15 Panzer Division. Such was the state of the defences that Kippenberger commented that 'no amount of shelling would do much harm'.[82] The undulating land meant that almost none of the battalion's posts were visible from the opposing front, which augured well if and when the enemy attack commenced.

On 6 March, less than two kilometres in front of the Māori Battalion, a line of 43 German tanks was advancing swiftly, followed by hundreds of trucks which were transporting German troops. However, Kippenberger rightly decided that the task of attacking this column was best left to the artillery (which was assisted by the Māori Mortar Platoon), which pounded it with shells, inflicting severe losses on the enemy, while the battalion's troops looked on. The Germans did attempt an infantry assault in the direction of the New Zealand 5th Brigade, but this was easily repulsed.[83] The first phase of Rommel's counter-offensive had failed. Sensing the opportunity for the enemy to be pushed back further, Montgomery decided to pierce the Axis defences in the vicinity of the coast, with the New Zealand forces assigned to break through the Tebaga Gap (a ten-kilometre passage), which lay about 80 kilometres east of Medenine.

Manahi was on the move again on 12 March, this time to join the troops of the 5th (New Zealand) Brigade. He was among those members of the battalion trucked east to Ben Gardene, and then south in a large loop, eventually moving north towards the Tebaga Gap, where the Allied plan was to encircle the Italian troops defending the Mareth Line. In Kippenberger's words, the function of the New Zealanders would be to 'smash a breach in a daylight attack'.[84]

The initial breakthrough at the Tebaga Gap was made by the 6th Brigade on 21 March. Five days later, Manahi was in the group of troops who relieved 26 Battalion, and was given the challenging order to take Point 209. C Company was involved 'in an epic struggle' against a battalion of Panzer Grenadiers on a rocky feature leading up to Point 209. This feature, nicknamed Hikurangi, was finally taken by C Company, with Second Lieutenant Te Moana-Nui-A-Kiwa Ngarimu leading the charge. It was a ferocious period of fighting, leading its commanding officer, Peter Awatere, to write about it afterwards, using the words 'slaughtered', and 'disembowelled', and explaining how one soldier was so determined to finish off the enemy that 'the only thing he did not do was eat their flesh'.[85] The most distinguished member of the battalion in this engagement was Ngarimu, who was recommended for, and awarded, the Victoria Cross (posthumously, as he was killed during an enemy counter-attack).[86] Not only had he led the attack on Hikurangi, but had displayed, in Bennett's estimation, 'courage and leadership of the highest order … personally annihilating at least two enemy machine gun posts'.[87]

The news of Ngarimu's exceptional bravery, and the award of a VC for his exploits, had a huge psychological effect on the entire battalion. Naturally, there was pride in a colleague for having earned the highest award for bravery, but it also set a new benchmark for valour, opening the possibility that even more audacious acts of fighting were possible in combating an enemy which was proving stubborn in retreat, and ferocious in combat.

The Germans had been terminally weakened by the latest Allied offensive, and by 28 March, they 'had effectively played their last hand'.[88] A total of 231 Germans had been taken prisoner by the end of that day, but the Māori Battalion had also suffered, with 22 of their number killed in the most recent fighting, and 77 wounded.[89] The defeat of the Germans at Point 209 was crucial. The Battalion's War Diary contains a buoyant assessment written in the immediate aftermath which portrayed the triumph at Point 209 as being something of a turning point: 'This marked the beginning of the end for the Hun as one PW [Prisoner of War] reported that his whole Bn [Battalion] was prepared to surrender'.[90] What remained was one final operation to squeeze them out of Tunisia in order for the North African campaign to be concluded successfully for the Allies.

## NOTES

1. Rommel took command of the Afrika Korps on 12 February 1941.
2. R Logan, 'Withdrawal from Crete', in *New Zealand 28 Maori Battalion Golden Jubilee Reunion*, Wellington, 28 Maori Battalion Association, April 1990.
3. Interview with Arthur Midwood, Rotorua, 7 September 2009.
4. Interview with Rau Manahi, Rotorua, 20 August 2009.
5. M Soutar, *Nga Tama Toa: The Price of Citizenship*, p. 156.
6. Ibid., p. 176.
7. Rau Manahi recalls no letters arriving from his father during the war.
8. Interview with Rau Manahi, Rotorua, 20 August 2009.
9. Interview with Arthur Midwood, Rotorua, 7 September 2009.
10. 28 (Maori) Battalion Routine Order no 21, 1 July 1941, in W Gardiner, *Te Mura o Te Ahi: The Story of the Maori Battalion*, p. 78.
11. M Soutar, *Nga Tama Toa: The Price of Citizenship*, p. 178.
12. J F Cody, *28 (Maori) Battalion*, p. 140.
13. W Gardiner, *Te Mura o Te Ahi: The Story of the Maori Battalion*, p. 78.
14. E W Westrate, *Forward Observer*. New York, Read Books, 1944, pp. 46–47.
15. W Gardiner, *Te Mura o Te Ahi: The Story of the Maori Battalion*, pp. 78–9.
16. J F Cody, *28 (Maori) Battalion*, p. 134.
17. Interview with Rau Manahi, Rotorua, 20 August, 2009.
18. J F Cody, *28 (Maori) Battalion*, p. 134.
19. L Sole, 'Memories of an Octogenarian', in *The Journal of the Sole Society*, December 2005, n. p.
20. A L Kidson, *Official History of New Zealand in the Second World War 1939–45: Petrol Company*, Wellington, War History Branch, Department of Internal Affairs, 1961, p. 150.
21. J F Cody, *28 (Maori) Battalion*, p. 135.
22. Op. cit.
23. Material supplied by R Manahi, 25 October 2010.
24. For an image of the terrain, see 'Baggush', unidentified photographer, 30 October, 1941, reference nunber:DA-01230-F, Alexander Turnbull Library.
25. J F Cody, *28 (Maori) Battalion*, p. 145.
26. B Freyberg to Minister of Defence, 13 December 1941, in *Documents Relating to New Zealand's Participation in the Second World War, 1939–45*, vol. 2, Wellington, War History Branch, Department of Internal Affairs, 1951, p. 87.
27. W Gardiner, *Te Mura o Te Ahi: The Story of the Maori Battalion*, p. 81.
28. The ineffectiveness of the Italian defence was attributed to the fact that Sollum was occupied by troops belonging to the 4th Italian Labour Unit – essentially men who provided logistical support and labour for the work gangs, as opposed to infantry men.
29. W E Murphy, *The Relief of Tobruk*, Wellington, War History Branch, Department of Internal Affairs, 1961, p. 129; W Gardiner, *Te Mura o Te Ahi: The Story of the Maori Battalion*, p. 81.
30. M Soutar, *Nga Tama Toa: The Price of Citizenship*, p. 191.
31. J F Cody, *28 (Maori) Battalion*, p. 152.
32. Between seven and nine prisoners were taken. W Gardiner, *Te Mura o Te Ahi: The Story of the Maori Battalion*, p. 82; J F Cody, *28 (Maori) Battalion*, p. 153.
33. R Royal to A Ngata, 6 December 1941, MS Papers 6919-0782, Alexander Turnbull Library. Also see *28th (Maori) Battalion 2007 National Reunion*, Whakatāne, 28 Māori Battalion Association, 5–9 April 2007, pp. 25–6.

34. Details provided by Rau Manahi, 19 January 2010.
35. Interview with Rau Manahi, 20 August 2009.
36. The probability that Manahi was a 'ratter' is based on accounts from Rau about his father's exploits in gathering German souvenirs. Interview with Rau Manahi, Rotorua, 20 August 2009.
37. J F Cody, *28 (Maori) Battalion*, p. 168.
38. W E Murphy, *The Relief of Tobruk*, p. 496.
39. W Gardiner, *Te Mura o Te Ahi: The Story of the Maori Battalion*, p. 85; M Soutar, *Nga Tama Toa: The Price of Citizenship*, p. 196.
40. B Freyberg to Minister of Defence, 13 December 1941, in *Documents Relating to New Zealand's Participation in the Second World War, 1939–45*, vol. 2, p. 87.
41. B Freyberg to Minister of Defence, 10 January 1942, in *Documents Relating to New Zealand's Participation in the Second World War, 1939–45*, vol. 2, p. 88.
42. Interview with Arthur Midwood, Rotorua, 7 September 2009.
43. Op. cit.
44. E Te K I Whakarau, 19 December 1941, in J F Cody, *28 (Maori) Battalion*, p. 176.
45. Interview with Arthur Midwood, Rotorua, 30 November 2009.
46. British units nearby expected a seaborne attack as a result of all the attention created by the Māori Battalion firing their weapons at this time. See A Ross, *A History of New Zealand in the Second World War, 1939–45, 23 Battalion*, Wellington, War History Branch, Department of Internal Affairs, 1959, p. 132.
47. This point is emphasised in W Gardiner, *Te Mura o Te Ahi: The Story of the Maori Battalion*, p. 88.
48. B Freyberg to Minister of Defence, 10 January 1942, in *Documents Relating to New Zealand's Participation in the Second World War, 1939–45*, vol. 2, p. 88.
49. J F Cody, *28 (Maori) Battalion*, p. 180.
50. Love died on 12 July 1942, S. Love De Miguel, 'Love, Eruera Te Whiti o Rongomai 1905–1942', in *Dictionary of New Zealand Biography*, Wellington, June 2007.
51. W Gardiner, *Te Mura o Te Ahi: The Story of the Maori Battalion*, pp. 92–3.
52. B Freyberg to Minister of Defence, 27 June 1942, in *Documents Relating to New Zealand's Participation in the Second World War, 1939–45*, vol. 2, p. 112.
53. B Freyberg to Minister of Defence, 1 July 1942, in *Documents Relating to New Zealand's Participation in the Second World War, 1939–45*, vol. 2, pp. 113–4.
54. B Freyberg to Minister of Defence, 5 July 1942, in *Documents Relating to New Zealand's Participation in the Second World War, 1939–45*, vol. 2, p. 114.
55. H Kippenberger, *Infantry Brigadier*, p. 139.
56. Ibid., p. 191.
57. B Freyberg to Minister of Defence, 14 July 1942, in *Documents Relating to New Zealand's Participation in the Second World War, 1939–45*, vol. 2, p. 120.
58. J F Cody, *28 (Maori) Battalion*, p. 205.
59. Interview with Rau Manahi, Rotorua, 20 August 2009.
60. Intelligence received by the British indicated that this was to be Rommel's final major offensive.
61. H Kippenberger, *Infantry Brigadier*, p. 200.
62. Ibid., p. 201.
63. Ibid., pp. 201–2.
64. Ibid., p. 202.
65. For details, see W Gardiner, *Te Mura o Te Ahi: The Story of the Maori Battalion*, pp. 101–2.
66. J F Cody, *28 (Maori) Battalion*, p. 212.
67. A Midwood, in H Mitchell to P Moon. 1 February 2010.
68. K Waaka, in ibid., p. 225.
69. K Ford, El Alamein 1942: *The Turning of the Tide*, Oxford, 2005, p. 73.
70. Some possible reasons for this are provided by Gardiner, see W Gardiner, *Te Mura o Te Ahi: The Story of the Maori Battalion*, p. 103.
71. M Soutar, *Nga Tama Toa: The Price of Citizenship*, pp. 236–7.
72. Kippenberger had informed the Battalion on 31 October that it would remain in its present location until Rommel's defensive line had been breached.
73. Which was part of the British 50th (Northumbrian) Infantry Division
74. B Montgomery, Personal Message from the Army Commander, Eight Army, 23 October 1942, in J F Cody, *28 (Maori) Battalion*, p. 228. Also see C Cruickshank, *Deception in World War II*, Oxford, Oxford University Press, 1979, pp. 26–33; B L Montgomery, *Memoirs*, London, Collins, 1958, pp. 121–2.
75. Attributed to H Von Moltke. See D Detzer, *Donnybrook : The Battle of Bull Run, 1861*, New York, Hoghton, Mifflin, Harcourt, 2005, p. 233.
76. Op. cit.
77. 'Report by Maj. C M Bennett', November 1942, in *War Diary of 28 Battalion*, WA II, I, DA 68/1/36, Archives New Zealand, p. 38.
78. B Montgomery, in J F Cody, *28 (Maori) Battalion*, p. 238.
79. 'Report by Maj. C. M. Bennett', November 1942, in *War Diary of 28 Battalion*, WA II, I, DA 68/1/36, Archives New Zealand, p. 38.
80. M Soutar, *Nga Tama Toa: The Price of Citizenship*, p. 241.
81. J F Cody, *28 (Maori) Battalion*, p. 256.
82. H Kippenberger, *Infantry Brigadier*, p. 271.
83. W Gardiner, *Te Mura o Te Ahi: The Story of the Maori Battalion*, p. 114.
84. H Kippenberger, *Infantry Brigadier*, p. 282.
85. P Awatere, in M Soutar, *Nga Tama Toa: The Price of Citizenship*, pp. 251–2.
86. K Findlay, and W Ngata, 'Ngarimu in Love and War', in *Mana Magazine*, no, 2, April–May 1993, pp. 78–83.
87. C Bennett, in W Ngata, 'Ngarimu, Te Moananui-a-Kiwa 1919 – 1943', in *Dictionary of New Zealand Biography*, Wellington, 22 June 2007.
88. W Gardiner, *Te Mura o Te Ahi: The Story of the Maori Battalion*, p. 117.
89. W G Stevens, *Bardia to Enfidaville*, Wellington, War History Branch, Department of Internal Affairs,1962, p. 233.
90. C Bennett, in Unit Diaries of the Maori Battalion in World War II [Archives Ref: WAII 1 DA 68/1/1-73], Saturday 27 March 1943.

*Haane Manahi, North Africa, 1943*

*Reference: DA-04139 Alexander Turnbull Library*

*Members of the Māori Battalion's swimming team photographed at the inter-unit swimming sports held in Egypt in July 1941. Left to right: Ruhi Pene, Rangi Logan, Ceylon Wikiriwhi, ?, Pine Timihou, Reuben Pene, Jack Mikaere, ?, Haane Manahi, ?. North Africa, c. 1942*

*Reference: DA-1371 Alexander Turnbull Library*

*The southern route up to Takrouna*

*Reference: DA-02197 Alexander Turnbull Library*

*View of Takrouna Heights, Tunisia, during World War Two, May 1943*
*Reference: DA-10929-F Alexander Turnbull Library*

*View from southern end of Takrouna hill, Tunisia, 1943*
*Reference: DA-09822-F Alexander Turnbull Library*

*General view of Takrouna, 1943*
*Reference: DA-02251-F Alexander Turnbull Library*

*Charles Bennett, a lifelong friend of Manahi and a commanding officer of the Māori Battalion*

*Reference: PAColl-5936-41 Alexander Turnbull Library*

*Reta Keiha, a commanding officer of the Māori Battalion, and the first officer to sign Manahi's VC citation*

*Reference: DA-04458 Alexander Turnbull Library*

*Freyberg and Kippenberger in Egypt, August 1942*

*Photographer: Sir John White, Reference: DA-03719-F Alexander Turnbull Library*

# CHAPTER 7: Takrouna

The Allied troops leading the charge against Rommel's remaining forces in North Africa were constantly stalked by danger. And just because the enemy was on the run, there was no room for laxity to creep in. In fact, quite the opposite seemed to be occurring. The men of the Māori Battalion in particular were becoming more daring, and were pushing themselves physically and psychologically further than possibly at any other period of the war. Ngarimu's formidable actions in March 1943 were, thus far, the peak of this growing demonstration of a hardening conquering spirit.

One of the things that the soldiers of the battalion, especially those like Manahi who had been with it from the start, had learned from experience was that the closer the proximity to an enemy, the greater the prospect for kills – an opportunity that carries with it an attendant risk of suffering the same fate as you are trying to inflict on your adversary. The only comparatively safe location in any battle is out of the range of enemy fire, and as the gap between combatants narrows, the accuracy of their fire increases and the conflict grows increasingly more deadly. In close fighting, the Māori Battalion had demonstrated that it was a fearsome body of men, and was a match for the finest enemy troops. Attaining this level of combat prowess was due to more than just good training. The will and the background of the battalion's men were two other crucial ingredients.

An army might march on its stomach, but it conquers by its will. The 'science' of victory – the calculus of troop numbers, terrain, equipment, supplies, and objectives – is dependent on the incalculable element of will. Montgomery could shuffle the deployment of his soldiers to points of strategic importance, but given that he did not have unlimited numbers of men, battles were being won largely on the calibre of those being committed to the fighting. This was where the Māori Battalion was developing such a notable reputation. Part of this can be attributed to its composition.

As a very general rule, volunteers make more effective soldiers than conscripts, and men of a common background more readily work with each other than strangers from different social, geographic, or ethnic groups randomly thrown together. This feature might be part of what one military historian wryly described as 'a moral confidence trick',[1] but it is a trick that undoubtedly works. In addition to this, by the time the Māori Battalion entered Tripoli, it contained some of the most battle-hardened men of the Allied 8th Army, who were now as much at home as anyone could be in this hostile environment. And while the boundaries of the battlefields in the desert could be vast, the companies of the Māori Battalion – bound by ties that few if any other battalions in the Allied army shared – appeared to operate best in compact settings, despite the concentration of firepower that tended to occur in these types of confrontations. The men of the companies had, at times, an almost intuitive sense of each other's movements, and this made them that much harder for an enemy to overcome.

Montgomery's plan to pound the enemy out of Africa involved the American 2 US Corps and the British First Army descending on the Tunisian capital of Tunis.[2] However, one of the lines of resistance that had to be broken in order for this to happen was in the Enfidaville area, around seventy kilometres to the south, and this was where the Second New Zealand Division was sent to. Montgomery did not necessarily require the New Zealanders to be successful in Enfidaville, but what he did need was for the Germans to think that this was where the main Allied advance was to take place, and therefore, would hopefully divert Rommel's attention from the main thrust that Montgomery was planning. While there were certainly dangerous periods of fighting still to take place in Africa, the Allies were confident of the eventual outcome, as Freyberg wrote: 'In my opinion, although he may fight hard, the enemy cannot long postpone final defeat in this theatre'.[3] Kippenberger was also buoyant about the attitude of the New Zealand troops as they prepared for battle in Enfidaville.

Bennett was told on 18 April by the Brigadier that the Māori Battalion would be responsible for taking Takrouna. 'That gave me the opportunity', Bennett recalled, 'to take my officers forward, which I did … and we moved up as far as we could towards Takrouna … and had a look at the ground features and familiarised ourselves as much as we could with what was there ahead of us'.[4]

The following day, Kippenberger visited the battalions as they readied themselves for action, and delivered detailed orders to the battalion commanders. 'I saw most of the company commanders, all cheerful and resolute, and my stout battalion commanders were all in their best form. None of us had any illusions about the difficulty of our task – we had had too many days to look at it – but we were all completely confident that the men would do it and satisfied that our plan was as good as we could devise'.[5]

Takrouna would be the key target for the Allies to take. It was the enemy's most forward position in this sector, and towered over the whole area, making its capture essential. It was described by one historian as 'a truly formidable position, perhaps the most formidable position ever stormed by New Zealand troops'.[6] If it was not taken, troops and artillery would not be able to advance any further, and would be exposed to enemy observation and fire at any time.[7] The Germans appreciated its strategic importance just as keenly. Their 90th Light Division war diary noted that 'Takrouna was the dominating point, flanking the enemy in both directions and must be held as long as possible', and the Italians suggested that the site 'be fortified as an advanced strong point not to be evacuated except under heavy pressure', with the commander of the First Italian Army, Marshal Giovani Messe emphasising its strategic value: 'I had immediately seen the importance which Takrouna hill could have in the general defensive scheme, though far advanced and almost detached from the main positions. I planned to make it an independent strongpoint whose function would be to break the first impetus of the enemy attack and divert it towards the re-entrants in the coastal and central sectors. I therefore gave orders for the small amount of material available to be used to strengthen the natural defences of this rock, and for enough food and ammunition to be dumped there to enable the garrison to hold out for a long time even if completely surrounded. I was certain that the defenders of such an outpost needed great tenacity and will to resist, and so in an endeavour to rouse the spirit of emulation I included a platoon of Germans in the garrison, gave orders to hold out to the last, and issued a statement to the German-Italian battle group entrusting the outpost to their honour as soldiers.'.[8]

Kippenberger's plan was for an attack which would be carried out in two phases. In the first one, 21 and 28 Battalions, would advance roughly three kilometres on either side of Takrouna. The Māori Battalion would be on the right side, close to a road that ran parallel to the front that Kippenberger established. The intention was that the Māori Battalion would capture Takrouna, with 21 Battalion offering assistance. This was to last precisely 68 minutes[9] after which 23 Battalion would advance to capture the neighbouring point – the 'ugly-looking features called the Gebel Foukr and the Gebel Cherachir'.[10] The region was described by the British as a 'tangled mass of mountains',[11] but was an area that none the less had to be taken.

There had also been some confusion about the role 21 Battalion was meant to fulfil in the attack. '21 Battalion was supposed to have given me assistance in the capture of Takrouna', Bennett noted, '[but] I was not fully made aware of that because I recall I made no arrangements with 21 Battalion about how we could co-ordinate our efforts. As far as I was concerned and as far as I can recollect, Takrouna was the sole responsibility of the Maori Battalion ... had I been made aware that 21 Battalion had equal responsibility, I would have ensured that 21 Battalion took its full share of that responsibility'.[12] According to the secret orders issued on 19 April, Takrouna would be the responsibility of the Maori Battalion, while '21 NZ Bn will prepare to assist if required'. This indistinct wording was probably the source of subsequent misunderstanding about the role of 21 Battalion.[13]

On paper at least, Kippenberger's plan looked feasible, but there were practical considerations which intruded on its smooth execution. The first of these was the nature of the Māori Battalion itself. In the previous weeks, there had been a great deal of juggling of troops within the Battalion in order to compensate for the high toll of casualties and the slow trickle of reinforcements arriving to fill their places. After the fighting at the Tebaga Gap, the Battalion's numbers had dropped from 714 men to 606, and by the time of the planned assault on Takrouna, the assaulting strength of the battalion had plummeted to just 319 men.[14] Yet, despite these losses, there was almost a sense of optimism as the men moved towards Enfidaville. The change of terrain certainly lifted the mood of some of the troops, as Bennett observed at the time: 'we had now entered that belt of fertile plains which extends in varying degrees from the Djebiniana to as far north as Enfidaville. Olive groves acutely reminiscent of Greece and Crete extended in orderly pattern for miles, interspersed at various points along the countryside with picturesque whitewashed homesteads typical of this part of the African coastline. With a background of changing landscape, travelling for once became a scenic adventure; the roads were good and water was readily available from the many wells dotted along the roadside. We had indeed bidden farewell to the sands and the barren wastes of the African desert'.[15] There had been the occasional skirmish along the route, but the main thing, as far as the commanders were concerned, was that the enemy was in retreat (something that made some of the troops overlook daily irritations, such as the fact that throughout the Takrouna operation, almost all the troops were infested with fleas because of the absence of any shower facilities).[16]

However, Takrouna was one of the locations where the Allied advance ran into a stone wall, almost literally. Bennett's portrayal of 'the Rock of Takrouna' gives a soldier's impression of this site as he and his men approached it. He described Takrouna as 'a pinnacle not unlike the Athenian Acropolis, rising to a height of over 600 feet [around 200 metres] and standing like a grim forbidding sentinel, nearly four miles to the west of the village of Enfidaville. On the very summit of the pinnacle, and commanding an interrupted view to the south were the remains of an old fort, a formidable stone structure of Berberan origin, used in former days to oppose French rule and administration. Resting as it did on a massive foundation of solid rock twenty feet deep, this fortress surveyed the plains below with an air of almost impregnable seclusion'.[17] The problem, as Bennett quickly discovered, was that Takrouna's height gave the enemy 'full view on to practically the whole of the Div[ision's] front', which left the Allies in the area 'handicapped to a certain degree by a lack of decent observation posts'.[18]

The village of Takrouna was perched halfway up the northern slopes of this feature. Before the war moved to Tunisia, it had been home to about 500 people, but was now deserted of its civilian inhabitants and occupied only by Italian and German troops[19] who were presumably confident in their ability to defend their position. Of the two main slopes of Takrouna, the southern end was steep and appeared impossible of an assault, while the northern side had a more gentle gradient, and contained a track leading down to the road, which the villages had used as their main means of access.

The northern side was therefore the obvious, and indeed, the only sensible point for an assault on Takrouna,[20] even though it would inevitably be the most heavily defended part of the feature. If the enemy positions could be worn down through constant and heavy fire, though, there might be an opportunity to gain a foothold there and use that as a base for an advance into the core of this enemy position. That was one option anyway, but it was still too early to consider details. The initial problem was to get through the surrounding terrain, which Bennett concluded gloomily was 'a natural death trap'. Radiating out from Takrouna's base were fields of olive trees, separated in several areas by 'walls of cactus so thick as to deny passage to a man's hands'.[21] These plants were such a threat (some grew to almost two metres high), that prior to the attack on Takrouna three Crusader tanks were despatched to the battalion to smash through them, while most of the troops were issued with machetes so that they could hack at this threatening vegetation whenever necessary.[22] It was only during this path-clearing exercise – which preceded the battle by just a few hours – that some of the men discovered that the cactus hedges had been mined by the enemy,[23] making them especially dangerous, and slowing down dramatically the infantry advance. And most worryingly for these approaching troops was the fact that 'there was not a single line of approach to the fort that was not covered by converged fire'.[24] So not only was taking the position going to be extremely difficult, even getting near it would be hazardous. The Allies had every right to anticipate a 'bloody struggle' ahead.[25]

Manahi was among those who were involved in nightly reconnaissance missions in the vicinity of the base of Takrouna,[26] where he witnessed the German and Italian occupiers of this elevated fort laying mines and digging defensive positions.[27] It was clear from these nocturnal observations that the enemy had no intention of a quick departure. On the contrary, if things went well for them, maybe they even conceived that Takrouna could become a turning point in the war in North Africa – the place where the Allied advance was halted long enough to allow the Germans and Italians to regroup. What was also learned during these covert moonlit expeditions was something of the layout of buildings on this bald outcrop of limestone: 'From various vantage points in the divisional area it was observed that buildings crowned the hill on three different levels: on the summit was a domed mosque at the south-east corner, with a square-towered building close by and a huddle of smaller buildings disappearing from sight over the crest – local inhabitants said that this was an old Berber fortress'.[28] The troops soon divided the feature into three distinct areas: the pinnacle (where the ruins of the fortress were), the ledge (made up of the buildings on the ridge extending from the mosque), and the village – sometimes called the lower village (which was the ramshackle collection of houses and huts located in the north, which lay on the lower shoulder, leading to the road).[29]

Had there been no time constraints, and sufficient forces, the Allies could have easily besieged Takrouna, slowly starving its occupiers out of their defences and take them captive. However, Montgomery was racing ahead with plans to take Tunis on 22 April, and so he needed a robust attack on Takrouna just before in order to draw enemy forces away from the Tunisian capital. The diversion would be useful to the overall offensive against the last remaining Axis stronghold in Africa, but would be a dangerous and costly one for those involved in what was looking like an almost impossible task, given the number of troops at the disposal of the commanders in the area, and the scale of the opposition, safely holed up in their seemingly impenetrable defence. Bennett conceded that even the highly risky reconnaissance missions usually 'gave little information of value', principally because of the difficulties in getting close enough to the feature.[30] 'The information that we got from Brigade was pretty limited, and we were not aware that Takrouna was held in the strength that we eventually found out it was held in', he later noted. This paucity of intelligence was in marked contrast to the useful details the battalion had received previously on Tebaga Gap and Point 209.[31] Takrouna was very much an unknown quantity, and prior to the attack, the battalion commander thought that 'it might be a bit of a cake walk'.[32]

There had initially been consideration given at brigade level to an attack sometime between 15 and 18 April, but on 15 April, instructions were received by the battalions in the area that the assault on Takrouna was 'postponed indefinitely'. During the day, some units were even withdrawn from the vicinity of the feature because of heavy bouts of enemy shelling that they had been subjected to in their forward positions.[33] On 17 April, the commanders of all the battalion's companies tried to get a closer look for themselves at Takrouna and study its features. The attack still had to proceed at some point as part of the Allied strategy, so any additional intelligence on the objective was crucial. However, yet again, efforts at approaching the rocky protrusion were frustrated by 'some very heavy concentrations of Arty [Artillery] fire on our fwd [forward] posns [positions]'.[34]

Zero hour for the assault on Takrouna was set for 11.00 in the evening of 19 April.[35] So vital was this operation that a higher-than-usual level of secrecy was maintained. Even on the day of the assault, Bennett reflected on 'how few if any realised what lay in store'. At 10.00 am, a Commanding Officers' conference was held at Brigade Headquarters where Kippenberger unveiled the plan to attack that evening. At 1.00 pm, the Commanding Officers assembled their officers and informed them of the details of the assault on Takrouna.

As soon as the sun set, intelligence officers from the 5th Infantry Brigade and the Māori Battalion unrolled white tape to mark the start line for the assault, but although working under the cover of darkness, they were intermittently fired on. By 8.15 that evening, Manahi was seated in a transport truck which formed part of a small convoy, carrying the men of the battalion from its rear position towards the area from which they would commence their attack. They disembarked just south of Wadi el Boul an hour and a half later, where a short church service was held.[36] One of the soldiers recalled that 'it was very sad. One of the first times ka tangi au [I wept]. We had a karakia about 9 o'clock, all the boys. We could hear the Battalion and they were singing Aue e Ihu. Padre Wanoa was the priest. And I knew there's somebody bound to get killed'.[37]

Zero hour was approaching, and the battalion waited for the intelligence officer to guide them to the tape. However, he had been delayed setting out the start line, and so these highly experienced troops made their own way to the front, causing some inevitable muddling of their formation.[38] The troops had barely settled down into their battle positions when they were given the order to advance closer to the position in readiness for the imminent commencement of the assault.[39] On the battalion's left flank was Manahi's company, which made good progress to an area close to the base of the eastern side of Takrouna, impeded mainly by the dangerous rows of cactus, which in a few cases pierced right through the bodies of some of the soldiers unfortunate enough to fall onto them.[40]

The first act in the set piece attack on Takrouna was an artillery bombardment,[41] which lasted for seven hours.[42] From his headquarters, Kippenberger left a depiction of the barrage as it appeared from his headquarters: 'we stood about, watching the flickering gun-flashes and the quick glow of bursts among the olive-groves and high on Takrouna, listening to the incessant screaming and sighing of shells overhead and the thunder and rumble of the bombardment and straining to hear the chatter of automatics. This ominous sound, the signal that the infantry were at grips, came all too soon, as did the nearer crunches of the enemy's defensive fire'.[43] These were the conditions for Manahi and his fellow B Company men – wedged in the thick of the firing, and steeling themselves for the forthcoming attack.

The fear of another advance into enemy fire had been mounting for the past few days, but the routines of the army helped sidetrack any excessive apprehension, as one of the battalion members noted: 'It's only when you're given notice that you're going to do a certain attack, you have fear … but there are so many things you have to do prior to that attack, you forget about fear – you forget it. By the time you get to the start line and you're ready to attack, you concentrate on what you have to do after that, with the result that you do the job without worrying. You do worry, but you keep on going'.[44] Bennett's tactic was to use three of the battalion's companies in the assault on Takrouna, and the fourth in reserve to mop up, and then take Takrouna from the rear, which was the only location from which it appeared to be accessible.

A serious problem emerged for B Company at this time, however, which threatened the final stages of preparation leading up to their assault. The contours of Takrouna meant that as Manahi and his comrades got closer to its base, they were left out of contact with the other companies. Within moments of moving into this isolated pocket, B Company came under a hail of machine-gun fire and mortar shells, with crossfire from the enemy position at Djebel Bir, around 600 metres away. To this perilous position was added the lethal hazard of land mines, all of which led to an early toll of casualties before the troops in B Company were forced to ground.

After about half an hour, an order got through the chaos to B Company. It was instructed to advance and link up with C Company, which was already on the verge of moving ahead. Bennett rushed over and told C Company to wait until B Company could join them, with the hope that 'some semblance of a battalion line' could be formed.[45] Bennett then scrambled back to B Company, and found that the fire they were under had intensified, and was pinning the men down. He managed to get a message back to headquarters for three of the available tanks to open fire against Takrouna to provide some cover for the infantry advance, and as soon as B Company was able to move forward (under the command of Captain Christopher Sorensen), Bennett returned to C Company to co-ordinate the advance, but in the process, tripped a box mine and was seriously injured.[46]

Bennett's incapacitation 'completed the disorganisation of the headquarters'.[47] According to the battalion's secret diary, the battalion's headquarters was 'temporarily non existent' due to the high number of officers and other staff who had become casualties.[48] However, the potentially chaotic effects of this were mitigated by the instinctive leadership offered by some of those in the ranks, and accepted by the other troops without question or dissent. As one corporal observed, 'Sgts were promoting themselves to Platoon commanders, Corporals to Sgts. and so on and in many cases they no sooner promoted themselves than they were wounded, but everyone stood their ground and there was no panic'.[49]

While one of B Company's platoons edged their way about 300 metres around part of the base of Takrouna, Manahi's platoon, led by Sergeant Johnny Rogers (another of Manahi's friends from Ōhinemutu and the first cousin of Martin McRae)[50] was charged with mounting a feigned attack on Takrouna's southern slopes as a diversionary tactic. Bennett had instructed these two sections of B Company to 'keep the enemy there engaged and to keep their heads down', while the rest of the company and the other battalions prepared to advance later on the rear of the feature.[51]

The attacking party that Manahi was in was made up of twelve men, including Sergeant W J Smith of 23 Battalion, who had lost contact with his own unit and had joined the Māori Battalion, just when it urgently needed any troops it could get hold of. Rogers and his second-in-command, Manahi (who had just been promoted to Lance-Sergeant),[52] crouched down together in a wadi (a small gully, probably part of a dried-up stream) and discussed how best to effect the attack. They considered the contours of the terrain, possible routes, and guessed what sort of resistance they might face at various points. They then decided to divide their forces, with one, led by Rogers, advancing from the south-east, while Manahi would lead the other group, which would launch its assault from the south-west. Just as the details were being worked out, Rogers and Manahi were momentarily joined by a reconnaissance officer[53] from 5 Field Regiment, who listened to the outline of the proposed attack, and offered a few suggestions before wishing the men well and departing.[54]

However, in deciding to launch themselves at the slopes of Takrouna and attack its enemy positions, rather than just giving the impression of an assault in order to fool the German and Italian troops defending it, both Rogers and Manahi were going against the orders they had received from Bennett. And to make their decision even harder to fathom was the fact that the battalion was suffering substantial casualties at this time. The idea of trying to take Takrouna with just a dozen men must have looked more like recklessness than bravery to the commanding officers when they heard about what was happening. But due to a breakdown in communication channels (exacerbated by radios failing in the extreme conditions and relying on batteries which were notorious for running down quickly), by the time headquarters learned of the decision Rogers and Manahi had reached, their platoon was already attacking this Axis stronghold.

The other factor mitigating the decision by Manahi and Rogers to go beyond their orders was that this was a night attack, and as Bennett conceded, assaults under the cover of darkness 'are the most difficult of attacks to control'.[55] This being the case, it was probably inevitable that soldiers in the field took it upon themselves to exercise greater initiative once the fighting commenced. On the other hand, though, Bennett emphasised the extent to which he went to make sure that his orders were understood: 'we always made it a point that before an attack, we held a … conference of all the men who were going to attack, right down to stretcher-bearers, and every man got the full story with regards to boundaries, to objectives, to the importance of maintaining contact with your right and with your left, and so that partly overcomes the lack of communication'.[56]

Forty years after that attack on Takrouna, Bennett asked Manahi directly: 'what made you decide, instead of this easy job of staying down the bottom and keeping the heads down of the enemy, what made you and your section, and Sergeant Rogers and his section decide to give the top of Takrouna a go?'[57] Manahi explained that he was initially concerned only with clearing out the enemy positions at the foot of Takrouna before sunrise, but that after this had been accomplished, 'there seemed to be no opposition … so Johnny Rogers decided to take what few men he had up the side there and try to get on to Takrouna, so I decided to bring my blokes up …'.[58]

Rogers and Manahi had probably estimated initially that there was some likelihood of their assault succeeding, based partly on the confidence they had in the other platoons of B Company making gains in their respective offensives (which they hoped would at the very least distract or divide the enemy's attention) and on the fact that the first stage of their assault had gone relatively easily, and that for a while, they had encountered no further resistance from the enemy on the position. Added to this was the fact that their plan to take Takrouna, especially with such a pitiful number of troops, was so implausible that the enemy occupying the feature could not have anticipated it, and therefore would be caught unprepared. However, 11 and 12 Platoons had got bogged down in heavy fighting as their men struggled through mortar and small-arms fire just to get to the base of a ridge at Takrouna, where they then faced grenades tossed at them from well-protected enemy pits, inflicting yet more casualties.

Even if the enemy was caught by surprise, there were hundreds of them on Takrouna, which made the prospects of success for the groups led by Rogers and Manahi extremely faint. The lack of communication with headquarters may also have been a factor in the decision of these two Ōhinemutu men to go beyond what had earlier been ordered. A Company had lost contact altogether with the rest of the battalion, and Brigade Headquarters 'had no clear picture of the confused battle'.[59] The only certain report that did reach Headquarters was that all of the battalion's company commanders had been injured. A crisis seemed to be unfolding around Takrouna, but revised orders could not be issued, and the commanding officers were having great trouble determining specifically how the battle was developing. Given these circumstances, some improvisation was inevitable. 'There was confusion, alright', one battalion member recalled, 'but at the same time, every man attacking would try to get into position as best he can'.[60] The Māori assailants were brave but certainly not mindless of the dangers the attack posed.

Kippenberger considered a withdrawal before daylight, when his men would be easily seen by the enemy. He was tempted to go directly to where the intense firing was taking place to organise the battalion to pull back, but thought he would be of more use if he remained at headquarters. Bennett's counsel had always been against changing plans: 'One of the important things about any plan ... is simplicity. I think once you've made up a plan, you should strive to stick with it right through. Otherwise you'll just create confusion, and in point of fact, you've got to be a bit of a superman to alter plans once you are committed to battle – particularly at night'.[61] Kippenberger then had another idea for dealing with the stubborn resistance from the feature: 'The guns were still out on the plain under direct observation from Takrouna and I started to work out a plan to storm the hill with the reorganised Twenty-first [Battalion] from the area occupied by the Maoris. But there was no need. At 8 a.m. we saw, to our relief and delight, a stream of prisoners coming down from the pinnacle, about 150 of them. After the battle, with much questioning, we discovered what had happened'.[62] What had happened was that just before dawn on 20 April, Manahi and Rogers had led their troops into position and then commenced their assault on Takrouna.

Manahi's group included Privates Hinga Grant, John Hamilton Ingram, Kamira Aranui, and John Takiwa,[63] and as the first rays of the morning's sun lit up the region, they had already clambered half way up 'the hill', as the troops called it, ducking and diving from enemy fire, sheltering behind one ridge before scrambling for cover at the next one,[64] and using the angle of the sun to blind the enemy to their movements.[65] It was an incline that got steeper the higher the men got, and was strewn with heavy boulders which dramatically slowed their ascent. As soon as the enemy got sight of this small force, it launched 'intense but ill-aimed fire',[66] forcing Manahi and his small unit to crawl for cover behind the nearest rocks. Being fired on from above by troops ensconced in well-protected positions ought to have forced Manahi and Rogers either to remain behind the rocks, shielded from the worst of the fire, or to withdraw from the feature altogether. Both men's determination was resolute, though, and having set an objective in their minds, there seemed nothing – short of being wounded or killed – that would divert them from their goal.

So instead of looking for sanctuary from the fire raining on them from the slopes above, Manahi led an assault on some of the lower enemy positions. It was 7.30 a.m. by now, and as he and his men got into some of the locations they had previously seen from the ground, they were able to angle themselves to fire into the deep enemy fighting pits, staking out those troops who had been firing on them with impunity for the previous few days.[67]

Getting to these set points was obviously central to the plan Rogers and Manahi had concocted. Several of the pits were now at the mercy of 10 Platoon and, realising that there was no hope in maintaining their defensive fire, their Italian occupants waved any white material they had on them and surrendered, allowing between 70 and 110 prisoners to be taken and escorted off the feature by those men who had been wounded but were still able to walk. This was the 'stream of prisoners coming down from the pinnacle' that had delighted Kippenberger. It was also a relief to the troops who had taken them, because they made the enemy captives march ahead of them and watch the route they took. The Italians had laid the minefields in the vicinity, and this was a good way of discovering where the safe passages were.

Again, the opportunity arose for Manahi and Rogers to withdraw. They had taken a huge haul of enemy troops captive, and their small number was further reduced as casualties in this intense fighting unavoidably occurred. Moreover, the sun was rising, illuminating all the men scaling the slopes of Takrouna, and making them clear targets for the German and Italian troops further up the feature. In addition to these obvious deterrents to continuing with the attack was a lack of intelligence about the number of enemy troops on Takrouna, the weaponry at their disposal, and the strength and dispersal of their defences. Then there was the practical problem of ascending further. The incline was too steep, even for skilled climbers, and as this was the 'wrong' side of Takrouna to scale, there was even reason to pull back to a safer location and await further orders. The magnitude of the opposition Manahi and Rogers faced was terrifying, yet neither man seemed the slightest bit terrified. They had set in their minds a complete victory, and none of these fleeting problems and obstacles, however daunting, was going to alter that.

From the enemy's perspective, this was potentially one of the turning points of the battle. Although these sorts of judgements are easy to make in hindsight, it is still a little surprising that with at least 200 troops on the feature, the Germans and Italians did not commit more men to fend off an assault that – with the surrender of the seventy Italians – had become much more than just an irritating diversion. It is likely that the enemy commanders calculated that because so few men were engaged in this attack, it was obviously meant to sidetrack their plans for the defence of Takrouna, and they were not going to allow that. Furthermore, the capture of the Italians could be put down to a stroke of luck on behalf of the attacking soldiers. Surely, no repeat of that feat was possible with the higher slopes of the hill much more strongly defended. All that the Axis soldiers had to do was to continue firing at these opportunist attackers and if the worst came to the worst, simply pick them off – even just with rifle fire – if they attempted to scale the walls at the points where the defenders were based. Thus, all the logical tactical calculations told the German and Italian commanding officers that the threat of this handful of assailants was now either at an end already, or would soon be extinguished.

What the enemy failed to include in its estimation, however, was the resourcefulness of this small band of attackers, their optimism that almost blinded them to the dire situation they were in, and their ability to survey quickly their terrain and make judgements about the best course to take. In short, it was a new style of attack – which later would be the preserve of commandoes – in which a small group of highly trained and seemingly fearless troops would operate without the need to wait for orders, in conditions that 'ordinary' soldiers could not manage, and with every man assuming much greater responsibility for leadership as the circumstances demanded.

As Manahi looked up, he saw the ledge as his next target. This was the lowest of the three sections of Takrouna, and was almost inaccessible from where he stood, especially as the final six or seven metres leading to its stone walls were almost sheer rock face. There were no steps cut in the rock, and no ladders, but Smith and Aranui found telephone cables from some of the pits they had just emptied of Italians. They used these to scale the side of Takrouna leading to the ledge before midday.[68] They climbed them not at great speed but deliberately, securing each foothold before pulling themselves up another arm-length. Despite the elation they must have felt at their successes to this point, they were hardly overwhelmed with satisfaction. They all knew that much more dangerous challenges were ahead of them, and so they could ill afford to lose a man, especially a 'cheap' death if he fell while climbing. Fighting spirit alone was of no value if any one of these soldiers was lost.

The improvised climbing rope proved invaluable, and enabled the men to get to the base of the rock face, where, one by one, they pulled themselves to the footings of an imposing wall. This detachment of Manahi's men then descended into a small courtyard slightly below their position and obtained the surrender of a startled German radio operator and another enemy soldier who was busy dictating. In the general din of the battle, neither of these two soldiers could have suspected that any Allied troops had penetrated this far into Takrouna, and so Manahi's group found the site lacking in any specific defences.[69] Most of Manahi's men then entered the maze of buildings and cleared out the remaining enemy troops there.

Meanwhile, Manahi – impatient to proceed with the advance – took four of his soldiers with him and managed to find a route that was climbable, and that led them to a narrow ledge on the pinnacle. They crept along it, looking down onto a square which measured roughly 30 metres by 30 metres. Into this area was crammed a hotch-potch of stone buildings, including a domed mosque which was one of the few distinctive structures on Takrouna. The immediate danger which they had to contend with, though, was their precarious hold on the narrow ledge they had climbed onto. As they moved along it, they would have seen how it fell away to a sheer drop from almost every point on its circumference, while along some stretches, the wall was built on an overhang.[70] A fall from here would result at the very least in serious injury. As Manahi and each of his men climbed over the wall, they lobbed grenades ahead of them,[71] and managed to scatter the enemy in this part of the feature. This was followed immediately by a period of frantic hand-to-hand fighting with the Italians among the huts and rubble, while the enemy shelling intensified in an attempt to finish off the attackers.[72]

Some of the earlier Māori casualties from the fighting had been placed in one of the huts for shelter. The combat turned ugly when the Italians managed to get close and lob grenades into this makeshift hospital. As soon as these grenades exploded, there was an abrupt change in attitude among Manahi and his troops, like a flock of birds suddenly changing direction in flight – 'that's when the boys turned around and started using the bayonet', was how Manahi put it.[73] Any Italian found, injured or not, was bayoneted, while those who ran out of reach of the blades had no option but to throw themselves off the walls and down the cliffs. The appearance was of the enemy soldiers being thrown off – an action that was given credence by Second Lieutenant Tom Keelan, who heard one of his men remarking 'Oh, B Company, they're throwing the Germans over the side. That fulla Rogers, he's throwing them over'.[74] This version of events was reinforced when it appeared in the official history of Takrouna, in which the historian Ian Wards confirmed to readers that the 'Italians were shot, bayoneted, and pushed over the cliff during one of those grim moments when all control is lost'.[75]

However, this impression was almost certainly a mistaken one. Even if there had been a deliberate intention by the Māori garrison to throw enemy soldiers off the edges of Takrouna as utu for the attack on their wounded comrades, the practicalities of this during the height of a battle make it highly improbable. Before anyone could be dispensed with in this way, they would have to be immobilised. The difficulty and danger of attempting to hurl someone over a precipice as they struggled to fend off such an attack preclude it as a possibility.[76]

Lieutenant Ronald Shaw, who had been assigned by Kippenberger to lead the platoon that relieved members of the Māori Battalion on Takrouna later recalled that 'there were several instances where the enemy themselves elected to jump over the cliff-face rather than be shot or bayoneted', and was adamant that 'under no circumstances were there any instances where the Maori soldiers were physically throwing the enemy over the cliff-face'.[77] A private from 21 Battalion claimed to have seen 'some of the enemy being thrown over the cliff by them [the Māori soldiers on Takrouna]', but rather than these victims being surrendered soldiers, they fell to their deaths directly as a result of being involved in hand-to-hand fighting.[78]

The other issue that arose in later accounts of this period of the battle was whether Manahi was responsible for killing Italian soldiers who were surrendering – something that went against the conventions of war. Most of the eyewitness accounts concede that enemy soldiers were killed with bayonets as well as from gunfire following the Italians throwing grenades and possibly shooting the hut where the wounded Māori troops were sheltering. However, no mention appears anywhere of the Italian soldiers surrendering, and every indication suggests that the deaths were the result of intense, close-proximity fighting.[79]

Bennett, who was not present at these events, described how the Māori involved in the fighting, on seeing their wounded colleagues attacked, 'turned upon the enemy with unbridled ferocity ... it was almost a massacre'.[80] While this may appear to indict Manahi, who was nominally in command of the platoon, Bennett's statement was a qualified one, and the reference to 'massacre' is best explained in the context of the number of enemy troops killed, rather than the circumstances of their deaths. Moreover, Bennett was adamant that the killing happened during 'some of the fiercest hand-to-hand encounters of the whole war', and not after the Italians had surrendered.[81]

Some later historians wrongly interpreted the 'intense kill-or-be-killed situation' on Takrouna as a grave misdemeanour rather than part of the 'instinctive reactions prompted by the demands of survival', as Bennett suggested. Certainly, no one involved in the action on Takrouna, or any of those troops in the vicinity, considered what had occurred to the enemy troops on the feature to be anything out of the ordinary. Bennett described it as 'a non-event hardly deserving a mention'.[82] Moreover, it appears that even the enemy perceived the fighting as unexceptional. If it had been considered as an atrocity, it would definitely have been used for propaganda purposes by the Italians, who would have 'publicised it, magnified it and reviled it'.[83] Yet, according to Marshal Messe, the Italians considered the aggression they directed at the Māori troops on Takrouna was much more robust than anything they received in return.[84]

The Italian Commander's report, written at the end of April 1943, described this portion of the battle: 'moving with vigour characteristic of our best shock troops, Folgore Battalion dislodged the enemy from house to house, pushed him back from rock to rock, hurled him down of the precipices on the eastern side of the [Takrouna] mountain and retook all the lost positions'.[85] If anyone was responsible for troops being thrown off cliffs, then according to this report, at least, it was the Italians. Finally, there is the evidence of the fact of hundreds of prisoners who were taken, which militates against the proposition that the men under Manahi's command were killing scores of enemy captives as some act of revenge.

However, the charge of an atrocity committed on Takrouna at this time by Manahi, or those immediately under his command, was an allegation that was not easily expunged. It surfaced in accounts of the battle written by Cody, Wards, and Gardiner,[86] but all of these versions of events overlooked the fact that at the specific time that the alleged killing of surrendered enemy troops was supposed to be taking place, Manahi had taken up a defensive position on the ledge on order to prevent the advance of a section of Italians, so could not have been a party to the rumoured atrocity.[87] Yet, the story managed to embed itself in later historical accounts. In a 1972 issue of the military magazine *Parade*, an article on the storming of Takrouna contained the following jingoistic portrayal of the reaction of Manahi's men following the Italian attack on their wounded colleagues: 'In an instant the Maoris reverted from disciplined soldiers to raging, charging warriors. With all the ferocity of their warlike ancestors they hurled themselves at the desecrators of their wounded. Neither the frantic firing of the Italians nor the deadly shooting of the Germans could check their vengeful onslaught. Sweeping to close quarters, the Maoris bayoneted, clubbed and in the mad mêlée, even seized men and flung them off the cliff. Nothing human could have withstood the almost primitive savagery of the frenzied attack'.[88]

Following on from this stance, in 1995, Major Richard Taylor, the director of the Waiouru Army Museum, repeated the allegation that 'Italians wanting to surrender later were shot, bayoneted and thrown off cliffs by Manahi's men'.[89] Once the story had entered the bloodstream of successive histories, it became accepted as fact, with little attention given to its underlying veracity, and with the occasional unsourced detail thrown in to give the impression of authenticity. Such was the case with one Italian publication which surveyed briefly the events at Takrouna. 'At one point with the battle out of control', its author wrote, 'Italian troops threw grenades into an aid station, prompting reprisals that included chasing Axis soldiers over the precipice at bayonet point and tossing two prisoners

*Takrouna Pinnacle with Takrouna village, 2007*

Norman Bennett

*Takrouna Pinnacle and fortification, 2007*

Norman Bennett

*Rugged terrain below the Takrouna Pinnacle with olive plantations below, 2007*

*Norman Bennett*

*Takrouna fortifications with cacti deterring intruders*

*Norman Bennett*

*Takrouna fortification*

Norman Bennett

*Takrouna fortification with village below*

Norman Bennett

*War Graves Commission cemetery at Enfidaville where many of the Takrouna battle dead lie, 2007*

*Norman Bennett*

after them'.[90] No reference for the provenance of this story was given, no names of the two alleged prisoners provided, and no account of how these men could have been captured as prisoners while all around them was frantic fighting at close quarters.

Perhaps the most instructive and concise appraisal of this phase of the fighting on Takrouna came from a later assessment, which observed that 'in the heat of battle what may be deemed excesses in normal times would have a different interpretation to those actually engaged in the struggle for life or death', and noted that it would be difficult to imagine 'that men of the calibre of Horrocks, Kippenberger, or Blundell would have initiated and strongly supported a VC recommendation for Manahi if there were any doubts in their minds about the moral fitness of Manahi for a Victoria Cross'.[91]

In the violent combat that had raged in the preceding hours, Manahi's force had been cut down to just four, with the remainder killed or wounded. Yet, on the other side of the balance sheet, there were now 150 enemy prisoners, and a further forty or fifty had been killed in the fighting.[92] This rate of advance, with the hugely disproportionate enemy losses, could not continue indefinitely. By mid-morning, Manahi knew that it would be reckless to proceed any further with just a few good men at his side, and he also anticipated that the entire enemy force on the feature would soon be organising frantically to launch a counter-attack. This was another inspired display of leadership. Like a seasoned gambler, Manahi knew when the risk was too great, and carefully weighed up how he would play his next hand.

What made the position of Manahi and Rogers so vulnerable now was that they were effectively trapped on the pinnacle. Initially, they had looked down towards Takrouna village – 'a stew of hovels'[93] on the western end of Takrouna – and relished the prospect of finally being able to fire on what appeared to be a soft target, especially early on, when the enemy had not yet realised that the pinnacle had been taken.[94] The element of surprise could not last, though, and so Rogers began to fire into the village to try his luck at taking out a few more of the enemy. The Italian troops there scrambled for cover (possibly one or two were killed), and Manahi and Rogers then began to implement a plan that they could not have conceived of even half an hour earlier. The village was separated from the pinnacle by a sheer rock wall which could be circumvented by a set of steps, and so they decided to block all access from the village to the pinnacle. To achieve this, some of the remaining troops managed to lever a large boulder to block the mouth of the entrance to the pinnacle, and were then posted to guard the steps leading to their position. This way, no enemy soldiers would be able to reach them.

Needing more men and ammunition[95] (and having created an opening for

Allied troops to ascend to this part of Takrouna), Manahi yelled out below to some of the stragglers of the Māori and 23 Battalion to join them, which they did.[96] A small garrison was now nestled at the top of Takrouna. It was a staggering achievement, but it was still not a triumph. The 5th Infantry Brigade's assault on the west of Takrouna had failed, leaving the enemy firmly in control of that part of the feature, and as the day dawned, 6 Field Regiment, which was in full view of the enemy in the village in Takrouna, had to pull back.

As the enemy had regrouped, it launched a sustained bombardment of the pinnacle. Casualties were heavy, and among the six killed that morning was Rogers, leaving Manahi in command of the small garrison on this portion of Takrouna. The defence held, due to some aggressive firing by Manahi and his men, and the defensive measures he had organised.

Rogers' death brought to an end an exceptional episode of bravery, and although the army offered no award in recognition of his feats at Takrouna, his brother proudly recalled the accomplishment on this feature. In a letter to their father, Private Winiata Rogers wrote 'you will probably have heard all about Johnny's exploits at Takrouna Heights … and we should all be very proud of him. He proved himself a man that day, and all the chaps who saw him in action that day leading his platoon up the sheer face of the Heights all say he did one of the bravest things ever performed in this war'.[97]

Back at Battalion Headquarters, the disorganisation had still not been fully overcome, due primarily to enemy incursions in the area. A planned tank advance had failed to proceed, and communications between all the companies had still not been fully re-established.[98] Kippenberger was considering an attack on Takrouna – which he presumed was still held by the enemy – by 21 Battalion but did not go ahead with this. And while 'the task of helping 28 Battalion was doubtless in the mind of the [21] battalion commander', no special action was taken 'and no reserve was available for the purpose'.[99] Manahi and his men were consequently marooned on Takrouna with no immediate prospect of being relieved.

As the day wore on, the enemy bombardment of the pinnacle and the ledge continued to blast away. However, even with the artillery odds loaded so heavily in favour of the Germans and Italians, Manahi's men managed (through highly accurate fire) to incapacitate two 25-pounders that the enemy had positioned on the northern slopes to attack the pinnacle. In the meanwhile, Manahi had made two attempts to communicate with the battalion, but these were unsuccessful. Yet again, a withdrawal was the most prudent course of action to take, and any conventional officer would probably have undertaken such a move. However, Manahi appears to have assumed personal responsibility for the entire Takrouna operation, and with men being killed all around him, including some of his closest friends, he decided to descend himself to seek reinforcements, and hope that the enemy did not choose that time to launch an assault. If it did, the garrison would almost certainly be wiped out, and the enemy once more would assume control of Takrouna. Manahi later recalled this episode: 'Well, I sent the first runner down to C Company [but] he never got back. The I sent another man down – Simkins – he never got back, he was wounded. So in the end, I had to come down to C Company, who were in the olive grove'.[100]

Manahi reached the base of Takrouna, dodging his way through heavy fire on the way down, and made contact with C Company's Lieutenant Wananga [Walton] Te Ariki Haig. He requested that the Lieutenant provide an infantry section, stretcher bearers, food and ammunition, to which he 'agreed straight away'.[101] As soon as this was arranged and the troops put at his disposal, Manahi returned to the pinnacle, with a section of soldiers – 'about a dozen, I suppose' as he put it[102] – following him through the dust and smoke churned up by the incessant enemy shelling of the position. Just before starting his ascent, Manahi encountered an artillery officer who was returning from the base of Takrouna, and who told him that the position on the pinnacle was doomed as another Allied shelling was about to be launched in anticipation of a new assault on the feature.[103] Manahi ought to have heeded this advice, because the intelligence was sound – or at least, he had no reason for doubting it. But he wanted to take Takrouna, and his instincts told him to ignore the warning, which proved to be fortuitous when Captain Catchpole of 5 Medium Regiment informed him a few moments later that the planned shelling had been cancelled, and that reinforcements were on the way (which was more of a hope than anything based on certain knowledge).[104]

The background to this cancellation of the proposed shelling involved Kippenberger, who just before midday had rejected a recommendation from both Corps and Divisional commanders that all troops in the vicinity of Takrouna be pulled back so that a fresh artillery assault on the hill could be launched.[105] Kippenberger was also not above gambling, and hoped that Manahi could hold the pinnacle until reinforcements secured the hold on this part of Takrouna.

Manahi rushed back up the hill, with his section following him, and as soon as he reached the pinnacle, he deployed the additional batch of men to bolster the defences to the utmost that the numbers at his disposal permitted. All he could do now was to wait for what he knew was the inevitable enemy effort to take back the pinnacle and the ledge. Finally, at 3.30 p.m., some more support arrived in the form of 15 Platoon of 21 Battalion under Lieutenant Shaw. Manahi briefed Shaw on the situation, and both men moved around as much of the feature as they could to get an impression of the location and preparations of the enemy. Shaw, as the senior officer, was to take over command from Manahi, but as they were walking around, assessing what form the enemy's counter-attack might assume, and while Shaw's men were taking up their positions, the enemy suddenly launched their assault. It was only in a discussion about Takrouna with Bennett forty years later that Manahi discovered – to his mild surprise – that there were two enemy companies (half a battalion) involved in the counter-attack. 'It was a big force alright', he acknowledged, and then, still taken aback by finally being told the size of the opposition, asked to make sure, 'was there really two companies?'[106]

Just as this enemy offensive commenced, Manahi caught sight of an additional group of enemy troops – twelve truckloads of them – approaching Takrouna. This force divided into two parties which attacked the north-west corner of the ledge. The first party endeavoured to lead a charge along the same track Manahi had used to return up Takrouna, but was beaten back in some of the most intense fighting Manahi had ever been involved in. As some of the Italians managed to get near to his position, Manahi, together with Corporal John Pani Bell, grabbed machine-guns and mowed down the advancing soldiers. Manahi's tactic at this juncture was crucial. Rather than just having his men firing constantly at the enemy as they approached, he let them get fairly close 'before we opened up' with fire from the Bren guns. 'They were like a mob of sheep being driven into us, then we opened up on them and not one escaped'.[107]

The second enemy party fought among the huts but was repulsed with the help of 15 Platoon, which was assisted by a small group of Māori led by Captain Muirhead, who had descended from the pinnacle to help fend off the assault. By 7.00 p.m., the enemy attack had been halted, and the mainly Italian troops retreated.[108] Shaw took over command of the Allied position on the hill, and Manahi and his exhausted band of men left Takrouna for some rest, having been involved in twenty hours of fighting. Shaw later wrote, 'I did not know who Manahi was at the time of the battle. He was obviously in charge as he introduced himself to me after the battle – and when order was finally restored on the ledge. I then took over command at this point and Sgt. Manahi showed me over the ledge and the area known as the pinnacle. Manahi then retired with his men, left the ledge at Takrouna and went down the cliff-face for a rest'.[109]

Two hours later, further reinforcements arrived on Takrouna[110] (much to Shaw's relief), and it was hoped that the night would be a quiet one after the intensity of the day's combat. No further ground had been gained, but at least the Allied foothold on the hill had remained, due chiefly to Manahi's extraordinary efforts in battle and his impressive leadership, which Shaw remarked was brilliant and valiant.[111]

However, shortly after 9.00 p.m., the enemy forces launched a surprise and risky attack, which resulted in them taking the pinnacle, and almost dominating the ledge. Stubborn New Zealand resistance prevented the ledge from being lost, though, but with the pinnacle now in German/Italian possession, the enemy was able to use its commanding height to fire continually on the New Zealand position. The resulting stalemate meant that 'neither party could remove the other, each endeavour being frustrated by a shower of hand grenades and small-arms fire'.[112]

In the early hours of 21 April, Shaw was wounded,[113] and so command passed over to Second-Lieutenant Ian Henry Hirst. However, the enemy was slowly consolidating its position, and its incessant shelling was beginning to have some effect. The situation was grave, but two developments occurred overnight that changed the course of the campaign. First, communications were restored between the New Zealanders on the hill and Brigade Headquarters, and second, Kippenberger – 'red-eyed and unshaven'[114] – arrived to take personal command of operations on Takrouna.

Kippenberger asked specifically for Manahi to lead a counter-offensive. Manahi hand-picked men from the battalion – twelve in all – and supplied with as much ammunition as the troops could carry, once more led soldiers up Takrouna. On reaching the New Zealand position, Manahi and Hirst conferred on the best tactic to employ to respond to the enemy's upper hand on the hill. Manahi recommended the use of mortars to soften up the enemy before any assault took place. The problem, however, was in the range of these weapons. Mortars positioned below Takrouna were ineffective because the distance of the target was too great, while the two-inch mortars on the ledge could not drop their shells in a range of just 100 metres, which was what was required.[115]

The solution was the use of heavier artillery, in the form of 25-pounders, which crept the barrage up the hill until they began to land shells directly on the pinnacle. By midday, three direct hits had been made on the mosque and, satisfied that the enemy had been weakened by this bombardment, three assault parties made their move towards the enemy position, with Manahi leading one of these groups in the attack on the pinnacle, while the second group was led by Sergeant Weepu. At first, though, Hirst had not been cooperative. Manahi asked him for another section of troops to lead the assault on the pinnacle, which he refused, so Manahi and Weepu got their own men together, and then Manahi told Hirst that he would not move until he gave him some troops to assist in retaking the pinnacle.[116]

The assault on the pinnacle was swift, with just one final barrage from the enemy positioned on the village,[117] after which Manahi and his men met with only small pockets of resistance as they encircled the buildings on Takrouna's highest point. But when they finally scrambled to the summit to confront the Italians, there was an unexpected sight that confronted Manahi and his men. Instead of corpses scattered around the ground as a result of the recent fighting, or well-concealed troops bursting out of their defences to fight off the assailants, there was no one on the pinnacle at all. Manahi was bewildered at this inexplicable turn of events. It was only after a quick but intensive search by his men that a secret escape tunnel was discovered (which had been so well concealed that none of the Allied troops who had been there the previous day had noticed it). The tunnel led to the lower village, and from there, the enemy deployed its mortars to fire on the pinnacle, just as Manahi had captured it. This inflicted further casualties, and threatened the hold the Allies had just secured on the pinnacle.

Artillery fire was then ordered on the lower village, which, as it was 'perched on a narrow ridge, huddled close to the abrupt face of the pinnacle … was a very difficult target'.[118] Eventually, the barrage had the effect of ending the mortar attacks, but it had taken 300 rounds being fired into the enemy stronghold. New, 17-pounder anti-tank guns were used, mainly because of the preferable angle of trajectory that they could achieve, and because they proved highly effective at pulverising the stone huts on the site, and interring their occupants in the process (it was perhaps partly because of their effectiveness that they were still on the secret list, to be used only in emergencies).[119]

While the Italians were at the receiving end of this bombardment, Manahi – again acting on his own initiative – led a group of men in neutralising enemy posts on the north-east slopes, with the intention of advancing on the village. He and his men – 'dodging and creeping among the boulders'[120] – again used bayonets and grenades to prise out enemy troops from their strongholds. Hirst complemented this action by leading a party to attack the village from the north. Initially, both Manahi and Hirst had to force out the enemy by driving them from house to house, but within half an hour, the Italians, together with a few Germans, saw the futility of further resistance, and surrendered. A further 323 enemy prisoners were taken, along with a huge haul of weapons and ammunition,[121] and Takrouna was finally in Allied hands – 'an outstanding military feat'[122] by any measure.

Manahi was physically shattered after such prolonged and intense fighting and as a result of having taken responsibility for several pivotal tactical decisions on Takrouna. These decisions unquestioningly made the difference between taking the hill, and relinquishing it to the enemy, and saved the lives of potentially hundreds of Allied soldiers (even though some of his closest friends were sacrificed in the process). Now that the remaining enemy troops had been taken into captivity, more Allied soldiers entered the Takrouna area and secured it. However, Manahi's sense of duty did not waver, and as night fell, he oversaw the collection of the dead from the pinnacle and the ledge, including the corpses of men he had fought with since Greece. Each body was wrapped in a blanket, tied up, and then carefully lowered over the edge and down the slopes by rope.

Strategically, Takrouna became the key to the firm line held by the Eight Army while the First Army delivered the final blows against the Axis forces in the north.[123] Manahi's role therefore contributed directly to a major element of Allied strategy in the final phase of the war in North Africa – and was the battle that Freyberg regarded as the hardest operation in the entire North African campaign.[124] It was also enormously costly to the Maori Battalion. Twelve of its 17 officers were either killed or wounded, while 104 of its 302 other ranks were made casualties.[125] Manahi's reaction to his astounding feats was typically understated. Shortly after returning to New Zealand in 1943, he was interviewed by a reporter for the *Rotorua Morning Post*, in which he gave just one statement about Takrouna: 'It was a hot scrap at the top. Our ammunition ran out and we had to use captured Italian and German rifles, machine guns and ammunition. We managed to hold on for the best part of the day and we were then joined by men of 'C' Company. Only three of us were left, (myself), Private Hinga Grant and Lance Corporal H. Ruha'.[126]

It took a day or two for the magnitude of Manahi's achievements on Takrouna to register with all the officers and troops in the vicinity. Years later, some of those present put their recollections in writing, offering first-hand accounts of the perception of Manahi's role in conquering this crucial feature. In 1992, Major-General W B (Sandy) Thomas, who was commanding the 23 (New Zealand) Battalion during the battle for Takrouna, described how he and his troops had attempted to penetrate the German defences on the flank of the main feature, but were pinned down by heavy enemy fire. Then, 'the fire abated [and] we became aware that the Maori's [sic] had captured the feature – and were shouting their triumph down to us. The lift to our morale was enormous and with the flank danger removed we were able to re-organise and consolidate our position. I cannot stress too much how great that particular action by the Maori's meant to my Battalion'. Once the battle was over, Thomas climbed up the slope of Takrouna 'and learnt that Sgt Manahi had commanded the small group who had seized the heights. When I saw the steep nature of the ground, the mass of enemy dug-outs and weapons I realised what an absolute epic the battle must have been: One could only look at the remnants of enemy dead – and the challenge of their seemingly impregnable position – with awe at the courage of Manahi and his few men. I was aware then, as I am now, that it must have needed the very highest order of personal bravery to have assaulted that final pinnacle .... I have been in many battles now but I have never in my experience seen or heard of an action more worthy of a Victoria Cross than Sgt Manahi's assault on the pinnacle of

Takrouna'.[127]

Brigadier Jack Conolly, who at the time of the assault on Takrouna was the Commanding Officer of the 24 (New Zealand) Battalion, noted that 'even from that distance [about two kilometres] we were able to assess the enormous physical difficulties, the almost impossible terrain and the stubborn, fanatical resistance of the defenders. It was an incredible display of initiative, leadership and courage. There was great jubilation and relief in the valleys and hills below when Takrouna finally fell'.[128] For the Allied soldiers within a growing radius of Takrouna, news of Manahi's feats rippled out, amazing men who were already well-experienced with heroism in battle.

Manahi and the men who fought with him at Takrouna brought with them talents for fighting that were the inheritance of a much older form of combat – one which had lasted in New Zealand longer than in most of the other countries which had sent troops to the war. This was an almost extinct quality, which one military theorist has characterised as 'a sort of empathy with one's adversary, lending the ability to anticipate his actions and forestall his blows, combined with a physical brazenness which would allow a man to look a stranger in the face and strike to fell him .... For direct, face-to-face, knock-down and drag-out violence is something which modern, middle-class Western man encounters rarely if at all'.[129] These traits, coupled with superb judgment, a highly-developed sense of the ebb and flow of battles, fearlessness in the face of anything the enemy could throw at him and any physical obstacles he encountered, and the ability to lead and command respect from his men, are what led to Manahi's triumph on Takrouna.

However, in the immediate aftermath of the victory, Manahi and the men of the battalion who had fought on the hill did not seek any sort of recognition or prestige. Rather, what they most craved for was rest, and the commanding officers saw to it that they received this. On 23 April, Major Keiha took up his appointment as the new commander of the Māori Battalion,[130] and that evening, led his men to the 5 Brigade bivouac area. For the final week of April, the men of the battalion 'were made as comfortable as possible', with hot showers provided for the first time since they had arrived in Takrouna, and daily visits made to the beach at Hergla.[131]

Manahi may now have finally had the urge to leave the fighting and return to New Zealand, or failing that option in the short term, at least have some more rest. However, the following week, there was a return to route marches. For the experienced troops, like Manahi, they knew this meant that the pause from the business of war was about to end. But, this was part of a major transition phase in the life of the battalion. 250 raw volunteers were heading towards Egypt to reinforce the battalion's numbers, while some of the 'old hands', including Manahi, were to be sent home on furlough, though he did not yet know it.[132]

After the church service on Sunday 2 May, Manahi was among those transported from their base to the beach at Hergla. Keiha described it as 'a good sandy beach and a calm sea [which] helped to make a very enjoyable afternoon for the men'.[133] The pressure of intense fighting finally seemed to be something in the past, and as the prospect of further conflict looked increasingly unlikely, the men of the battalion took every opportunity they could to unwind and relax. The following morning, the men were ordered to pack up their bivouacs as the battalion prepared to move to a new temporary location, at Djebel. The war in North Africa was not yet over, though, and so when the troops established their new camp, they returned to the familiar routines of digging slit trenches, stationing sentries, mounting their Bren machine guns, and more marching. Their role during the early weeks of May was, in Harding's all-embracing phrase, to be 'passive-offensive'.[134] There were skirmishes with the enemy in the following days (with few casualties), but A and D Companies were the ones committed to these engagements, while Manahi and the others of B Company were kept in reserve. By 11 May, the battalion had returned to the beach at Hergla, and were receiving some rare luxuries, including more hot showers, plus dental inspections, fresh sets of clothing, Canadian beer, and were even shown films in the evenings. The result was 'plenty of fun and noise … in the camp'.[135]

On 13 May, the Italians in North Africa surrendered unconditionally, bringing about the end of the war in the region, and giving rise to General Alexander's pronouncement that 'we are masters of the North African shores'.[136] Two days later, Manahi and the men of the Fifth Brigade began the long and tedious journey from Tunisia back to Egypt, arriving in Maadi – on the outskirts of Cairo – during the final week of May. (The route back to Egypt was easier because, apart from the absence of any direct threat from enemy forces, the trucks were able to use their headlights at night, making progress much swifter.)[137]

The announcement that so many of the troops were waiting to hear came at 4.00 p.m. on Monday 24 May: 6000 men from the New Zealand Division were to go home for three months' leave. The battalion was still making its way back to Egypt, but the atmosphere must have changed markedly after this news. On the morning of 31 May, Colonel Keiha ordered a full muster parade of the battalion where he read out the names of 182 officers and men – 'practically all that was left of the original Battalion' – who had been chosen to return to New Zealand for a three-month furlough.[138] The men in this group, which included Manahi, were then domiciled in separate quarters, and whiled away their last two weeks in Egypt by visiting Cairo, and relaxing. For Manahi, three of the most intense years of his life, in the service of his country, were coming to an end. On 15 June, he boarded the former cruise ship and now troop transporter, *Nieuw Amsterdam*, which had berthed in Egypt few days earlier. The war was finally behind him.

## NOTES

1. J Keegan, *The Face of Battle: A Study of Agincourt, Waterloo, and the Somme*, pp. 295–6.
2. W Gardiner, *Te Mura o Te Ahi: The Story of the Maori Battalion*, p. 118.
3. B Freyberg to Minister of Defence, 11 April 1943, in *Documents Relating to New Zealand's Participation in the Second World War, 1939–45*, vol. 2, p. 174.
4. C Bennett, interview with R A Cairns, in *Takrouna: 28 Maori Battalion Engagement, 19–21 April 1943*, video recording, c. 1983.
5. H Kippenberger, *Infantry Brigadier*, p. 303.
6. T D M Stout, *New Zealand Medical Services in Middle East and Italy*, Wellington, War History Branch, Department of Internal Affairs, 1956, p. 437.
7. I McL Wards, *Takrouna*, Wellington, Historical Publications Branch, Department of Internal Affairs, 1951, pp. 5–6.
8. I McL Wards, *Takrouna*, p. 29.
9. Kippenberger got his times wrong, because he was calculating based on desert conditions. The olive groves and cactus hedges slowed down the advance around Takrouna. See H Kippenberger, *Infantry Brigadier*, p. 304.
10. H Kippenberger, *Infantry Brigadier*, pp. 303–4.
11. *Supplement to the London Gazette*, 5 February 1948, p. 879.
12. C Bennett, interview with R A Cairns, in *Takrouna: 28 Maori Battalion Engagement, 19–21 April 1943*.
13. 5 NZ Inf Bde Operation Order no. 18, Copy no. 3, 19 April 1943, in Secret War Diary of the 28 NZ (Maori) Battalion, 1 April – 31 May 1943, appendix 3, Archives New Zealand, ref WAII 1, DA 68/1/40.
14. H Kippenberger, *Infantry Brigadier*, p. 304; M Soutar, *Nga Tama Toa: The Price of Citizenship*, p. 260.
15. C Bennett, in J F Cody, *28 (Maori) Battalion*, p. 286.
16. T D M Stout, *New Zealand Medical Services in Middle East and Italy*, p. 451.
17. C Bennett, in J F Cody, *28 (Maori) Battalion*, p. 290.
18. C Bennett, in Unit Diaries of the Maori Battalion in World War II [Archives Ref: WAII 1 DA 68/1/1-73], Wednesday 14 April 1943.
19. The battalion guessed that Takrouna was guarded by an Italian garrison. See W G Stevens, *Bardia to Enfidaville*, p. 305.
20. This was the normal approach to the village on Takrouna. See W G Stevens, *Bardia to Enfidaville*, pp. 304–5.
21. C Bennett, in J F Cody, *28 (Maori) Battalion*, p. 290.
22. Report on operations for period night 19/20 April 43, 28 NZ (Maori) Bn 30 April 43, in Secret War Diary of the 28 NZ (Maori) Battalion, 1 April – 31 May 1943, appendix 4, Archives New Zealand, ref WAII 1, DA 68/1/40.
23. Trip-wires were used to detonate the mines, and on exploding, they revealed the position of the attacker to those defending Takrouna.
24. C Bennett, in J F Cody, *28 (Maori) Battalion*, p. 291.
25. *Supplement to the London Gazette*, 5 February 1948, p. 879.
26. Interview with Arthur Midwood, Rotorua, 7 September 2009.
27. C Bennett, interview with R A Cairns, in *Takrouna: 28 Maori Battalion Engagement, 19–21 April 1943*.
28. I McL Wards, *Takrouna*, pp. 3–4.
29. Ibid., pp. 4–5; W. G. Stevens, *Bardia to Enfidaville*, pp. 304–5.
30. C Bennett, in Unit Diaries of the Maori Battalion in World War II [Archives Ref: WAII 1 DA 68/1/1-73], Thursday 15 April 1943.
31. C Bennett, interview with R A Cairns, in *Takrouna: 28 Maori Battalion Engagement, 19-21 April 1943*.
32. Op. cit.
33. C Bennett, in Unit Diaries of the Maori Battalion in World War II [Archives Ref: WAII 1 DA 68/1/1-73], Thursday 15 April 1943.
34. C Bennett, in Unit Diaries of the Maori Battalion in World War II [Archives Ref: WAII 1 DA 68/1/1-73], Saturday 17 April 1943.
35. The code word for the operation was 'Oration'. The orders for the assault were only issued that morning. See C Bennett, interview with R A Cairns, in *Takrouna: 28 Maori Battalion Engagement, 19-21 April 1943*. Takrouna was code-named 'Tinker', see 'Oration', Main H.Q., 10 Corps, Ref 134, 7 April 1943, in Secret War Diary of the 28 NZ (Maori) Battalion, 1 April – 31 May 1943, appendix 3, Archives New Zealand, ref WAII 1, DA 68/1/40.
36. Report on operations for period night 19/20 April 43, 28 NZ (Maori) Bn 30 April 43, in Secret War Diary of the 28 NZ (Maori) Battalion, 1 April – 31 May 1943, appendix 4, Archives New Zealand, ref WAII 1, DA 68/1/40.
37. M Parkinson, in M Soutar, *Nga Tama Toa: The Price of Citizenship*, p. 262.
38. W G Stevens, *Bardia to Enfidaville*, pp. 314–6.
39. Report on operations for period night 19/20 April 43, 28 NZ (Maori) Bn 30 April 43, in Secret War Diary of the 28 NZ (Maori) Battalion, 1 April – 31 May 1943, appendix 4, Archives New Zealand, ref WAII 1, DA 68/1/40.
40. M Soutar, *Nga Tama Toa: The Price of Citizenship*, p. 262.
41. Aided by recently-arrived American Sherman tanks.
42. I McL Wards, *Takrouna*, p. 29.
43. H Kippenberger, *Infantry Brigadier*, p. 303.
44. Cited in T Stevens (Director and Producer), *Maori Battalion March to Victory*, Television New Zealand documentary, 1990.
45. W G Stevens, *Bardia to Enfidaville*, p. 317.
46. Op. cit.
47. Op. cit.
48. Report on operations for period night 19/20 April 43, 28 NZ (Maori) Bn 30 April 43, in Secret War Diary of the 28 NZ (Maori) Battalion, 1 April – 31 May 1943, appendix 4, Archives New Zealand, ref WAII 1, DA 68/1/40.
49. W S Smellie, in A Ross, *23 Battalion*, p. 259.
50. Their mothers were sisters. F McRae to P Moon, 9 February 2010.
51. C Bennett, interview with R A Cairns, in *Takrouna: 28 Maori Battalion Engagement, 19-21 April 1943*.
52. Manahi had his promotion to Lance-Sergeant confirmed on 21 April 1943.
53. Captain S F Catchpole.
54. W G Stevens, *Bardia to Enfidaville*, p. 327.
55. C Bennett, interview with R A Cairns, in *Takrouna: 28 Maori Battalion Engagement, 19-21 April 1943*.
56. Op. cit.
57. Op. cit.

58. H Manahi, interview with C Bennett, in *Takrouna: 28 Maori Battalion Engagement, 19-21 April 1943.*
59. J F Cody, *28 (Maori) Battalion*, p. 299.
60. Cited in T Stevens (Director and Producer), *Maori Battalion March to Victory*, Television New Zealand documentary, 1990.
61. C Bennett, interview with R A Cairns, in *Takrouna: 28 Maori Battalion Engagement, 19-21 April 1943.*
62. H Kippenberger, *Infantry Brigadier*, p. 308.
63. J F Cody, *28 (Maori) Battalion*, p. 300.
64. H Manahi, interview with C Bennett, in *Takrouna: 28 Maori Battalion Engagement, 19-21 April 1943.*
65. Interview with R Manahi, 25 February 2010.
66. H Kippenberger, *Infantry Brigadier*, p. 309.
67. Report on operations for period night 19/20 April 43, 28 NZ (Maori) Bn 30 April 43, in Secret War Diary of the 28 NZ (Maori) Battalion, 1 April – 31 May 1943, appendix 4, Archives New Zealand, ref WAII 1, DA 68/1/40.
68. Forty years later, Manahi was vague on the exact timing. H Manahi, interview with C Bennett, in *Takrouna: 28 Maori Battalion Engagement, 19-21 April 1943.*
69. W G Stevens, *Bardia to Enfidaville*, p. 327.
70. H Kippenberger, *Infantry Brigadier*, p. 309.
71. Op. cit.
72. B Freyberg to Prime Minister, 27 May 1943, in *Documents Relating to New Zealand's Participation in the Second World War 1939 – 45*, vol. 2, p. 179.
73. H Manahi, interview with C Bennett, in *Takrouna: 28 Maori Battalion Engagement, 19-21 April 1943.*
74. T Keelan, in M Soutar, *Nga Tama Toa: The Price of Citizenship*, p. 265.
75. I McL Wards, *Takrouna*, p. 25.
76. The mention of Rogers in the story is suspect in so far as when the alleged throwing off the cliffs occurred, Rogers was already dead.
77. Letter from R A Shaw, Mt Maunganui, 20 January 1993, p. 2, author's collection.
78. W L Richards (21 Battalion), statement Sworn on Oath in the Field, 9 May 1943, author's collection.
79. See report of M Carew in M Taylor, 'Memorandum Re: Sergeant Hoane [sic] Manahi', Woodward Law Offices, 4 February 2000, n. p. author's collection.
80. Op. cit.
81. C Bennett, in op. cit.
82. Letter from C Bennett, Te Puke, 19 January 1993, author's collection.
83. Op. cit.
84. Op. cit.
85. G Messe, April 1943, cited in Petition presented by the Manahi Victoria Cross Committee, 1993, p. 13.
86. J F Cody, *28 (Maori) Battalion*; W Gardiner, *Te Mura o Te Ahi: The Story of the Maori Battalion*; I McL Wards, *Takrouna*, p. 25; J F Cody, *Official History of New Zealand in the Second World War 1939–45, 21 Battalion*, Wellington, 1953, p. 260.
87. See report of M Carew in M Taylor, 'Memorandum Re: Sergeant Hoane [sic] Manahi', Woodward Law Offices, 4 February 2000, n. p. author's collection.
88. H C Baker, 'The Modest hero', in *Parade*, February 1972, p. 30.
89. N Reid, 'Push for Maori Hero Gets Celebrity Backing But Atrocities May Taint Valour', in *Sunday News*, 8 January 1995.
90. California Historical Group, 'The "FOLGORE" : The 285th Paracadutisti Battaglione in Tunisia', information sheet published by the CHG re-enactment society, 1992, n. p.
91. Statement from Manahi VC Committee, 1 December 1992, author's collection. Also see Waitangi Tribunal, *The Preliminary Report on the Haane Manahi Victoria Cross Claim*, Wai-893, Wellington, 2005, p. 8.
92. H Kippenberger, *Infantry Brigadier*, p. 309.
93. J F Cody, *28 (Maori) Battalion*, p. 302.
94. W G Stevens, *Bardia to Enfidaville*, pp. 327-8.
95. Running low on ammunition was a frequent problem for Manahi while on Takrouna. H Manahi, interview with C Bennett, in *Takrouna: 28 Maori Battalion Engagement, 19-21 April 1943.*
96. Just before 6 a.m., Kippenberger sent part of Notts Yeomanry forward to clear up any pockets of resistance on the east side of Takrouna, and to give what help it could to either battalion. See W G Stevens, *Bardia to Enfidaville*, p. 329.
97. W Rogers, Cairo, 3 August 1943, letter, pp. 3-4, courtesy of D. Rogers.
98. The signal cables had not withstood the heavy shell fire.
99. W G Stevens, *Bardia to Enfidaville*, p. 306.
100. H Manahi, interview with C Bennett, in *Takrouna: 28 Maori Battalion Engagement, 19–21 April 1943.*
101. Op. cit.
102. Op. cit.
103. He did not yet know that this policy had been dropped.
104. W G Stevens, *Bardia to Enfidaville*, p. 333.
105. Op.cit.
106. H Manahi, interview with C Bennett, in *Takrouna: 28 Maori Battalion Engagement, 19-21 April 1943.*
107. Op.cit.
108. 'The attackers were believed to be all Italians, but 90 Light Division mentions a few Germans from 47 Regiment', op. cit.
109. Letter from R A Shaw, Mt Maunganui, 20 January 1993, p. 2, author's collection.
110. 14 Platoon (21 Battalion) under Lieutenant Hirst.
111. Letter from R. A. Shaw, Mt Maunganui, 20 January 1993, p. 2, author's collection.
112. I McL Wards, *Takrouna*, p. 26.
113. He was evacuated with great difficulty.
114. I McL Wards, *Takrouna*, p. 27.
115. W G Stevens, *Bardia to Enfidaville*, p. 337.
116. H Manahi, interview with C Bennett, in *Takrouna: 28 Maori Battalion Engagement, 19-21 April 1943.*
117. Op. Cit.
118. I McL Wards, *Takrouna*, p. 27.
119. Op. cit.
120. Op. cit.
121. Report on operations for period night 19/20 April 43, 28 NZ (Maori) Bn 30 April 43, in Secret War Diary of the 28 NZ (Maori) Battalion, 1 April – 31 May 1943, appendix 4, Archives New Zealand, ref WAII 1, DA 68/1/40.
122. W G Stevens, *Bardia to Enfidaville*, p. 340.
123. I McL Wards, *Takrouna*, p. 28.
124. Op. cit.
125. Op. cit.
126. H Manahi, in *Rotorua Morning Post*, 19 July 1943.

127. Letter from W B Thomas to C Bennett, 20 June 1992, author's collection.
128. Letter from J Conolly to C Bennett, 12 June 1992, author's collection.
129. J Keegan, *The Face of Battle*, p. 314.
130. A position he held until 11 September 1943 when he was admitted to hospital and relinquished the role.
131. J F Cody, *28 (Maori) Battalion*, p. 311.
132. As part of the second furlough draft.
133. K A Keiha, in Unit Diaries of the Maori Battalion in World War II [Archives Ref: WAII 1 DA 68/1/1-73], Sunday 2 May 1943.
134. R W Harding, in Unit Diaries of the Maori Battalion in World War II [Archives Ref: WAII 1 DA 68/1/1-73], Wednesday 5 May 1943.
135. K A Keiha, in Unit Diaries of the Maori Battalion in World War II [Archives Ref: WAII 1 DA 68/1/1-73], Friday 14 May 1943.
136. H Alexander to W. Churchill, 13 May 1943, in J F Cody, *28 (Maori) Battalion*, p. 314.
137. K A Keiha, in Unit Diaries of the Maori Battalion in World War II [Archives Ref: WAII 1 DA 68/1/1-73], Thursday 20 May 1943.
138. J F Cody, *28 (Maori) Battalion*, p. 317.

# CHAPTER 8: From VC to DCM

There is another trail associated with Manahi from April 1943 that can be followed in relation to his actions at Takrouna. This involves the fate of the recommendation made that he receive the Victoria Cross (VC). The VC was instituted in 1856,[1] and could be awarded to both officers and non-commissioned ranks of the Royal Navy and the Army [and later the Airforce] who, in the presence of the enemy 'shall have performed some signal act of valour …'. Since its inception the VC has remained the British Empire's premier award for gallantry in face of the enemy and was worn before all other orders, decorations and medals.[2]

The starting point for the award of the VC is the citation. This is the document (usually written by a commanding officer) which specifies what it is that the nominee has done to earn the medal. It is signed by the relevant commanding officer (who collects supporting statements from other military personnel involved in the act for which the award is being recommended), and then is passed up the ranks of the armed force (in Manahi's case, the army) until it is finally approved by the VC Committee (usually comprising the Permanent Under Secretary and Service Chiefs of Staff) in London. From there, the decision to award the VC is published in the *London Gazette*, and is thus officially confirmed. The wording accompanying the VC confirms that its recipient has been awarded it 'for most conspicuous bravery, or some daring or pre-eminent act of valour or self-sacrifice, or extreme devotion to duty in the presence of the enemy'.[3] The following extract is the full text of Manahi's citation for the VC, written in the desert in Tunisia within a few days of his actions on Takrouna:

> On the night 19/20 Apr 1943 during the attack upon the TAKROUNA feature L/Sjt MANAHI was in command of a Section. The objective of his platoon was the pinnacle, a platform of rock right on top of the feature. Early in the advance his platoon came under heavy enemy fire which caused many casualties, including the Platoon Commander. First light on 20 Apr 43 found the platoon reduced in strength to ten and pinned to the ground a short way up the feature by heavy Mortar and SA fire. The platoon continued to advance towards their objective, L/Sjt MANAHI leading

a party of three up the WESTERN side. During this advance they encountered heavy MG fire from posts on the slope and extensive sniping by the enemy actually on the pinnacle. In order to reach their objective L/Sjt MANAHI and his party had to climb some 500 feet the last 50 feet being almost sheer and during the whole time they were under heavy fire. L/Sjt MANAHI personally led the small party and silenced several MG posts in turn. Eventually by climbing hand over fist they reached the pinnacle and after a brief fight some 60 enemy, including an OP officer, surrendered.

They were then joined by the remainder of the platoon and the pinnacle was captured.

Within a short time the small area was subjected to intense Mortar fire from the considerable enemy force still holding the village of TAKROUNA and the NORTHERN and WESTERN slopes of the feature, and later to heavy and continuous shelling. The platoon Sgt was killed and other casualties reduced the party then holding the pinnacle to L/Sjt MANAHI and two Pvts. An Arty [Artillery] OP offr who had arrived ordered L/Sjt MANAHI to withdraw but he and his men remained and held the feature. This action was confirmed by Bde HQ as soon as communications were established.

The end of the morning 20 Apr 43 found the party short of men, rations, and water. L/Sjt MANAHI himself returned to his Bn at the foot of the feature and brought back supplies and reinforcements, the whole time being under fire. During the afternoon the enemy counter-attacked in force some of them gaining a foothold. In face of grenades and small arms fire L/Sjt MANAHI personally led his men against the attackers. Fierce hand to hand fighting ensued but eventually the enemy were driven off. Shortly after this the party was relieved.[4]

On the morning of 21 Apr 43 urgent and immediate reinforcements were required and L/Sjt MANAHI again led up a party consisting of 15 men. At this time the enemy had once more gained a foothold on the pinnacle.

L/Sjt MANAHI led one of two parties which attacked and drove back the enemy. This attack was made under

> concentrated Mortar and heavy MG fire. All that day the feature was heavily shelled, Mortared and subjected to continual MG fire from in and about TAKROUNA.
>
> Late in the afternoon of 21 Apr 43 L/Sjt MANAHI on his own initiative took two men and moved round the NORTH WESTERN side of the feature. In that area were several enemy MG and Mortar posts and two 25 prs operated by the enemy. With cool determination L/Sjt MANAHI led his party against them, stalking one post after another and always under shell and MG fire. By his skill and daring he compelled the surrender of the enemy in that area.
>
> This courageous action undoubtedly led to the ultimate collapse of the enemy defence and the capture of the whole TAKROUNA feature with over three hundred prisoners, two 25 prs, several Mortars and 72 MGs.
>
> On the night 21/22 Apr 43 L/Sjt MANAHI remained on the feature assisting in the evacuation of the dead and wounded and refusing to return to his Bn until this task was completed. During that time the area was being heavily and continually shelled.
>
> Throughout the action L/Sjt MANAHI showed the highest qualities of an infantry soldier. His cool judgement, resolute determination and outstanding personal bravery were an inspiration to his men and a supreme contribution to the capture and holding of a feature vital to the success of the operation.

This citation was signed by Lieutenant-Colonel Keiha – who had recently been appointed as Commander of the Māori Battalion – and then moved its way up the ranks. The next signature was that of Brigadier Ralph Walden Harding, Commander of the 5th New Zealand Infantry Brigade, followed by Major-General Kippenberger, who was Commander of the Second New Zealand Division. From here, it went to Lieutenant-General Freyberg, General Officer Commanding of 10 Corps and the New Zealand Expeditionary Force, then to General Montgomery, General Officer Commanding of the Eight Army. The final name that appeared on the document was that of General Harold Alexander, who was commander of the 18th Army Group. The other apparent endorsement placed on the first page of this recommendation was the stamped (not signed) name of General Henry Maitland Wilson, who was Commander-in-Chief, Middle East Forces.[5]

Within a week of Manahi's triumph on Takrouna, work had started on the wording of the commendation, and it was typed on the relevant form and received by Lieutenant-Colonel Keiha for signing probably on the last few days of April. On 2 May, it arrived at Brigade Headquarters, where Brigadier Harding endorsed it before despatching it to Major-General Kippenberger the following day. It finally arrived at Army Headquarters on 7 May, where Montgomery put his name to it, before it was sent on through the army bureaucracy the next day.[6]

Endorsements were needed for a recommendation as important as this, and they were duly collected. On 9 May, Private William Lawson Richards, a member of Shaw's 15 Platoon of 21 Battalion which arrived on the pinnacle in the afternoon of 20 April, gave his evidence. Richards was an eyewitness to Manahi's feats, and his testimony was therefore of vital importance. Richards recalled, 'particularly noticing L/Sjt MANAHI. With the assistance of him and other Maoris some enemy who had regained a foothold on the pinnacle the previous night and remained in the buildings all day were driven back. I then saw L/Sjt MANAHI and other MAORI leave the pinnacle and move down around the North Western slopes. They had said they were going to have a look a[t] what was there. This was from where a lot of the Mortar and MG fire had come. I saw them disappear in the direction of the enemy positions and before long there was the sound of considerable firing … I know that as a result of the action by L/Sjt MANAHI and the other MAORI the enemy positions in that area were cleared and many prisoners captured. Not long after this the enemy in the village surrendered and the TAKROUNA feature was captured'.[7] This statement was sworn before Captain Denis Blundell (who was later to become a New Zealand Governor-General, and who was the author of Manahi's citation).

Private Hinga Grant, a recipient of the Military Medal for his actions on Takrouna, and who assisted in the capture of Italian prisoners from the feature, volunteered his statement before Lieutenant-Colonel Keiha on 3 May. In it, Grant wrote how he was 'one of a party of four led by L/Sjt MANAHI up the slopes. We were trying to reach the pinnacle. On the way up we were fired on by enemy from posts below and on the pinnacle. L/Sjt MANAHI was always in front of us and personally attacked and captured MG posts. To get onto the pinnacle itself we had to climb up almost sheer rock face and hand over hand. After brief fighting there, the enemy surrendered and we took approximately 60 prisoners …. After capturing the pinnacle we came under heavy mortar and shellfire and also fire from MGs sited in and about TAKROUNA below us. Towards the end of the morning our party holding the pinnacle had been reduced to three. L/Sjt MANAHI returned to the coy and bought back supplies and a few reinforcements. In going down and up the hill he was under fire the whole time.

'In the afternoon further reinforcements arrived, this time from 21 NA Bn. The enemy counter-attacked and some of them gained a foot-hold on the feature. L/Sjt MANAHI led an attack against them. There was fierce hand-to-hand fighting but eventually the enemy withdrew … the remainder of that day we were subjected to steady fire. After dark I returned to my unit with L/Sjt MANAHI. Of the original party from my platoon who attacked the pinnacle on 20 Apr 43 L/Sjt MANAHI and myself were the only ones not casualties'.[8]

The final contemporary statement from a participant in the Takrouna assault came from Lieutenant Hirst of 21 Battalion, who led a party of 45 soldiers (with one other officer) in relieving a section of the feature from Manahi's unit. Hirst, who also swore his statement before Lieutenant-Colonel Keiha on 3 May, was the only officer who witnessed some of Manahi's feats on the feature, and his supporting comments were important in giving weight to the recommendation, especially if more senior officers were expected to endorse it.

Hirst wrote that while he was on Takrouna on the night of 20 April, 'the village and the western slope were strongly held by the enemy. At about 2200 hrs enemy troops fired on us from some of the houses on the pinnacle. It was later found that they had gained a foothold by using a secret and covered approach. Fierce fighting ensued and the position was desperate. Reinforcements were asked for and at about 0800 hrs 21 Apr, L/Sjt MANAHI in charge of fifteen Maoris arrived. I discussed a plan of attack with him. This included bringing our own Arty [artillery] to bear on the feature. After a concentration during which we took cover, L/Sjt MANAHI personally led four men in an attack on some of the houses. They came under the heaviest Mortar fire we experienced there and also considerable MG fire but the attack was a complete success. The enemy withdrew by the same means as they had used earlier to gain a footing and the entire pinnacle feature was once again in our hands. Following this we were heavily shelled and mortared and fired on by MGs … Later in the afternoon of 21 Apr L/Sjt MANAHI and one or two of his men, on their own initiative, moved out from cover on the pinnacle and I saw them stalking enemy section posts on the North Western slopes of the TAKROUNA feature. They stalked post after post capturing them in turn. When I saw the number of enemy surrendering I realised they were cracking and took a party down to the village which was captured. But for the action of L/Sjt MANAHI and his men, the capture of the whole feature would have been delayed considerably. During these operations L/Sjt MANAHI and his men were continually under shell fire and small arms fire'.[9]

Yet, despite the supporting evidence, and the endorsement of officers right up to the level of Field-Marshal, Manahi's VC was denied him, and in its place, he was promptly awarded the Distinguished Conduct Medal (DCM). The VC recommendation, signed by Lieutenant-Colonel Keiha, Brigadier Harding, Major-General Kippenberger, Lieutenant-General Freyberg, and Generals Montgomery, Alexander, and Wilson, was received at brigade level on 2 May and had reached the army level five days later.[10] So while statements were still being prepared and sworn for Manahi's VC, the decision to award the DCM had already become fixed in the army's mind in London.

The swiftness of this decision to downgrade the award can be seen in the fact that the VC recommendation and the DCM recommendation both appear to have been received at brigade level on the same day (2 May 1943). The first form had the letters 'VC' typed on it. This was crossed out (by an unknown person in the army hierarchy) and replaced with the handwritten letters 'DCM'. The second form (the one recommending that Manahi be awarded the DCM) had the names of the assenting officers typed, and a space at the top of the 'Honour or Reward' column, where 'DCM' was hand-written, with no mention of a VC. This second form bore no signatures (just their typed names) and so while its recommendation of a DCM for Manahi stood, it was not what three generals had recommended for the Lance-Sergeant.

The identity of the person who crossed out the letters 'VC' has perplexed everyone who has sought to explain this decision, particularly as the axiomatic alteration was not initialled by its author, does not appear to be in the handwriting of any of the officers who signed the document, and the ink and the nib size differ from any of the other samples on the page. According to William Spencer, a specialist in historical records from the Public Record Office in Richmond who analysed this matter in 1997, the downgrading 'was done in the UK, either at the VC Committee stage or by the Secretary of State of Defence Level. As the original eye witness statements are amongst the surviving documentation, I doubt if the recommendation was downgraded in theatre as I am sure the paperwork would have been destroyed there'. The problem, however, is that no documentation appears to have survived to confirm where and when the downgrade was decided on.[11]

Once General Wilson reviewed the supporting evidence, and no doubt discussed Manahi's deeds with other senior officers to confirm the extent of the bravery of his actions at Takrouna, Wilson gave his assent to the VC recommendation. It was then despatched, with the accompanying testimony of the eyewitnesses, to the Army Council in London.[12] The fact that the supporting eyewitness statements were also sent is significant in so far as the VC is the only British military decoration that requires three sworn testimonies from military personnel present at the action for which the award is to be considered. That three such statements were sent with the citation suggests that there was unanimity of feeling in favour of Manahi receiving the VC at the highest levels of the army in the North African theatre.

It is most likely, then, that it was once the recommendation was assessed in London that the army's VC Committee considered the matter and struck out the VC in favour of the DCM. As for possible individuals who could have been responsible, at this juncture, one candidate emerges: Lord Alanbrooke. Alanbrooke was Chief of the Imperial General Staff during the Second World War, and a member of the Army Council during this period.[13] Although, quite appropriately, no mention is made in his diaries of the deliberations that took place in VC Committee,[14] the single circumstance that points to Alanbrooke as being the most probable individual responsible for the downgrade of Manahi's VC recommendation is that only Alanbrooke would have the seniority to overturn the endorsements of several generals and a field-marshal. The suggestion that it was some unknown official is implausible on the basis that no such official would have the authority. Moreover, the lack of any protest when those who had signed the recommendation for a VC found that their opinion had been overturned, suggests that they accepted the decision had been made by someone with higher authority than themselves, which in the case of Wilson and Montgomery's endorsement leaves Alanbrooke as the most feasible candidate.

No paper trail linking Alanbrooke directly to the decision to downgrade Manahi's VC exists. Neither is there any firm evidence of the signatories (even the most senior ones) on Manahi's VC citation knowing that Alanbrooke might have been responsible for the downgrading of the award. However, informal channels of communication in the army were well-established, and could have been the route by which Alanbrooke choose to inform his subordinates of his decision. This would certainly explain the muted response by some of the officers (and the absence of any response at all by the more senior ranks who endorsed the citation) at having their decision overturned. At the same time, this informal means of advising others of the decision to alter the VC recommendation would also account for the difficulty in pinpointing with absolute assuredness the identity of the individual responsible for the alteration – the written material simply does not exist.

On 4 June 1943, a pre-printed but personally-signed certificate was sent to Manahi from Freyberg, in which the Lieutenant-General congratulated the Lance-Sergeant for 'gallant and distinguished service in the field'.[15] The award was formally confirmed on 12 June.[16] When Manahi's DCM was gazetted in London in July 1943,[17] the wording of the citation was almost identical to that contained in his original VC recommendation, but with one important amendment. The phrase 'His cool judgement, resolute determination and outstanding personal bravery were an inspiration to his men' was omitted.[18] As with the crossing out of the letters 'V.C.' in the original citation, the identity of the person who deleted this sentence is not recorded in any of the official records. However, this sleight-of-hand did not remain concealed completely. When Manahi's DCM was announced in the press, this phrase was not excluded, and appeared verbatim for everyone to read.[19]

When made public, the decision to award the DCM to Manahi was not received with universal acclaim. Among his fellow soldiers in particular, the failure to grant Manahi the VC for which he was recommended left a 'sour taste'.[20] Teasing open the responsibility for the removal of this segment of the citation relies on a strong element of conjecture, but the extraction of this phrase from the final DCM citation indicates that the person responsible had sufficient knowledge of the nuances of the wording of citations to realise that its inclusion would have made the subject of the citation seem more eligible, or at the very least more deserving of a VC. If this was the case, then a circumstantial connection could be made between the person who downgraded the original recommendation to a DCM, and the person who subsequently edited the wording of the citation that Blundell had composed for Manahi. It is feasible that the same individual was responsible for both alterations, and that it was more likely a senior officer rather than a clerical or administrative staff member of the army that gave the instructions for this change to be made. The liability for this, at least in some ancillary way, again seems to lie with Alanbrooke.

In the scrutiny given to the possible identity of the individual who crossed out the 'V.C.' on Manahi's citation, the existence of another piece of unidentified handwriting in the first page of the citation has gone unnoticed. At some point, Manahi's incorrectly-listed army serial number that was typed on the citation (39009) was crossed out and above it was written the correct number (39099). Who made this alteration is almost impossible to determine now, but when it was made can possibly be narrowed down. The error in the citation appears to have gone unnoticed until at least 22 July 1943, when the incorrect number appeared in the official announcement of his DCM in the *London Gazette*.[21] The typesetters at the *London Gazette* correctly copied the mistaken number, and so it was presumably after its publication that the error was spotted and corrected by hand on the original citation.

The greatest difficulty in determining with more precision who was responsible for Manahi's VC being downgraded to a DCM, and why the decision was made rests with the absence of any additional documentation around the VC decision-making process, other than the citation forms themselves. In 1997, an official from Britain's Ministry of Defence confirmed that 'unfortunately, on the question of individual VC case files, it was long ago concluded by the Records Management Branch of the Ministry of Defence (MOD) [that] these files had been destroyed. The VC Committee never kept minutes – each case is minuted in its own file – so there appears not to be any other source to which you can refer in the case of Lance Sergeant Manahi'.[22] The answer as to who made the decision to change the citation, and why, therefore may once have lain in a Ministry of Defence file, but was now no longer in existence.

How the downgrade of Manahi's award was viewed by officers is only known in a few instances. Neither Lord Alanbrooke, nor Generals Montgomery, Wilson, and Alexander left any direct reference to the matter of Manahi's VC, most probably because it would have been regarded (if at all) as an administrative matter, and one of trivial importance when considered in the scope of the whole of the Second World War. However, a few of those more closely associated with the New Zealand campaign in North Africa did leave behind opinions on the way the army treated Manahi on this issue.

One of the most insightful and fair assessments from a senior officer was made by Major-General Brian Horrocks, who was a commander in North Africa from August 1942, and who was highly regarded by fellow officers and subordinates alike.[23] Horrocks developed a very clear impression in his mind of the significance of Manahi's actions at Takrouna. 'Of all the magnificent achievements of 2 NZ Div', he wrote, 'I have always felt that the capture of Takrouna must surely have been one of the finest. I went up there myself during the battle just after the 51st Highland Division had taken over, and I cannot, to this day, imagine how it was captured in the face of tenacious enemy resistance'.[24]

Horrocks later included a section on the Allied victory at Takrouna in his autobiography, *A Full Life*. This book was first published in 1960 – long after the dust had been able to settle on the issue of Manahi's VC downgrading. Yet, despite the passage of seventeen years, Horrocks was clearly still riled by the treatment Manahi had received after his acts of supreme valour: 'A platoon of Maoris was given the final task of capturing Takrouna, but by the time it reached the foot of the pinnacle, only two sergeants and seven other ranks were left. Somehow or other these few men scrambled up one at a time led by a most gallant sergeant called Manahi, and captured the whole feature .... A few days later I visited Takrouna myself and it was all I could do to physically get to the top. How the Maoris did it wearing full equipment and in the face of tough enemy opposition, I simply do not know .... I have mentioned this fight in some detail because in my opinion it was the most gallant feat of arms I witnessed in the course of the war, and I was bitterly disappointed when Sergeant Manahi, whom we had recommended for a VC, only received a DCM'.[25]

Kippenberger, on the other hand, hardly seemed troubled at all by the downgrading of Manahi's award. In his memoirs of the war, written in 1949, all he had to say on the matter was that 'Manahi was recommended for the VC and got an immediate DCM'.[26] This overly nonchalant response to the rejection of Manahi's VC was in stark contrast to how Kippenberger felt on the morning after the battle. At a meeting with Freyberg, he wrote how 'I started to tell him [Freyberg] what had happened & found myself speechless. Our men have never shown more devotion'.[27]

The reasons for Kippenberger's later reluctance to uphold his earlier recommendation are open to conjecture, but certainly, as stories about the alleged atrocities on Takrouna gained more currency in the post-war years, Kippenberger may have decided to distance himself from his earlier position. In addition, if Alanbrooke had been the person who reduced Manahi's award to a DCM, Kippenberger would have been disinclined to speak out against a superior. In this respect, his indifference can be interpreted as a case of 'just following orders', and not wishing to stir up the sediment on this matter.

There can be little doubt that charges of impropriety affected the eligibility of soldiers to receive certain awards. Bennett later referred to the allegation of 'certain skeletons in Manahi's cupboard', which remained the impediment to the VC being granted.[28] However, this was a comment given when reflecting on allegations made long after the triumph at Takrouna. If there were any skeletons in Manahi's cupboard, they were put there by someone else. Bennett's observation about the circumstances that prevailed at the time that Manahi's VC citation was written are especially instructive on this issue: 'We all know that Manahi would not have been recommended for a Victoria Cross in the first place if it was thought by his superior officers that he was guilty of a grave misdemeanour'.[29]

Even relatively balanced accounts of Manahi's role at Takrouna were tarnished on some occasions by writers who attempted to imply that there had been something untoward that had taken place during the fighting. One account plays subtly on Manahi's well-known humility and reluctance to discuss anything of his time in the war. Although this was a trait common to many soldiers, the writer framed his description of Manahi in a manner that was bound to insert some small sliver of suspicion in the minds of readers: 'He [Manahi] was such a humble and in a way strange man, that whenever Takrouna was mentioned he would either clam up or try to change the subject'[30] – as though he was eager to conceal something. Corporal Te Kuru Waaka, from Whakarewarewa, also recalled Manahi's quiet disposition. On one occasion, when the battalion was stationed outside Cairo, Waaka was officer of the day, and Manahi his 'bat man' – responsible for waking him for reveille and other tasks. However, on that day, Manahi slept in, and later showed no signs of concern at having failed at carrying out his orders. But when Manahi was aroused for battle, Waaka described how 'he had this look – a steadfast stare .... It was quite uncanny to reconcile the two in the same man'.[31]

Kepa Ehau, who was an expert on whakapapa in Rotorua, attributed part of Manahi's reluctance to talk about his extraordinary feats in the war to his ancestry. 'In Jack Manahi's family'. He observed, 'you will find sources for his normal quietness and gentleness and for his once-in-a life time terrible fury. His father's father was Te Rauawa 'The Peacemaker', a saintly man remembered for his quelling of tribal strife. But another ancestor on the father's side was Tunohopu, a warrior chief of Ngati Whakaue sub tribe of the Arawa, and a man to be feared'.[32]

In fact, there was an occasion, in 1983, when Manahi did participate in an interview which dealt in details with events at Takrouna,[33] but otherwise, he was reluctant to mention the war, in part because he was naturally disinclined to anything that could even resemble boasting, and because for him, as for most soldiers who had fought in such circumstances, it could be traumatic revisiting the events of that period.

The critical point about the influence of these allegations on the downgrading of the VC recommendation is that they arose well after Manahi received the DCM. They therefore could not have had a bearing on the decision, although their later circulation may well have served the interests of anyone in the British and New Zealand military hierarchy (together with some politicians) who were inclined to prevent Manahi receiving his VC.

The other, more probable reason for Manahi's VC recommendation being shunted to the side in favour of a DCM is the fact that Ngarimu had received a VC just three weeks earlier. Two VCs to men from the same battalion, and from the same ethnic group, within a month, might have possibly looked to the army hierarchy as though the awards were being given too easily. Rather than the merits of each potential recipient being the sole consideration, senior officers also took into account the currency of the VC, and were conscious that awarding them in a higher frequency could have a devaluing effect, and might even lead to others demanding VCs. For this reason, the act of bravery of those proposed for a VC was not the only criterion for the award being granted. According to one historian, there was 'a feeling' in the British High Command that another Victoria Cross to a member of the Maori Battalion, so soon after the first one, would somehow be inappropriate or unwarranted.[34]

Of course, the evidence for such a view is largely circumstantial. It would be unusual to find, among the documentation of generals, statements which explicitly revealed such considerations. However, not only is the circumstantial evidence compelling for its own logic, it is also supported by the suppositions of officers who were prepared to put pen to paper on the matter. In the Māori Battalion's 1984 Reunion Magazine, Blundell revealed that the close proximity in time between Ngarimu's award and the recommendation for Manahi to receive the VC was a fact that was taken into consideration in the higher echelons of the Army: 'I wrote the citation for V.C for Sgt. Manahi and like the rest of the DIVISION was disgusted when he was awarded an immediate D.C.M. I feel sure that here was an example that even in the realm of bravery, politics played a part, and that the award to 2nd Lieutenant Ngarimu only some three weeks previously influenced the final decision. This for me was confirmed when later at the Gezira Sporting Club, Cairo, our Military Secretary, Brigadier Rudd asked me to tell the story to a Senior British General. The General's comment was that, "We did make a mistake".'[35] Unfortunately, Blundell did not name the general, but it is the most direct contemporaneous evidence of why Manahi's VC was not granted.

There is also the consideration of what the military historian Christopher Pugsley has described as the 'quota system' for the allocation of VCs. In the Second World War, 'each brigade and battalion got its allocation, and recommendations for the Victoria Cross were carefully monitored before final approval in London'.[36] However, while Pugsley's argument may have some general application, the fact that Freyberg, Montgomery, and Wilson endorsed Manahi's VC recommendation must imply that these very senior generals believed that his receipt of the VC would be in accordance with the 'quota system' as they understood it to operate at the time. A factor which could have had a bearing on this is the probability that the VC Committee considered Manahi's and Ngarimu's VC citations at the same meeting. With only 182 VCs awarded during the entire course of the war in all theatres,[37] and with all the other demands on the members of the committee, it is very probable that the VC citations for Ngarimu and Manahi were considered at the same meeting.[38] If this was the case, then it would give more credence to the possibility that a de facto quota system was applied in Manahi's case. The anomalous position Manahi was therefore placed in is revealed by the fact that he was the only New Zealand serviceman in the Second World War to have the original recommendation for a VC turned down in favour of a 'lesser' award.[39]

The matter obviously irked Ngata, because at Ngarimu's VC investiture at Ruatoria on 6 October 1943, a song he had composed especially for the event made specific reference to Manahi. The third verse was in equal measure a tribute to Manahi's bravery and a protest for the VC being plucked from him:

Aotea and Waipounamu!
Here are the honours they earned,
Risking their lives regardless,
Striving with might and main.
Moana, son! Manahi too,
And Te Tuahu! Ha!
Heroes who have by doughty deeds
Lifted my fame on high![40]

The day after this investiture, Ngarimu's kuia died, but 'beforehand she had willed herself into a state of whakamomori, not just because of the death of her favourite moko, but because of what happened to Haane in being declined the VC. It was decided then that the Ngarimu family would have to bear this cross in acknowledgement of Haane's rebuff'.[41] This account is suggestive of the extent to which the battalion and the whānau who had members in it felt about Manahi having had his VC taken away from him. And beneath the friendly rivalry between the battalion's companies, it also reveals how firm the links really were among the whānau, hapū and iwi. It was truly a 'Māori' battalion in every sense of the word.

The prospect for Manahi to be awarded a VC seemed to have come to a definite halt when King George VI issued instructions that there be no further awards or decorations after 1949 for the actions of soldiers in the Second World War.[42] From this point on, little consideration was given – at least publicly – to what many of Manahi's comrades and members of his hapū and iwi felt was an injustice.

## NOTES

1. Instituted by Royal Warrant on 29 January 1856, Original Royal Warrant, signed by HM Queen Victoria, instituting the award for meritorious distinction, with drafts of conditions, requirements etc., of those eligible for the award, WO 98/1, The National Archives, Surrey, United Kingdom.
2. W Lennox, *The Victoria Cross: The Rewarded and their Services*, London, John Mitchell,1857, pp. 3–4; J G Smyth, *The Story of the Victoria Cross, 1856–1963*, London, Frederick Muller,1963, pp. 21ff.
3. Ministry of Defence (UK) , 'Military Awards and Honours, Fact Sheet', London, 2009, n. p.
4. Recommendation for VC for Haane Manahi, 2 May 1943, W7670/M2618, 2000m, 9/17s, 191, G&S, E. 1733, Army Form W. 3121/5, pp. 449–51.
5. Op. cit.
6. This information is contained in Recommendation for VC for Haane Manahi, 2 May 1943, W7670/M2618, 2000m, 9/17s, 191, G&S, E. 1733, Army Form W. 3121/5, p. 1.
7. W L Richards (21 Battalion), statement Sworn on Oath in the Field, 9 May 1943, author's collection.
8. H Grant, statement Sworn on Oath in the Field, 3 May 1943, author's collection.
9. I H Hirst (21 Battalion), statement Sworn on Oath in the Field, 3 May 1943, author's collection.
10. Recommendation for DCM for Haane Manahi, 7 May 1943, W7670/M2618, 2000m, 9/17s, 191, G&S, E. 1733, Army Form W. 3121.
11. Letter from W J G Spencer, Specialist Reader Adviser: Defence Policy and Military History Records, Public Record Office, Richmond, to S Hart, 4 March 1997, author's collection.
12. Manahi Victoria Cross Committee and Te Arawa Confederation of Tribes, 'Lance Sergeant Haane Manahi: Award of the Victoria Cross. Informal Submission', Rotorua, 1993, p. 3. If the recommendation had not been sent to London and had been downgraded in the theatre to a DCM, it would not have appeared in the National Archives in Britain. Interview with Norman Bennett, Auckland, 11 January 2010.
13. For Alanbrooke's membership, see signed group photographs of [Army Council meeting, 1942–1945], in Alanbrooke: 13/12 [1942–1957], Liddell Hart Centre for Military Archives, Kings College, London. Alanbrooke was also the foremost military advisor to Winston Churchill for most of the war.
14. Danchev, A, and Todman, D (eds.), *War Diaries 1939–1945: Field Marshal Lord Alanbrooke*, London, University of California Press, 2001.
15. B Freyberg, 2NZEF, Certificate for Lance-Sergeant Haane Manahi, 4 June 1943, facsimile in author's collection.
16. New Zealand Army Headquarters, 'Details of Decoration for Investiture Purposes', presented 18 December 1945, author's collection. 18 June 1943 is the date that appears on Record of Promotions, Reductions, Transfers, Casualties, Punishments, Etc., 'Particulars of Will', New Zealand Defence Forces

Archives, 14 February 1944.

17. Distinguished Conduct Medal for Haane Manahi, in *Supplement to the London Gazette*, 22 July 1943, p. 3314.
18. See Waitangi Tribunal, *The Preliminary Report in the Haane Manahi Victoria Cross Claim*, Wai-893, Wellington, 2005, p. 6.
19. The report came from the New Zealand Expeditionary Force Official War Correspondent in Cairo, and was published in various newspapers on 13 June 1943.
20. M Soutar, in I McGibbon (ed.), *The Oxford Companion to New Zealand Military History*, Auckland, Oxford University Press, 2000, p. 311.
21. Distinguished Conduct Medal for Haane Manahi, in *Supplement to the London Gazette*, 22 July 1943, p. 3314.
22. Letter from R G Bird, (MoD), London, to N Bennett, 8 April 1997.
23. P Warner, *Horrocks: The General Who Led from the Front*, London, Hamish Hamilton, 1982, p. 76.
24. B Horrocks, in J F Cody, *28 (Maori) Battalion*, p. 282.
25. B Horrocks, *A Full Life*, London, Collins, 1974, pp. 162–3.
26. H Kippenberger, *Infantry Brigadier*, p. 315.
27. H Kippenberger, in D McLean, *Howard Kippenberger: Dauntless Spirit: A Life of an Outstanding New Zealand Leader*, Auckland, Random House, 2008, p. 247.
28. Letter from C Bennett, Te Puke, 19 January 1993, author's collection.
29. C Bennett to W McKinnon, 19 January 1992, in Waitangi Tribunal, *The Preliminary Report in the Haane Manahi Victoria Cross Claim*, Wai-893, Wellington, 2005, p. 8.
30. Attributed to D Stafford, in file on Manahi, author's collection.
31. K Waaka, cited by H Mitchell, 1 February 2010.
32. K Ehau, in item reprinted in *NZ 28 Maori Battalion Reunion, Rotorua, April 1992, p. 52.*
33. The interview was conducted in the main by Captain R A Cairns, New Zealand Army, see letter from R A Cairns to H Manahi, Waiouru, 29 August 1983, author's collection.
34. V O'Malley and D Armstrong, *The Beating Heart: A Political and Socio-Economic History of Te Arawa*, p. 295.
35. D Blundell, in item reprinted in *NZ 28 Maori Battalion Reunion, Rotorua, April 1992, pp. 51–2.*
36. C Pugsley, 'Manahi: Was he Cheated?', in *New Zealand Defence Quarterly*, Spring, 1998, p. 30.
37. Awarded to 181 recipients, Victoria Cross Registers, vols. 3 and 4, WO/98, National Archives, Richmond, United Kingdom.
38. Although no documentary evidence survives to confirm this one way or the other.
39. See P McDermott, *For Distinguished Conduct in the Field: The Register of the DCM, 1920–1992*, Suffolk, Uckfield, 1993, and A J Polaschek, *The Complete New Zealand Distinguished Conduct Medal*, Christchurch, Medals Research Christchurch, 1983, in letter from N. Bennett, Manahi Victoria Cross Committee to The Executive Committee, Te Arawa Maori Returned Services League (Inc.), 12 September 1997, p. 2, author's collection.
40. A Ngata, Theme Song for Ngarimu's VC investiture, in M Soutar, *Nga Tama Toa*, p. 279.
41. Monty Soutar, oral source.
42. I McGibbon (ed.), *The Oxford Companion to New Zealand Military History*, Auckland, Oxford University Press, 2000, p. 295; 'For God! For King! For Country!', in *Army News*, issue 365, 17 October 2006.

# CHAPTER 9: Back Home

On 7 July 1943, Freyberg arrived in Rotorua, ahead of the contingent of the Māori Battalion (including Manahi) that was on furlough, and was shortly due to reach the town. The locals had frequently read about Freyberg in the newspapers, and had seen him occasionally on newsreel segments at the movies. Popular recognition of his leadership had escalated as the war progressed, and particularly as the news of the achievements in North Africa (filtered, as they were at the time, by military censors) were regularly relayed in the press. It was no surprise, then, that on that day, a mass crowd gathered in Rotorua to hear the general deliver a speech in which he paid tribute to the men of the region who had served under him so far during the war.[1] Six days later, the train carrying the troops of B Company that were on leave pulled into the Rotorua train station. They had been away from home since January 1940, and in the case of Manahi, the last time he saw his son Rau, he was just three-and-a-half years old. Now, he was almost seven, and was about to meet the man he knew more from photographs than in person. 'When the old man came back from the war, I remember it clearly', Rau recollected. 'I was with my grandfather [Manahi Ngakahawai]. He was where the Queen Victoria Memorial is. A big crowd was there. Then the boys came marching in to Tama[tekapua], and they all sat in front of Tama, and I could pick out some of them. But then I thought 'Where the hell's my father?' I never saw my father. Then about three quarters of an hour later, he came down and stood outside the old place, behind Tama, then he came down. I said 'where's he been?' and my auntie said that he had broken rank before the Catholic Church. He had grabbed my auntie's arm and grabbed my mother's arm, and walked up the hill, to where the hospital is now. My father took them up to this big tree that was there, and he knelt on the ground and stayed there for about half an hour. All that time, we were wondering, 'What the hell, where is he?' Well, he was acknowledging Makawe, the guardian spirit of Ngati Whakaue. I supposed he was mixed up with the old tohungas when he was young, so that's what he knew he had to do. Under that tree was the placenta, the whenua, of the old tohunga Ngahihi. This is going right back many generations. And when that tohunga was born, Makawe appeared like a shooting star over the lake'.[2] Makawe was a celestial being in Ngāti Whakaue's history (often appearing as a comet) who was called on to aid warriors as they entered battle,[3] and who was said to appear when Ngāti Whakaue people were in danger.[4] Manahi went to give thanks to Makawe for guiding him through the minefields and up the precipice of Takrouna.[5] It had led him right up to the enemy line and then disappeared.[6] Makawe had previously appeared to Kepa Ehau – the Ngāti Whakaue historian, orator and First World War soldier – during a night-time wiring repair party at La Basseville, in Flanders, in August 1917.[7]

Rau and Neil reminisced about Manahi and his comrades going to the lake later that day. After the men had got together outside Tamatekapua, 'the next minute, all the old boys from Ohinemutu disappeared. They went down to the lake. They had gone to get some fish .... We were the beaters, us kids. After all the ceremonies and whatever, we went down to the lake. And we used to go around the edges, where all the weeds were, and splash with our hands. And of course, what we caught was the morihana – that's a carp. They would swim out into the deep water, then all the uncles would dive for them. And the men were meant to be going to a formal dinner, but they all went for a feed of morihana. That was special to them'.[8]

Manahi underwent a standard army medical examination at the end of October 1943, which revealed him to be in excellent health,[9] which perhaps was unsurprising, considering the amount of physical exercise he had undergone since the beginning of 1940. However, when he was formally discharged from the army on 22 August 1946,[10] a final medical inspection was carried out, which showed not only that he remained in good physical condition, but that the only wound or injury he had ever suffered was a broken right wrist before the war. There was no mention whatsoever of the wounds he received in Crete,[11] which had been so serious that his next of kin had been notified at the time.

The small trickle of troops returning to places such as Rotorua in 1943 was something of a dress rehearsal for the government for the much bigger demobilisation expected in a few years when it was hoped the war would end. Preparations for this had been in motion almost since the start of the war, with authorities looking at the surge of returning troops as a strategic opportunity for the country – a chance to create a more skilled workforce. The emphasis was on trade training for the returning troops, which was based in part on the belief that there would be an increased demand for housing in the immediate post-war years[12] that would require more skilled construction workers than existed in the country at the time. To assist in this, and in the integration of soldiers back into civilian life, the government initiated the Rehabilitation Board. Its main trade training activities emerged from the earlier scheme for trade training centres which had commenced in 1940 as a means of providing workers to replace those who had entered the armed forces. The Rehabilitation Board took over control of these centres in February 1944, and limited entry into the scheme to ex-servicemen.[13]

Carpentry training had begun in 1941 for the small flow of returning soldiers, but gradually, the type of training being offered evolved: 'instead of aiming to produce semi-skilled men quickly to meet an industrial crisis, it was designed to produce tradesmen able to hold their places permanently. When the Rehabilitation organisation developed from 1942 onward, its policy was to use existing machinery wherever possible. The emergency trade training schools, ready-made for its purpose, were taken over during 1943 and their courses extended'.[14] This was the sort of course Manahi entered when he returned to Rotorua in 1943, which conveniently was where one of seven of the country's carpentry courses was located at the time.[15] Neil recollected that Manahi 'went to the big carpentry school they set up in Whittaker Road. Then he got a carpentry job at Rotorua Hospital for a while. Hiwa [Haane's uncle] was head of the hospital's painting team, so he got the job through him'.[16]

Manahi's involvement in the armed services was not quite over, though. In 1946, his final act was to participate in the New Zealand Victory Contingent[17] – a group of servicemen and women which made up an official party that went to Britain as part of celebrations of the Commonwealth's role in the war. On 17 April, he travelled to Trentham, where a mass of soldiers, sailors, airmen, and support personnel were assembling in preparation for the voyage to England to commemorate the victory over the Axis powers the previous year. They sailed out of Wellington Harbour on 20 April on the troop transport ship HMNZT *Maunganui*. On the way to England, they stopped off at Tahiti, before going through the Panama Canal and on to London.[18] Incidentally, despite all Manahi's previous sea travel in the previous six years, this was the first time he had left the country without a naval convoy or the fear of being attacked by an enemy while en route.

The main event for which everyone was gathering was the Victory Parade, which was held on Saturday 8 June, and was a sort of homage paid by Britain to those nations which had contributed to defeating the enemy during the war. A senior sergeant from the RNZAF described the events of that day, of which Manahi was a part: 'Were up at 6 am. Had breakfast ten in convoy of 50 trucks … into London. Lined up in Kensington Gardens – the march was wonderful. By Big Ben when it struck midday …. It started to rain about 1 pm …. To bed at 9 pm …. Too many people in town to venture out'.[19] London was certainly packed as troops representing all the countries of the Commonwealth, along with members of the armed forces of other countries that had fought against the Axis powers, amassed in the British capital.[20]

Manahi was among the group of Dominion troops that was near the front of a huge procession. They marched from Marble Arch, then past Oxford Street, Charing Cross Road, Trafalgar Square, Northumberland Avenue, the Embankment, Parliament Square, Whitehall, The Mall (where King George VI took the salute), Constitution Hill, and Hyde Park Corner.[21] By early afternoon, the march-past was over, having taken two hours for all the servicemen and women to complete the route.[22] Manahi was then able to enjoy the entertainments on offer during the rest of the day with those of his comrades who had also made the trip to London. It was a moment of euphoria, but the next day, there was also a sense of nostalgia that began to settle on some of those involved as they realised that this was the last obligation to the Great Cause that they would fulfil collectively. Afterwards, there would be small-scale reunions, and in New Zealand, Anzac Day parades, but this was the final occasion that such a mass gathering of armed forces personnel for the Allied nations would be together.

Following this monumental show of camaraderie and the spirit of triumph, Manahi remained in England for a further four weeks with the rest of the New Zealand contingent. After this sojourn, he returned to New Zealand on the *Maunganui*, passing through the Suez Canal before steaming to Colombo, and then Fremantle, finally reaching Wellington on 13 August 1946.[23] What emotions he experienced when sailing past the Mediterranean and Egypt in particular are impossible to know for sure, but based on the testimony of many former servicemen, thoughts of fallen colleagues, buried in the sand in makeshift cemeteries in various parts of North Africa were often prominent in their minds.

Swimming remained a passion for Manahi, and after the war, he coached a number of swimmers from the Rotorua region. His community involvement also extended into other areas. He was also a foundation member of the Springfield Golf Club (in November 1947), a patron of the Rotomahana Anglers Club, and a vice president of the Waikite Rugby Football Club.[24] Above all, though, he placed great emphasis on his whānau: 'He was a family man', Neil noted, 'He just cared about the family. I think that got instilled in all of us. The family came first. 'He visited all his relations around the lake [Rotorua]. He was not one of those guys who says, 'I have cousins over there', but never sees them … [and] he had a lot to do with us. He took us hunting and fishing'.[25]

Increasingly, however, work and inclination drew Manahi away from his family. 'After a while', Rau explained, 'he got mixed up with his mates, with his pakeha mates, then he went over to the Ministry of Works. He became a traffic inspector, checking all the meters around the whole of the Bay of Plenty. So he had a cushy job then'. Still, though, Manahi's leisure pursuits were prominent in his life: 'He loved fishing, so he'd go off to work and sometimes take his fishing rod with him .... He played golf – he was quite a good golfer – but the only thing that stopped him was that he suffered gout'.[26]

One feature of Manahi's character that remained constant throughout his life was his modesty. From the late 1940s and into the 1950s, Sir Bernard Freyberg would seek out Manahi whenever he was visiting Rotorua (usually in his official capacity as Governor General), as did Sir Howard Kippenberger when in the area. Yet, although they were his former commanders, Manahi shied away from meeting them. 'He hated things like that', Rau explained. 'The boys from here had to more or less haul him down here to meet someone. He hated the fuss'.[27] Sometimes, he would even head out into the lake to go fishing to avoid attracting any attention from visiting dignitaries. And if anyone managed to corner Manahi and ask him specifically about Takrouna, his response was to downplay its significance. 'Crete was a hell of a lot tougher', he would say, and then change the subject to anything but the war.[28]

In August 1976, Manahi's wife, Rangiawatea, passed away. By this stage, however, he had already had relationships with two other woman: Gela Florence Thomas, which started in 1958 (and from which partnership, Manahi's second child, Geoffrey, was born); and then from 1971, Mate Pene.[29] Following the death of his estranged wife, though, Manahi decided to move to Maketū, and two years later, in 1978, retired. From the mid-1970s, as age left him less active physically, and as he had more time available him following retirement, Manahi found himself spending more time at the Rotorua RSA.

After three years of fighting battle after battle, and particularly following the extraordinary events at Takrouna, Manahi had done his best to meld back into civilian life in the decades after the war – something that outward appearances suggested he succeeded in. Yet, for those who had been in heated combat, from that point on, there was always going to be something that separated them from everyone else in the community. As a result, many of the returned soldiers found that their closest companions were those who shared similar experiences of being in war. Meeting for a drink and a chat at the RSA became a frequent ritual for Manahi, and on retiring, the camaraderie it offered became an even bigger part of his life.

Over the years, Manahi's friendship with Charles Bennett grew closer, and when Bennett retired to Te Puke, Manahi considered moving to the area too. Neil noted how 'the family had land at Maketu, and a lot of his [Manahi's] mates were there. Charlie Bennett was at Te Puke. Uncle used to travel to Wellington, up to the far north, but mainly all around the Bay of Plenty. He loved to go around and visit all his old war buddies'.[30]

Rotorua remained one of Manahi's favourite haunts, though, and he would regularly visit the local RSA, which was about a forty-minute drive from the home he had retired to at Maketū. He certainly enjoyed his beer – 'I think we get it from our Scottish side',[31] Rau joked – and would look forward to catching up with the slowly shrinking group of former war comrades. On one typical occasion – on Saturday 29 March 1986 – Manahi had spent the afternoon at the Rotorua RSA with some of his friends, sharing some drinks and conversation. Normally, he would have stayed in Rotorua, but, as Rau recalled ruefully, 'That night, I told him to stay here, but he wanted to go home'.[32]

This was not out of character, however. Neil remembered how Manahi generally 'wouldn't stay with any of us. He was very private. Many times I would go to the RSA to pick him up and tell him to stay with me, but he'd say, "Nah, you take me back to Maketu", so I'd have to take him back to Maketu. He wouldn't stay with anybody. I think that was his nature', and on that particular evening, 'what happened was that none of us was around to take him home'.[33] So he climbed into his car to make his own way back to Maketū.

Around quarter to eight that night, Constable Bartlett Meihana received a call that there had been an accident on State Highway 33. He arrived at the scene – about 9 kilometres south of the settlement of Paengaroa, towards Rotorua – at 8.00 pm. The crash had occurred approximately half an hour earlier, when Manahi's Honda Civic crossed the centre line and collided with another vehicle.[34] A witness in the other car gave an account of final moments before the crash: 'As I was rounding this right hand bend I saw a car coming towards me from the opposite direction. It was well onto my side of the road. I slowed right down and pulled right over into the shingle on my left side of the road. I was about to change down a gear, when this other car struck the right hand front of my car. The impact was enough to push my car backwards, slightly. The other car glanced off mine and rolled on down the road for a short distance before stopping'.[35] The two occupants of this car ran towards Manahi's vehicle and tried to get the door open. The passenger in the other car gave evidence of what were the closing moments of Manahi's life: 'I could see that a male person was the driver and the only occupant. The steering wheel was up against his chest, and I thought he might be dead. He didn't respond when I spoke to him'.[36] As Manahi lay dying in the gloom of the early evening, a busload of players and supporters from the Waikite Rugby Football Club – of which Manahi had been vice-president – crawled past the accident site. No-one on the bus could make out any of the people involved in the accident, and seeing that the police were already there, they continued back on their way to Rotorua.[37]

An ambulance arrived at the scene of the accident shortly afterwards, and

*L/Sgt Haane Manahi standing at the poutokomanawa inside the tupuna whare, Tamatekapua at Ōhinemutu, Rotorua.*

*Geoffrey Manahi family collection*

[MS3-2] W7670/M2618 2000m 9/17s 191 G & S E.1733. Forms/W.3121/5

Army Form W. 3121.

Date Recommendation passed forward.

| | Received | Passed |
|---|---|---|
| Brigade | 2.5.43 | 8.5.43 |
| Division | | |
| Corps | | |
| Army | 7 May 43 | |

5 NZ INF BDE Brigade. 2 NEW ZEALAND Division. Corps.

| Schedule No. (to be left blank) | Unit | Regtl. No. | Rank and Name (Christian names must be stated) | Action for which commended (Date and place of action must be stated) | Recommended by | Honour or Reward | (To be left blank) |
|---|---|---|---|---|---|---|---|
| | 28 NZ (MAORI) BN | ~~39009~~ 39099 | MANAHI, Haane<br>L/Sjt. | On the night 19/20 Apr 43 during the attack upon the TAKROUNA feature L/Sjt MANAHI was in command of a Section. The objective of his platoon was the pinnacle, a platform of rock right on the top of the feature. Early in the advance his platoon came under heavy enemy fire which caused many casualties, including the Platoon Commander. First light on 20 Apr 43 found the platoon reduced in strength to ten and pinned to the ground a short way up the feature by heavy Mortar and SA fire. The platoon continued the advance towards their objective, L/Sjt MANAHI leading a party of three up the WESTERN side. During this advance they encountered heavy MG fire from posts on the slope and extensive sniping by the enemy actually on the pinnacle. In order to reach their objective L/Sjt MANAHI and his party had to climb some 500 ft the last 50 ft being almost sheer and during the whole time they were under heavy fire. L/Sjt MANAHI personally led the small party and silenced several MG posts in turn. Eventually by climbing hand over fist they reached the pinnacle and after a brief fight some 60 enemy, including an OP officer, surrendered.<br>They were there joined by the remainder of the platoon and the pinnacle was captured.<br>Within a short time the small area was subjected to intense Mortar fire from the considerable enemy force still holding the village of TAKROUNA and the NORTHERN and WESTERN slopes of the feature, and later to heavy and continuous shelling. The platoon Sjt was killed and other casualties reduced the party then holding the pinnacle to L/Sjt MANAHI and two Ptes. An Arty OP offr who had arrived ordered L/Sjt MANAHI to withdraw but he and his men remained and held the feature.<br>This action was confirmed by Bde HQ as soon as communications were established. The end of the | [signature]<br>T/Lt-Col<br>Comd 28 NZ (MAORI) BN<br><br>R W Harding<br>Brigadier.<br>Comd 5 NZ Inf Bde.<br><br>H K Kippenberger<br>Major General<br>Comd 2 NZ Div<br><br>B Freyberg<br>Lt Gen<br>GOC. 10 Corps &<br>NZEF | ~~VC~~ DCM.<br><br>(Sd.) H. M. WILSON, General, Commander-in-Chief, Middle East Forces | 449<br>13500 |

This page and next: The citation for Manahi's Victoria Cross, with the letters 'VC' crossed out and replaced with 'DCM'.

Paul Moon

[M3425] W7670/M2618 2000m 9/17s 191 G & S E. 1733. Forms/W. 3121/5

- 2 -

Date Recommendation passed forward.

| | Received | Passed |
|---|---|---|
| Brigade | | |
| Division | | |
| Corps | | |
| Army | | |

Army Form W. 3121.

Brigade. Division. Corps.

| Schedule No. (to be left blank) | Unit | Regtl. No. | Rank and Name (Christian names must be stated) | Action for which commended (Date and place of action must be stated) | Recommended by | Honour or Reward | (To be left blank) |
|---|---|---|---|---|---|---|---|
| | | | | morning 20 Apr 43 found the party short of amn, rations, and water. L/Sjt MANAHI himself returned to his Bn at the foot of the feature and brought back supplies and reinforcements, the whole time being under fire.<br>During the afternoon the enemy counter-attacked in force some of them gaining a foothold. In face of grenades and small arms fire L/Sjt MANAHI personally led his men against the attackers. Fierce hand to hand fighting ensued but eventually the enemy were driven off.<br>Shortly after this the party was relieved.<br>On morning of 21 Apr 43 urgent and immediate reinforcements were required and L/Sjt MANAHI again led up a party consisting of 15 men. At this time the enemy had once more gained a foothold on the pinnacle.<br>L/Sjt MANAHI led one of two parties which attacked and drove back the enemy. This attack was made under concentrated Mortar and heavy MG fire. All that day the feature was heavily shelled, Mortared and subjected to continual MG fire from in and about TAKROUNA.<br>Late in the afternoon of 21 Apr 43 L/Sjt MANAHI on his own initiative took two men and moved round the NORTH WESTERN side of the feature. In that area were several enemy MG and Mortar posts and two 25 prs operated by the enemy. With cool determination L/Sjt MANAHI led his party against them, stalking one post after another and always under shell and MG fire. By his skill and daring he compelled the surrender of the enemy in that area.<br>This courageous action undoubtedly led to the ultimate collapse of the enemy defence and the capture of the whole TAKROUNA feature with over three hundred prisoners, two 25-prs, several mortars and 72 MGs.<br>On the night 21/22 Apr 43, L/Sjt MANAHI remained on the feature assisting in the evacuation of the dead and | | | |

[M3425] W7670/M2618 2000m 9/17s 191 G & S E. 1733. Forms/W. 3121/5

-3-

Date Recommendation passed forward.

| | Received | Passed |
|---|---|---|
| Brigade | | |
| Division | | |
| Corps | | |
| Army | | |

Army Form W. 3121.

Brigade. Division. Corps.

| Schedule No. (to be left blank) | Unit | Regtl. No. | Rank and Name (Christian names must be stated) | Action for which commended (Date and place of action must be stated) | Recommended by | Honour or Reward | (To be left blank) |
|---|---|---|---|---|---|---|---|
| | | | | wounded and refusing to return to his Bn until this task was completed. During that time the area was being heavily and continually shelled.<br>Throughout the action L/Sjt MANAHI showed the highest qualities of an infantry soldier. His cool judgement, resolute determination and outstanding personal bravery were an inspiration to his men and a supreme contribution to the capture and holding of a feature vital to the success of the operation. | | | |

Sd) B.L. Montgomery
Gen.,
G.O.C. Eighth Army.

(SGD) H.R. ALEXANDER.
GENERAL.
COMMANDER. 18th ARMY GROUP.

*General Sir Alan Brooke (Later Lord Alanbrooke) at his desk, 1942*

*Wikimedia Commons, Imperial War Museum No. TRISI Collection 4905-03 IP UK Government. War Office official photographer*

*Geoffrey and Rau Manahi, Te Papa-i-Ouru Marae, Ōhinemutu, Rotorua, 17 March 2007*

*Geoffrey Manahi family collection*

*Arthur Midwood holds the 'Te Arawa Sword of Gallantry for Haane Manahi'. On his left is HRH Prince Andrew, and on his right is Rau Manahi, Anaru Rangiheuea and Geoffrey Manahi, Te Papa-i-Ouru Marae, Ōhinemutu, Rotorua, 17 March 2007*

*Geoffrey Manahi family collection*

Manahi – who was critically injured – was rushed to Tauranga Hospital, where he was pronounced dead at 9.35 pm as a consequence of blood loss caused by multiple chest and abdominal injuries.[38] The next day, Manahi's body was formally identified by one of his grand-nephews, John Fitzgerald,[39] and the arrangements for the tangi commenced. The tangi was held a few days later at Ōhinemutu, where an already large crowd was augmented by men of the Māori Battalion who had been at a reunion at Gisborne, and who travelled to Rotorua as soon as they had heard of Manahi's passing.

## NOTES

1. D M Stafford, *The New Century in Rotorua*, p. 239.
2. Interview with Neil and Rau Manahi, Rotorua, 20 August 2009.
3. T R Hiroa, *Medicine Amongst the Maoris, in Ancient and Modern Times*, Doctor of Medicine Thesis, Otago Medical School, Dunedin, 1910, p. 44.
4. H Mitchell to P Moon, 1 February 2010.
5. Donna Hall's mother Bonita Morehu recalled Manahi's tribute to Makawe sometime in the 1990s. Bonita's mother was one of the women who accompanied Haane up to Makawe's tūāhu. H Mitchell to P Moon, 1 February 2010.
6. G Manahi to P Moon, 25 February 2010.
7. Personal comment to H Mitchell by Hamuera T Mitchell nephew of Kepa. H Mitchell to P Moon, 1 February 2010. Also see M H Pene, 'Ehau, Kepa Hamuera Anaha 1885–1970', in *Dictionary of New Zealand Biography*, 22 June 2007. Also see H Mitchell, 'Tribute Speech to Celebrate Award to Haane Manahi DCM', Tamatekapua, Ōhinemutu, 7 October 2006, author's collection.
8. Op. cit.
9. New Zealand Military Forces, 'Record of Medical Board', NZEF Furlough Draft, Manahi, Haane, Rotorua, 26 October 1943.
10. New Zealand Military Forces, 'Victory Contingent', History-sheet, Haane Manahi , 39099, War Form N.Z. 307.
11. New Zealand Military Forces, 'Proceedings of Medical Board, Haane Manahi, 13 August 1946, New Zealand Defence Forces Archives.
12. *New Zealand Herald*, 26 March 1943.
13. J V T Baker, *War Economy*, Wellington, Historical Publications Branch, Department of Internal Affairs, 1965, p. 512. The last of the full-time Trade Training Centres closed in 1953, and at that stage 7300 men had received full-time training.
14. N M Taylor, *The Home Front*, vol. 2, Wellington, Historical Publications Branch, Department of Internal Affairs, 1986, pp. 1271–2.
15. *The Press*, 17 April 1944, p. 3, in ibid, p. 1277.
16. Interview with Neil Manahi, Rotorua, 20 August 2009.
17. Letter from A N V Dobbs, Army Secretary, to H C Baker, Fairfield, New South Wales, 10 March 1959, New Zealand Defence Forces Archives..
18. Union Steam Ship Company of New Zealand. Union Line New Zealand, England. New Zealand Victory Parade Contingent, June 8th 1946. HMNZT Maunganui, Dinner adieu. At sea, August 11th, 1946. [Menu]Reference Number: Eph-A-WAR-WII-Peace-1946-01Alexander Turnbull Library.
19. Diary of RNZAF Senior Sgt. Judith Copeland for 8 June 1946 describing the day she marched in the Victory Parade. Facsimile in author's collection.
20. His Majesty's Stationery Office, *Official Programme of the Victory Celebrations*, London, 8 June 1946, p. 1.
21. Op. cit.
22. W Webster, *Englishness and Empire 1939–1965*, Oxford, Oxford University Press, 2005, p. 55.
23. Record of Promotions, Reductions, Transfers, Casualties, Punishments, Etc., 'Particulars of Will', New Zealand Defence Forces Archives.
24. Interview with Rau Manahi, Rotorua, 20 August 2009.
25. Interview with Neil Manahi, Rotorua, 20 August 2009.
26. Interview with Rau Manahi, Rotorua, 20 August 2009.
27. Interview with Rau Manahi, 19 January 2010.
28. Interview with Rau Manahi, 25 February 2010.
29. Details contained in death certificate for Haane Te Rauawa Manahi, Department of Internal Affairs, 1986.
30. Interview with Rau Manahi, Rotorua, 20 August 2009.
31. Interview with Rau Manahi, 19 January 2010.
32. Interview with Rau Manahi, Rotorua, 20 August 2009.
33. Interview with Neil Manahi, Rotorua, 20 August 2009.
34. Sworn Deposition of Bartlett Meihana, Tauranga, 6 June 1986.
35. Sworn Deposition of Rose-Anne Marie Smith, Tauranga, 6 June 1986, in Findings of Coroner (M J Cooney) at inquest completed on 6 June 1986 in Tauranga, Ministry of Justice file, Coronial Services.
36. Sworn Deposition of Mark John Ebert, Tauranga, 6 June 1986, in Findings of Coroner (M J Cooney) at inquest completed on 6 June 1986 in Tauranga, Ministry of Justice file, Coronial Services.
37. Interview with Neil Manahi, Rotorua, 20 August 2009.
38. Findings of Coroner (M J Cooney) at inquest completed on 6 June 1986 in Tauranga, Ministry of Justice file, Coronial Services. Also see New Zealand Police, Deceased Person Certificate and Identification Form, 29 March 1986, in op. cit.
39. Op. cit.

# CHAPTER 10: Revival

After the war, Manahi ensured that there was little mention of his triumph in North Africa. His instinctive humility and aversion to any public displays of gratitude saw him retreat into relative anonymity. It was therefore only following his death that those who felt he had been deprived of the appropriate recognition for his feats launched a succession of campaigns focussing on having his Victoria Cross reinstated. The first of these took the form of the Manahi VC Committee. It was established in 1987 – within a year of Manahi's death – and determined to resolve what it saw to be unfinished business regarding the VC that Manahi had originally been awarded, but that had subsequently been downgraded. Its membership at various times included Sir Charles Bennett, Ernie Dix (a retired SAS soldier), Norman Bennett (VC researcher), Anthony Horton (President of the Rotorua RSA), Captain (retired) Maxwell Rolston (Secretary of the Rotorua RSA), Brigadier (retired) Ian Thorpe, Major (retired) John Marsh, Major (retired) Alfred Voss, Donna Manahi Morrison Grant (one of Manahi's nieces), Donna Hall (solicitor and one of Manahi's nieces), and was supported by Professor Laurie Barber, the Right Honourable Sir Peter Tapsell, retired Generals McKinnon, Pierce, and Thomas (New Zealand Defence Force),[1] and Manahi's eldest son, Rau. Additional evidential support was provided by the then last two surviving veterans of Takrouna – Arthur Midwood and Maiki Parkinson, and other veterans of the war, including Sonny Sewell and Sonny Mitchell.[2] It was a pantheon of supporters which in itself was an imposing testament to the esteem that Manahi was held in.

Rau explained why it took more than four decades after Takrouna, though, for action to be taken on the issue of Manahi's VC: 'The whole thing for the VC started straight after he [Haane] died, because he didn't want to have anything to do with it. He wasn't even interested. Whenever we spoke to him about the war, he would just change the subject'.[3] For many of those around him, and those familiar with the circumstances of the denial of his VC though, it was not as easy to dismiss what they felt was a wrong that had been perpetrated against Manahi. As one former serviceman described it, 'Haane not getting that VC was, for us, like getting a stone on your shoe. You can keep walking, but it still annoys you, and the only way to fix it is to get rid of the stone – to sort out the problem – and that's how a lot of us felt about Haane. While he was alive, we respected that he didn't want any fuss, but later on, we felt we had to do something, for Haane and for all the other boys who were with him'.[4]

Despite the early enthusiasm and determination of the Manahi VC Committee, their initial efforts at lobbying the government met with official reluctance for the matter to be reconsidered. At the beginning of the 1990s, informal talks were held between two former New Zealand governors-general and Buckingham Palace, and although the content of these discussions remains confidential, the lack of any evident progress in advancing the Manahi case indicates that they bore little fruit for the committee. The New Zealand Government was at least not overtly opposed to the idea of the reinstatement of the VC, and had been behind the semi-official feelers that had been put out to the Palace to test the response.[5] At the time, it was believed by officials that a direct approach, in the form of some official recommendation for Manahi to be posthumously granted the VC, might not have elicited the desired response, and so the government maintained an informal and gradual method, testing the waters at every stage to gauge the reactions from the Palace.

Initially, just the fact that communication channels had been opened up with the Palace was reason for cautious optimism, but any thoughts of a quick resolution dissolved when the government received a response from the Queen's Private Secretary, Robert Fellowes, which suggested that the period of time that had elapsed since the award of the DCM and this 'appeal' would incline the Queen to be reluctant to consider the reinstatement of Manahi's VC.[6] The main objection by the Palace was that the Queen would not view it as right to consider upgrading the award because so much time had elapsed since Manahi received his DCM, and thus there could be 'no substitute for a careful assessment of the facts at the time'.[7] Given this softly-worded but unambiguous rejection, the New Zealand government concluded that no further progress was possible.

During 1993 and 1994, there was an exchange of correspondence between the committee and members of the New Zealand government, petitioning for an official request to be made to the Queen to reinstate Manahi's VC. At the same time, the committee engaged in further research, especially regarding the circumstances of the downgrading of the initial award, but as Charles Bennett conceded, at the start of the decade, 'we were very short on supporting material'.[8]

On 7 December 1993, Charles Bennett (on behalf of the Manahi VC Committee) wrote to the Prime Minister, Jim Bolger, with a summary of the facts surrounding the Manahi case, and with an accompanying petition seeking the reinstatement of Manahi's VC. There had already been one setback with the campaign, as the committee noted: 'The Committee were [sic] actually on the point of sending a strong delegation to Wellington last year (4 December 1992), when it was decided to cancel because in a private interview with our chairman, Sir Charles Bennett, given a few days before the meeting [25 November 1992], Defence Minister, Warren Cooper made it clear he was not prepared to recommend our petition favourably to Cabinet and that would also be his stance to any delegation we might be sending down to see him'. According to the committee, Cooper's two main objections to further efforts directed at the Palace were that the Queen had already twice declined informal suggestions to reconsider the case, and that Manahi's own cause had not been helped by the allegations of acting in an 'unmilitary' manner on Takrouna.[9]

Bennett later expressed regret at having seen Cooper privately. 'I now realised that I committed a tactical error in agreeing to see the Minister on my own', he wrote to a colleague.[10] From this point onwards, the need for a strong delegation, matched with more abundant evidence, was seen as vital by the committee.

It appears as though the New Zealand Government, from its standpoint, however, did not wish to appear simply as a deferential agent of the Crown. Thus, when Cooper received the request for reconsideration of the Manahi case, instead of simply referring to the advisory statement from the Palace, he regurgitated the allegations of improper conduct relating to the treatment of prisoners on Takrouna as a barely-veiled message to the committee that Manahi's own alleged conduct was the reason why the Palace had rejected the reinstatement of Manahi's VC, and why the New Zealand Government was bound to follow a similar line in its stance.

The sense of injustice was hardly likely to subside, though, just because the government had concluded that the matter was over. If anything, the feeling that Manahi had been 'short-changed' by the Crown only intensified in the aftermath of this phase of the campaign for the VC reinstatement. Charles Bennett responded point-by-point to the government's position, carefully laying out the areas where the government's arguments were either at odds with the historical evidence, or wrong on points of law or procedure. His next planned tactic was to seek a third consideration by the Palace of the Manahi case, this time based on substantially more historical data that had been unearthed since the two earlier approaches. This was a plan with very slim chances of even getting government backing, but Bennett felt it was the only good option remaining. He sought this further 'consultation' with the Queen by the New Zealand Cabinet 'because of the most unusual nature of the Manahi case and of the wide support now given to the Manahi petition by some very famous people and by his own Maori tribe'.[11]

On 7 December 1993 the Manahi VC Committee submitted a formal request to the government that it, in turn, ask for the Queen's approval to grant a posthumous VC to Manahi. Unlike previous approaches, though, this submission was firmly propped up with evidence and precedents which the committee believed strengthened enormously the case they were making, and which were partly in response to the points on which the earlier pleas for reconsideration were denied.[12] These are worthwhile considering in that they show the extent to which the justification for the reinstatement of Manahi's VC had grown during the preceding two years. First, Charles Bennett referred the Prime Minister to the Heaphy Case, in which Major Charles Heaphy (a member of the New Zealand Militia)[13] was recommended for a VC for his actions in February 1864. However, even though the recommendation was initially rejected because members of the Colonial Forces at the time were ineligible for the award, following representations from the New Zealand Government and senior military officers, Heaphy eventually was granted his VC.[14] Following on from this, the committee and Bennett argued that the lapse of time between the initial downgrade, and the request for the VC reinstatement ought not to be a material consideration, and that the rights and wrongs of the award were at the heart of the matter.

Bennett also provided evidence of the precedent for DCMs to be upgraded to VCs, citing the case of Sergeant Wright of the Coldstream Guards, whose DCM, awarded in January 1944 was cancelled and replaced by a Victoria Cross in September the same year.[15] To these strands of the case were bound the existing fibres of the earlier request for the government to recommend to the Queen that Manahi's VC to be reinstated.

This was by far the most convincing plea yet put before the government, so it was with much disappointment that the reply from the Prime Minister was issued on 30 March 1994.[16] Bolger and his officials went through the letter from the Manahi supporters, and rather than giving it due consideration, made every effort to counter the arguments. The Heaphy precedent was rejected outright (though with no explanation), and great stress was placed on the fact that the Queen had already rejected two informal approaches to reinstate Manahi's VC, and there was therefore no point in approaching the Palace for a third time, despite the additional evidence the committee had accumulated by this time.[17]

Bolger and those who pieced together his reply were also careful to rebut all the other precedent arguments that Bennett and his committee had presented, before heading into the most unusual aspect of the prime minister's response, in which he suggested what he considered a possible reason why Manahi was not awarded the VC: 'A reason, not cited, why a DCM, rather than a VC, was recommended may have been that Manahi was in command of, and supported by, a party of soldiers. He was not acting alone and was supported by others. In other words he made a contribution to what was a collective action under his command and therefore it may have been seen as somewhat invidious to single him for a VC. It should also be borne in mind that no individual has a 'right' to a particular honour'.[18]

This intemperate section of the prime minister's response negated entirely Manahi's leadership of his troops, and also flew in the face of the specific details of the citation, which emphasised his singular role on the victory at Takrouna (and which was endorsed by the most senior military commanders in the North African theatre). This statement was nothing short of an attempt to rewrite history, and betrayed a deep lack of understanding of the nature of military awards, as well as concluding with a snide and similarly inaccurate observation regarding Manahi's 'right' to the VC. Even a cursory look at the relevant documentation would have revealed that there was no question of Manahi's entitlement to the award – an opinion backed by some of the most senior Allied commanders in the war. Evidently, an official in the prime minister's office felt it fit to insert this didactic assessment in the response to Bennett's letter. And in a later submission to the government, the counsel acting for the committee and for Te Arawa made clear the absurdity of this argument by pointing out that the failure to award Manahi the VC 'was seen as a failure to recognise the huge efforts of not just Lance Sergeant Manahi but the whole of Te Arawa'.[19]

In his conclusion, Bolger summarised that it would be 'fruitless to pursue this matter any further', and suggested to Bennett and his committee that they consider 'another appropriate manner in which to commemorate in perpetuity the bravery of the late Haane Manahi, such as a public memorial or a prize of some form to assist Maori'.[20] A subsequent appraisal of Bolger's letter by the Manahi VC Committee (produced for their own records) identified over a dozen errors in fact or false arguments used to reject the appeal for Manahi's VC to be reinstated.[21]

In all, it was a deeply disappointing response, and temporarily left the Manahi VC Committee wondering what course of action it could possibly take next. Initially, Bennett toyed with the idea of replying to Bolger's letter with a detailed rebuttal of the several dubious points that it contained. A draft along these lines was prepared, but realising the futility of engaging in such a tit-for-tat debate with the prime minister's office, Charles Bennett opted not to send the reply. 'It would have served no purpose', Bennett wrote to Bolger on 5 July 1994, 'for quite clearly the Government and its advisor, in our view, had already formed rock-firm opposition to the Manahi VC Request – an opposition first expounded by Defence Minister Warren Cooper'.[22] Bennett had spelt out what the government had never conceded publicly – that it had long since decided not to offer any support for Manahi's VC reinstatement.

The ongoing campaign by the Manahi VC Committee was supported extensively by the RSA, Te Arawa, and the wider community in general. However, there were the odd outbursts of dissent over the lobbying efforts of the committee. In 1998, military historian Chris Pugsley offered a caustic assessment of the motive behind the campaign to have Manahi's VC reinstated. 'What makes Manahi more important than the other New Zealanders', he wrote in a defence journal, 'so that his cause should now be readdressed? To suggest that it is because he is a Maori would have me labelled as racist, but I can see no other reason'.[23] Pugsley's main thesis was that many other New Zealand soldiers since the Boer War had not been granted the medals they should have been awarded, and Manahi was just one of possibly hundreds in this category. However, Pugsley's reasoning was deficient. Manahi had been recommended for the VC (after which it was mysteriously downgraded to a DCM). There was never any campaign for Manahi to be given a medal he had not actually received. Pugsley mistakenly claimed that Manahi, 'like 525 New Zealanders, was awarded the DCM .... He follows a consistent New Zealand tradition of inadequate recognition that continues to the present day'.[24] The main point that campaigners working for Manahi's VC award argued was precisely that he was not like the 525 New Zealanders who received the DCM, on the basis that none of the others had been recommended for a VC.

Pugsley then went on to chastise some of those who supported the awarding of Manahi's VC, suggesting that 'it is unfortunate that the many former military men who support the Manahi case do not reflect on their own experience with honours and awards. Had they done so they would know that the granting of awards, like death and wounding in combat, has always been a lottery, where often the most deserving die and are not honoured, while the undeserving live ... fate and circumstance led to Lance Sergeant Haane Manahi being awarded the DCM instead of the Victoria Cross'.[25] Again, Pugsley seems to have misrepresented the Manahi VC campaign as some sort of crusade to boost the recognition Manahi received from the military, whereas its main thrust was consistently to rectify an error made by the military.

In spite of the occasional flare-up of opposition such as that from Pugsley, the campaign to have Manahi's VC reinstated maintained its momentum, and in 2000, the Manahi VC Committee received a legal opinion from the public law firm of Chen and Palmer, which it hoped would be able to advise them on the best route to advance their cause. However, Chen and Palmer's conclusions on the matter were bleak. Having surveyed a number of experts, the assessment of the chances of Manahi receiving a VC were slim. One of the firm's partners and a former prime minister, Geoffrey Palmer, concluded that 'I judge it unlikely that the Government will ever make a formal recommendation in this case, given the Queen's attitude'.[26] This assessment was based in part on the responses of various people interviewed by the law firm. Rebecca Ketteridge, for example, who was a solicitor in the cabinet office, had stated that the cabinet office would be 'very strongly' against the government making such a recommendation; Philip O'Shea, an expert on royal honours and decorations, similarly said that there was little the government could do; and Ian Wards, former chief historian at Historical Publications Branch of the Department of Internal Affairs, went as far as to argue that it would be 'seriously improper' to make the award to Manahi.[27] With this apparent consensus of opposition to the suggestion that Manahi be awarded the VC, Palmer advised the Manahi VC Committee that, in his view, the government's position was unalterable.[28] The only faint flicker of hope in the legal opinion was the observation that 'There is nothing in the [Royal] Warrant to prevent the Government from recommending to the Queen that Manahi be awarded a VC and his DCM be annulled',[29] but this was a technicality which on its own offered no remedy.

Given this grim appraisal of official opinion on the matter, the supporters of the Manahi VC campaign could have taken Palmer's advice given to Norman Bennett and his colleagues that 'perseverance on your behalf, while honourable, will not change the Government's mind in our judgment and as such will end up only being a drain on both your time and energy'.[30] But the push to have the VC awarded to Manahi reached a new high-water mark that same year with the submission of a claim to the Waitangi Tribunal.[31] The Tribunal was established in 1975 as a permanent commission of enquiry to investigate and report to the government on breaches (by action or omission) of the Treaty of Waitangi (1840) by the Crown. While the Tribunal is unable to make binding decisions in most cases, it does provide recommendations for the government to consider when resolving grievances.

The Manahi claim was filed by Arapeta Tahana, who was then chairman of the Te Arawa Maori Trust Board, which had already submitted claims to the Tribunal on other matters. As a result, there was very limited time for the Tribunal to hear the concerns specifically about the Manahi case, but such was the importance with which Ngāti Whakaue and others viewed the need for the reinstatement of Manahi's VC that they shortened the hearing time for other issues so that the Manahi case could be adequately heard.[32]

Te Arawa argued that 'they have supported the Crown steadfastly in war, and that the culture of both Crown and claimants requires due recognition of outstanding contributions made in the service of our nation', and that the government had not handled adequately the earlier requests to restore the original VC recommendation. The Tribunal acknowledged that 'There is merit to the argument that this claim is damaging the relationship between the Crown and Te Arawa', and that some resolution of the whole issue was needed.[33]

What the claimants sought was for the Crown to consult with Te Arawa and 'present a fully researched and agreed proposal to the Queen for her consideration'.[34] In the case of the Manahi claim, the Tribunal issued a preliminary report in November 2005, which did not make general recommendations or findings, but rather, suggested 'a path forward' in the matter.[35]

The first issue that had to be confronted, though, was one of jurisdiction. This was not a claim that was internal to New Zealand, but rather, one that involved the British Crown. The Tribunal's jurisdiction was confined to the Crown in New Zealand, and so consequently, although the actions of the British authorities could be considered by the Tribunal, it was not in a position to issue recommendations to the British Government with respect to Manahi's VC recommendation. All that it could do was to recommend a course of action for the New Zealand Government to pursue.

The basis of the claimants' submission was that the alteration of the original citation from recommending a VC to a DCM was a 'miscarriage of justice', and that the way in which the New Zealand Government had subsequently dealt with the matter represented a lack of good faith.[36] The claimants were prudent enough, however, to avoid the temptation of comparing Manahi's acts of bravery and valour with those of other VC recipients. The intention was not to argue that Manahi had been hard done by as a result of his bravery not being appropriately recognised, but that the processes first of the British Army, and later the New Zealand Government, were prejudicial to Manahi, and by implication, to all of Te Arawa.[37]

In support of the submission, evidence was provided of precedents for reconsidering VC cases, and throughout, the claimants emphasised that they were not seeking an upgrade of an original award, but quite the opposite – the reinstatement of the medal that Manahi had initially been recommended for.[38] Also contained in the claim was the observation that the Queen had it within her discretion to grant the VC on the recommendation of a government, and yet the New Zealand government had failed to present such a recommendation directly to her. Cooper's remarks about the alleged ill-treatment of Italians by Manahi and his men during the fighting on Takrouna were raised in the claim, and were evidently a sore point for the claimants, particularly, as has been noted, because there was and remains no evidence that confirms any breaches of the conduct of war were committed at Takrouna, and certainly nothing that implicates Manahi in the involvement of any such acts.[39]

Te Arawa and the Manahi VC Committee concluded their submission with three proposed means of remedy. They sought for the Tribunal to recommend that the Crown (that is, the New Zealand Government): 'Undertake a thorough and open inquiry into the Manahi VC case, including findings of fact as to Manahi's actions, the importance of the case to Te Arawa, and allegations of ill treatment of prisoners. The inquiry would also cover the steps already undertaken by the Government to reopen the case, the approaches that have been made to the Palace, and the information placed before the Palace; Reopen the dialogue with the Queen and Palace after the inquiry, based on agreed statements of fact. If convention demands that a formal approach not be made without permission, then a further informal approach, fully informed and agreed with the committee, should be undertaken; [and] Undertake 'all reasonable steps' to have due recognition given to Haane Manahi within New Zealand and the Commonwealth'.[40]

On 11 May 2005, the Tribunal held a hearing at Te Papa-i-Ouru Marae at Tamatekapua, where much of this detailed evidence, assembled over the preceding eight years (primarily by members of the Manahi VC Committee) was presented. Historical evidence was heard from Norman Bennett and Ernie Dix – both of whom had explored issues surrounding Manahi's DCM in great detail – and oral submissions were made by some of the surviving members of the battle at Takrouna, along with Rau's account of details of the battle. The New Zealand Returned Services Association (RSA) lent its support to the claim at this hearing, and a haka created especially for Manahi in 1998 by Uenuku Fairhall (and arranged by Howard Morrison jnr. and Inia Maxwell) was performed. The lyrics reveal something of the popular conviction that a wrong existed that needed to be righted:

### Haane

| *Kua Ea Te Nama* | *The Price Has Been Paid* |
|---|---|
| Haane! E koro e! | Haane! Oh, koro! |
| Ka rongo, ka rongo! | We heard, we heard! |
| 'He iwi kotahi tātou'. | 'We are one people'. |
| Ahakoa ko wai, ahakoa nō hea | And no matter who, or from where |
| He tangata! He tangata! He tangata! | We are people, we are people! |
| Koina tā rātou i kī ai! | Well, that's what they had said! |
| Ka horihori ngā ngutu tere! | But fast lips tell lies! |
| Nā, ka rarapa te mura o te ahi. | Then the flames of hell burst forth |
| Kia hiwa rā! Kia hiwa rā! | Arise! Arise! |

| | |
|---|---|
| Ka rongo te iwi Māori! | The Māori people heard |
| Ka rongo, ka rongo! | We heard! We heard! |
| Muia ngā tari hoia e te tini | The recruitment offices were swamped with the many |
| O ngā uri o Tū-matauenga. | descendants of Tū. |
| | |
| He aha koa! He aha koa! | But what of it! But what of it! |
| Ko tā rātou i whakarite ai mō te pokai tara? | What did they arrange for these warriors? |
| He ngārahu Pākehā! | Pākehā commanders! |
| Mā te karoro ngā kākā e arataki? | Does the seagull lead the forest's parrots? |
| Mahi kūware! Mahi tinihanga! | How ignorant! How underhanded! |
| | |
| Engari tō Apirana mō te Niu Tirenitanga! | What of Ngata's talk of citizenship? |
| He aha tā rātou i utu ai? | What price had they paid? |
| Rātou i haere konihi mai i te maru o te Tiriti! | They who snuck in under the shadow of the Treaty! |
| | |
| Ahakoa tō tātou kaha e kore e ea! | No matter how strong, we can never pay enough! |
| Kore...Kore rawa! | Never, never! |
| He utu nekeneke! He utu nekeneke! | It is an ever-inflating price! |
| | |
| Haane! E koro e! | Haane! Oh, koro! |
| Tangata wehi kore, tangata maia! | A fearless man, a brave man, a brave man! |
| Tītoko-o-te-rangi, whakawhiti-o-te-rā. | Sky-propper, sun-raiser. |
| Ka haruru te whenua i Takaruna! | The land shook at Takrouna! |
| | |
| He aha koa! He aha koa! | But what of it! But what of it! |
| He taumata anō tō te toa Pākehā! | Pākehā bravery is of another level! |
| He kāpō nō te karu, he turi nō te taringa! | The eyes are blind and the ears are deaf! |
| Ka ngoto rawa te mamae me te whakamā! | The pain and shame are intense! |
| Kōhukihuki kau ana! | Making themselves keenly felt! |
| | |
| Toronā tītaha – tītaha! | Turning to the side – to the side! |
| Nā rongo, nā kite, ko mōhio | Hearing and seeing begat knowledge |
| Rokohanga atu ko whakamā-whakaingoingo | And he came across the whimpering shame |
| | |
| Ata! Aitia rawatia | Ata! She was roughly taken |
| Kia puta ki waho ko whakatakariri | And so grave birth to anger |
| Ko Tū-ka-riri! Ko Tū-mata-uenga! | To the angry! Tū the red-eyed one! |
| | |
| Tēnā! Karu-kāpō – titiro mai! | So! Blind-eyes – look at us! |
| Taringa-turi – whakarongo mai! | Deaf-ears – listen to us! |
| Ka kite, ka kite! | And you'll see, you'll see! |
| Ka rongo, ka rongo! | And you'll hear, you'll hear! |
| Ko whakatakariri e haka atu nei! | The angry one who dances here! |

| | |
|---|---|
| Waewae takahia! | The stamping feet! |
| Ringaringa pākia! | The slapping hands! |
| Ko te iwi Māori e ngunguru nei! | It is the Māori people who rumble! |
| Kare rawa mātou e noho tamariki! | We will no longer be as children! |
| Kua ea pai te nama! | The price has been paid! |
| Kei hea te rihiti?! | So where is the receipt?! |
| Kua ea pai te nama! | Give it! Give it! Give it here! |
| Kei hea te riihiti | |
| Arā! Ko te tohu Wikitōria | |
| Tēnā! Hōmai! Hōmai! | |
| Hōmai rā! | |

During the hearing, a church service was held at the side of Manahi's grave by the claimants and representatives of the RSA. Tony Horton, the President of the Rotorua RSA, delivered a eulogy which captured much of the sentiment of those supporting the claim, and which reminded everyone present of the reason for the submissions to the Tribunal: 'We stand here today at Muruika Services Cemetery surrounded by the mana of many a warrior who served their King and country. A number of those that we mourn today were not so fortunate and lie in battle fields far away in foreign countries. As I stand at the foot of the tomb of Haane Manahi I am inspired by his bravery and his absolute courage in the face of a fearsome enemy. We as the foremost organisation for Returned Servicemen within New Zealand fully support the call for a full inquiry into the circumstances surrounding the downgrading of the highly recommended citation for the Victoria Cross and feel that this matter needs to be given the highest priority given the frailness of those around us who served with this gallant hero'.[41] For the Tribunal members present, the church service and eulogy, together with all the testimony presented during the hearing, impressed on them the depth of feeling within Te Arawa and among returned servicemen regarding the need for Manahi's VC to be reinstated.

The Crown's submission to the Tribunal – in response to the claim of Te Arawa and the Manahi VC Committee – was largely an attempt by the government to argue that it had met its obligations to Te Arawa under the Treaty, and that there was nothing more, practically, that it could do to change the stance of the Palace. The Crown alleged that the claimants' submissions 'overstate the symbolic importance of the claim and underestimate the Crown's acknowledgement of Te Arawa's contribution to New Zealand's participation in the Second World War'.[42] Moreover, in counter to the suggestion that it had taken insufficient action to have Manahi's VC reinstated, the Crown submitted that it had taken 'all reasonable steps to recognise the valour of Lance-Sergeant Manahi', and in essence argued that while not the highest honour, the DCM was still a fitting tribute, and that in addition to this medal, other forms of recognition of Manahi's achievements had subsequently been made, including a room being named after him at the Rotorua RSA, the naming of a barrack at Waiouru military camp after Takrouna, and that the claim 'may best be resolved by further recognition of this kind'. The Crown was thus directing its argument towards its own proposed remedy – that some form of recognition outside of the formal honours system might be the most appropriate way to satisfy the affected parties.[43]

The Crown also provided some more insight into the informal negotiations that had been carried out with the Palace. The unfavourable response from the Palace, according to the Crown's submission, came about because 'It was now general policy in Britain not to consider cases of upgrading awards for gallantry where long periods of time had elapsed, because there can be no substitute for a careful assessment of the facts at the time'. In addition, the Crown raised the failure by anyone to identify who had altered Manahi's citation as a possible impediment preventing the Queen from reinstating the original award of a VC.[44]

Finally, the Crown attempted to draw attention to what it saw as the reality of the whole situation. It claimed that further attempts to lobby the Queen would be 'futile', and that it would therefore be 'disingenuous' of the government to offer to make such a request without any prospect of success. In this light, 'the making of a further request cannot be required of the Crown as a responsible Treaty partner'.[45] In essence, the Crown was arguing that its hands were tied because of the protocols of the Palace, and that having exhausted all avenues to seek a remedy to the situation, there were no further options available to it as far as the formal honours regime was concerned.

Having heard the evidence from both parties, the Tribunal deliberated and in November 2005, offered its analysis of the matters that made up the claim. The Tribunal considered that at the core of the claim was the relationship between Te Arawa and the Crown, and how the Manahi issue affected this relationship. It found that there was 'no indication of official discrimination against Maori receiving military awards for gallantry', and that no evidence had been presented 'about the existence of any policy during the Second World War, on the part of either the British or the New Zealand authorities, to restrict the numbers of Maori who might receive gallantry awards'.[46]Although certainly correct that there was no racial discrimination applied in the awarding of VCs, the Tribunal's position in rejecting the possibility of a quota system appeared to go against the consensus of opinion of senior army officers during the war that such a system did exist. Moreover, no other better explanation was provided by the Tribunal to explain the downgrading of Manahi's VC to a DCM. The Tribunal could have reached a reasonable conclusion that a de facto policy restricting the number of VCs awarded to a battalion existed, but instead adopted a slightly more pedantic approach to the evidence in this aspect of the claim.

The main thrust of the Tribunal's analysis was that 'the available evidence does not indicate that the process of alteration involved a miscarriage of justice *in Treaty terms*'.[47] This was an inevitable conclusion, especially as nothing done by the New Zealand government during the war had prejudiced Manahi – rather, it was the actions of British authorities that were responsible for Manahi not receiving the VC he had been recommended for.

The New Zealand Government might have acted in good faith during the war, but what about afterwards –especially when responding to the compelling pleas of the Manahi VC Committee? This was also mulled over by the Tribunal, which summarised the nub of an element of estrangement between Te Arawa and the Crown relating to the Manahi VC downgrade: 'Government actions to date concerning the reopening of the case have disappointed the tribe. Further, by not involving Te Arawa more fully (through the VC Committee), the informal approaches have ironically revived just the sort of speculation that the claimants feel occurred in the wake of the original unexplained alteration of the award. This, in turn, has prolonged Te Arawa's distress, rather than resolving the issue'.[48] However, the Tribunal's responsibility in this facet of the claim was to determine whether the actions that the New Zealand Government took in the early 1990s were those appropriate to its role as a Treaty partner.

The Tribunal was broadly defensive of the government's actions in this period, and again noted that the obstacle to Manahi's VC reinstatement lay in London, not Wellington. This had not been directly disputed by the claimants, but they had been concerned that they had undertaken almost all the research on the case, and yet, when the New Zealand Government made its informal approaches to the Palace, they had been substantially excluded from the process.

Another important element of the claimant's case was the possibility of VCs to be awarded long after the action occurred. Throughout the twentieth century, limitations were gradually put in place restricting aspects of VC awards, including King George's instruction that no more VCs be given for actions during the Second World War. However, the Tribunal reached the opinion that 'the claimants are correct when they argue that these rules do not prevent the reinstatement of an earlier recommendation (rather than the making of a fresh one). In any case, neither the claimants' nor the Crown's view has been put to the test of a formal approach to the Queen'.[49]

In its concluding statement, the Tribunal members made it clear that they felt it 'unlikely' that the New Zealand government had breached the principles of the

Treaty in its dealings with the Manahi VC issue.[50] 'Nevertheless', the Tribunal's report noted, it 'seems clear to this Tribunal that, while the Crown has attempted to resolve the issue and has acted in good faith in doing so, the issue has not been adequately resolved and is still causing hurt to Te Arawa and difficulties for their relationship'.[51] What the Tribunal did not mention, though, was that George VI's stricture on the issuing of VCs after 1952 for actions in the Second World War was not written into the Royal Warrant itself, and therefore, there was no legal or procedural impediment to the Queen making such an award.

Instead of making recommendations on what should happen regarding the government's responsibility for advising to the Queen that Manahi's VC be reinstated, the Tribunal issued three 'suggestions', which were not binding, but which they expected the parties to the claim to act on in good faith. The first of these was that the claimants could 'take heart' that the Crown publically recognised Manahi's bravery, and that through public pronouncements of this, there was the opportunity for speculation about events surrounding the downgrading of the award to be removed. The second suggestion was a more practical measure, but one which if not pursued, could lead to cause for further possible action. The Tribunal proposed 'that the Crown and the committee work together on a joint submission to provide the basis for a formal approach to the Palace, following an informal approach if convention again requires it. If this suggestion is not followed, we may need to consider whether a Treaty breach has taken place. However, we trust that this will not be needed. If an approach by the parties is ultimately unsuccessful, the Tribunal may need to consider the ramifications of this'.[52]

Finally, the Tribunal observed that there remained a lack of certainty over the reason why Manahi's VC was downgraded. His acts of bravery were unquestioned, but the subsequent alteration of his citation remained mysterious. Consequently, more research was needed, and the Tribunal suggested that the Crown and the claimants 'facilitate a joint research effort … to assist with any future agreed submission to the Palace'.[53] There was nothing in this preliminary report which in itself looked like a solution to the apparent impasse that the Manahi VC Committee had reached. Rather, the Tribunal set out avenues for the Crown and the claimants to pursue in order hopefully to budge the Palace into reconsidering and ultimately reinstating Manahi's VC.

Although alternative forms of recognition were certainly possible, what frustrated the committee most was that the provision for Manahi's VC to be reinstated was explicit in the Royal Warrant of September 1999 on the New Zealand Gallantry Awards.[54] Not only did the Royal Warrant allow for VCs to be awarded posthumously,[55] but under section 20, the Crown had the right, 'on a recommendation by Our Prime Minister of New Zealand or by a Minister of the Crown acting for Our Prime Minister .... Where the conferment of an Award or a Bar to an Award, or both, on any person has been cancelled or annulled, to restore the Award or the Bar, or both, to that person, and to restore the person's name to the register'.[56] The appearance was thus given, at least from one angle, that the Queen might be able to confer Manahi with a posthumous VC, but that the obstacle to this lay with New Zealand Government ministers, who were holding back from making the necessary recommendation.

Six months after the Tribunal issued its Preliminary Report, Te Arawa responded with an informal submission to the government, led by lawyer and Manahi's niece, Donna Hall. Its backers hoped to capitalise on the renewed interest in the Manahi case, and the fact that the Tribunal had issued statements which suggested that it would be prudent for the New Zealand Government to reconsider its position on the matter – especially in light of the fact that the existing state of affairs was proving harmful to relations between Te Arawa and the Crown. The timing also seemed fortuitous as 2006 was the 150th anniversary of the Victoria Cross being instituted, and it was the year designated by the government as 'The Year of the Veteran'. On making this announcement, the Minister of Veterans' Affairs, Rick Barker, noted that 'it's time for us to recognise the massive contribution veterans made in our communities and townships as well as our cities and indeed to New Zealand's free and democratic society'.[57] As far as Te Arawa was concerned, the belated award of the VC to Manahi would be the most fitting tribute possible, and 'a superb example to the Military, to Maori, and to the wider New Zealand community, of the difference that can be made by personal commitment "to God, to King and to Country"'.[58]

The informal submission delivered to the government was the summation of all the research and preparation for the reinstatement of Manahi's VC that had been carried our in the preceding two decades. There was little that was new in its content, but by building on the enthusiasm for the cause that had been quickened by the Preliminary Report of the Tribunal, it was the last best hope for those advocating that Manahi receive the award he was originally recommended for.

Finally, the government appeared as though it had been swayed by the strength of the case, and the persistence of its advocates. This manifested itself in a trip to London in May 2006 by Minister of Defence Phil Goff, who was accompanied by Donna Hall and Norman Bennett. The trio, led by Goff, delivered a joint submission in person to the Queen's private secretary, Sir Robin Janvrin. Initially, Goff seemed optimistic about the outcome: 'I took the opportunity today to visit London … to make representations to the Palace on behalf of the Manahi VC Committee and the Te Arawa people, whose representatives accompanied me. The government has been in discussion with Te Arawa and the Manahi VC Committee. We believe that, on the best evidence, the actions of Haane Manahi were worthy of the award of the Victoria Cross for his bravery at Takrouna Ridge in North Africa in 1943. In my view, he won the VC not just once, but time and again. Given that the entire chain of military command recommended him for the Victoria Cross, it is hard to understand why he received the DCM. The original citation and supporting sworn statements are compelling evidence of Lance-Sergeant Manahi's conspicuous bravery. We are exploring with the Queen's advisors whether his case can be reconsidered, mindful of the fact that the consistent position of the monarch since the late 1940s has been not to revisit such decisions. We had a positive meeting with the Queen's Private Secretary this afternoon. We are grateful to him for making the time to see us, and for giving us a sympathetic hearing'.[59]

Hall, Bennett and Goff met with Janvrin as a group on 26 May, but after less than fifteen minutes minutes, Goff requested that he speak in private with Janvrin, with Hall and Bennett left waiting outside the office. This meeting went on for around half an hour, at the conclusion of which, the Palace's position was noticeably less supple.[60] Bennett was unaware at the time of the Palace visit that SAS Corporal Willie Apiata's Victoria Cross recommendation for gallantry in Afghanistan in 2004 was also in the process of being forwarded by the New Zealand Government to the Palace for approval. On 28 July, Janvrin advised that the Queen had turned down the request to have Manahi's VC recommendation restored. Just four days later, the Queen was 'pleased to approve' the VC for Willie Apiata. Bennett later queried whether Goff was also in discussions with Janvrin over two VCs (both for Māori soldiers) at the Palace meeting in May 2006.[61]

The Queen evidently would not be budged, as New Zealand's *Army News* later reported: '"Sir Robin said that Her Majesty had asked him first to reiterate Her great admiration for Lance Sergeant Manahi's remarkable bravery", said Mr Goff. The reports of witnesses and commanders at the time said there was evidence that a recommendation for the award of the Victoria Cross was by no means unjustified and that Lance Sergeant Manahi was clearly deserving of the Distinguished Conduct Medal, a significant decoration in its own right. However, he said that Her Majesty places great store by King George VI's decision shortly after the Second World War that no further awards for service during the war should be considered'.[62]

However, a compromise of sorts was worked out in the ensuing weeks. As Goff put it 'In communicating her view, however, the Palace expressed The Queen's wish that careful thought be given to alternative ways in which further recognition could be given to the gallantry of Lance Sergeant Manahi, and indicated that The Queen would be pleased to be personally associated with it'.[63] This suggestion – of an alternative form of recognition – was probably raised by Goff when he had met privately with Janvrin in London in May, and was certainly an idea that was not looked on favourably at first by the Manahi VC Committee. 'It was never our thought that there be an alternative' was Norman Bennett's response to Goff's announcement.[64]

In October 2006, Goff announced what the compromise arrangement would be. It was to be a triumvirate of items presented to Te Arawa – something unique, and imbued with great significance from a number of perspectives. The basis of the presentation would derive from the motifs 'for God, for King, and for Country': '"For God" will be marked by the presentation of an altar cloth, for Saint Faith's Church … "For King" will take the form of a letter from The Queen, acknowledging the gallantry of Haane Manahi, to be framed and hung in the Tamatekapua Meeting House alongside photos of Haane Manahi and The Queen. "For Country" will be represented by a sword to be gifted on permanent loan to Te Arawa by The Queen. Te Arawa would in turn present the sword to the Chief of Defence Force along with a patu in memory of Haane Manahi. The sword would be displayed in the office of the Chief of Defence Force. The patu would be worn, on appropriate occasions as part of the dress of the Chief of Defence Force. These gifts would be a tangible link between Haane Manahi, The Queen, Te Arawa and all serving members of the Defence Force'. Goff concluded by noting that 'The Queen has expressed Her gratitude for the sensitive and imaginative manner with which Her offer of recognition has been handled'.[65]

Finally, after two decades of concerted effort, the Palace was seen by the people of Te Arawa as paying homage to Manahi, although the response offered by the Queen was not met with unanimous endorsement. On 17 March 2007, a ceremony was held at Te Papiouru Marae in Ōhinemutu, where the Queen's second son, His Royal Highness the Duke of York, Prince Andrew, offered the gifts to Te Arawa as the token of the Queen's recognition of Manahi's accomplishments at Takrouna. Draped in a korowai, Prince Andrew presented the gifts and spoke of Manahi's bravery. 'When one listens to the words of those that were actually there', he told the crowd, 'the extraordinary actions of Lance Sergeant Haane Manahi become abundantly clear. His leadership, devotion to duty and outstanding courage are beyond question. His gallantry bring great honour to his descendants, to the 28$^{th}$ Maori Battalion and to the Te Arawa people'. He went on to say how the Queen had personally commanded him to convey her admiration for Manahi's bravery, and 'to express her appreciation of the long history of service of the Te Arawa people'.[66]

The Queen's letter, which was displayed in the Rotorua RSA, stated how she was 'pleased to renew my personal admiration for the remarkable bravery shown by Lance Sergeant Haane Manahi in the course of his service with the 28th (Maori) Battalion during the Second World War', and that 'Throughout his life, he embodied the enduring tradition of dignified and loyal service associated with the Te Arawa people. To them, and to us all, I trust that Lance Sergeant Manahi's gallantry will serve as a powerful inspiration for many generations to come'.[67]

Te Arawa then presented the sword to the Chief of Defence Force, Lieutenant-General Jerry Mateparae, along with a patu in memory of Haane Manahi. Mateparae, responded, reminding the audience that those who had fought with Manahi were also being honoured by this gesture from the Queen: 'Recognising Haani in this way is a tribute to Te Arawa and the men of 28 Battalion. The presentation of a sword to Te Arawa, in particular, signifies the esteem in which he was held, and the mana of Haani Manahi, and it is a great honour for the Defence Force to accept the sword from Te Arawa. It will remind us often of his gallantry, the contribution of the 28 Battalion, and [it will] be a tangible link with Maoridom, Te Arawa, and the attributes that were so conspicuously demonstrated by Haani Manahi'.[68]

Once the ceremony was over, there was a meal, and by the end of the day, most of the attendees had made their way to their homes. Manahi's place in the consciousness of Te Arawa was as strong as ever, but it was now complemented by tokens of royal recognition that are unique in New Zealand military history.

## NOTES

1. N Bennett, 'Background Information on the Manahi Victoria Cross Committee', undated, author's collection.
2. Te Puni Kōkiri, *Haane Te Rauawa Manahi 1913–1986*, Wellington, Te Puni Kōkiri, 2007, p. 4.
3. Interview with Rau Manahi, Rotorua, 20 August 2009.
4. Interview with ex-serviceman (name withheld on request), Auckland, 21 December 2009.
5. Letter from C Bennett to W McKinnon, 19 January 1992, author's collection.
6. Waitangi Tribunal, *The Preliminary Report on the Haane Manahi Victoria Cross Claim*, Wai-893, Wellington, 2005, p. 8.
7. R Fellowes, London, 1992, in N Bennett, et al., 'Informal Submission of the Government of New Zealand and the Manahi Victoria Cross Committee', Appendix 2, undated, author's collection.
8. Letter from C Bennett to W McKinnon, 19 January 1992, author's collection.
9. N Bennett, 'The Manahi Victoria Cross Case: Notes on the Petition', Tauranga, undated, author's collection.
10. Letter from C Bennett to W McKinnon, 19 January 1992, author's collection.
11. Op. cit.
12. Letter from C Bennett and Manahi VC Committee to J Bolger, 7 December 1993, author's collection.
13. Heaphy was in the Auckland Rifle Volunteers.
14. See *London Gazette*, issue 23217, 8 February 1867, p. 696.
15. See *Second Supplement to the London Gazette*, issue 36690, 5 September 1944, p. 4197.
16. Letter from J Bolger to C Bennett, 30 March 1994, author's collection.
17. Op. cit.
18. Op. cit.
19. Woodward Law Office, 'Informal Submission Seeking Award of Posthumous Victoria Cross to Haane Manahi on Behalf of Te Arawa Confederation of Tribes', Lower Hutt, May 2006, p. 5.
20. Letter from J Bolger to C Bennett, 30 March 1994, author's collection.
21. N Bennett, 'An Updated Extended Commentary on Prime Minister Jim Bolger's letter dated 30 March 1994 to Sir Charles Bennett on the 1993 Manahi Victoria Cross Petition, Auckland, 8 August 2005, Norman Bennett collection.
22. Letter from C Bennett to J Bolger, 5 July 1994, author's collection.
23. C Pugsley, 'Manahi: Was he Cheated?', in *New Zealand Defence Quarterly*, Spring, 1998, p. 31.
24. Op. cit.
25. Op. cit.

26. Letter and accompanying legal opinion from G Palmer to N Bennett, 12 May 2000, author's collection.
27. Op. cit.
28. Letter from G Palmer to N Bennett, 27 June 2000, author's collection.
29. Letter and accompanying legal opinion from G Palmer to N Bennett, 12 May 2000, author's collection.
30. Letter from G Palmer to N Bennett, 27 June 2000, author's collection.
31. Waitangi Tribunal, *The Preliminary Report on the Haane Manahi Victoria Cross Claim*.
32. Woodward Law Office, 'Informal Submission Seeking Award of Posthumous Victoria Cross to Haane Manahi on Behalf of Te Arawa Confederation of Tribes', p. 10.
33. Waitangi Tribunal, *The Preliminary Report on the Haane Manahi Victoria Cross Claim*, p. 2.
34. Ibid., p. 1.
35. Ibid., p. 2.
36. Ibid., p. 9.
37. Op.cit.
38. Ibid., pp. 9–10.
39. Ibid., p. 10
40. Ibid., p. 11.
41. T Horton, in ibid., appendix II, p. 22.
42. Waitangi Tribunal, *The Preliminary Report on the Haane Manahi Victoria Cross Claim*, p. 11.
43. Ibid., p. 12.
44. Op. cit.
45. Ibid., pp. 11–12.
46. Ibid., pp. 13–14.
47. Ibid., p. 14.
48. Ibid., p. 16.
49. Ibid., p. 17.
50. Op. cit.
51. Op. cit.
52. Ibid., p. 18.
53. Op. cit.
54. Issued under the authority of the Acts and Regulations Publication Act 1989, published in the Gazette on 23 September 1999. Also see M J Crook, *The Evolution of the Victoria Cross: A Study in Administrative History*, London, Midas Books, 1975, pp. 302–5.
55. S. 8, Royal Warrant on The New Zealand Gallantry Awards, September 1999.
56. Ibid., s. 20.
57. R Barker, Minister of Veterans' Affairs, speech delivered in Queenstown, 30 December 2005, cited in Woodward Law Office, 'Informal Submission Seeking Award of Posthumous Victoria Cross to Haane Manahi on Behalf of Te Arawa Confederation of Tribes', p. 22.
58. Woodward Law Office, 'Informal Submission Seeking Award of Posthumous Victoria Cross to Haane Manahi on Behalf of Te Arawa Confederation of Tribes', p. 23.
59. P Goff, in 'Manahi Submission Presented to Palace', media release, New Zealand Government, 26 May 2006.
60. Interview with N Bennett, Auckland, 11 January 2010.
61. N Bennett to P Moon, 4 February 2010.
62. 'For God! For King! For Country!' in *Army News*, issue 365, 17 October 2006, n. p.
63. P Goff, 'God, King and Country' recognition from Queen for Manahi', speech delivered 9 October 2006.
64. Interview with N Bennett, Auckland, 11 January 2010.
65. Op. cit.
66. Speech by HRH. the Duke of York, Prince Andrew, KG, KCVO, Rotorua 17 March 2007, in Te Puni Kokiri, *Haane Te Rauawa Manahi 1913–1986*, p. 23.
67. Letter from HRH Queen Elizabeth II, gifted to the people of Te Arawa to mark the settlement of the Haane Manahi VC Quest during the visit of HRH the Duke of York, Prince Andrew, KG, KCVO, Rotorua 17 March 2007, RSA, Rotorua.
68. J Mateparae, in *Army News*, 27 March 2007, p. 4.

# EPILOGUE

Not everyone was convinced of the adequacy of the recognition that the Queen bestowed on Manahi in March 2007. There was no doubt that it was well-intentioned, but at the same time, the feeling – for some – that it was still a compromise was difficult to overlook completely. One B Company veteran – 84-year-old Sonny Sewell – boycotted the ceremony because he said 'it was an insult that Manahi was never given the VC'.[1]

Moreover, in talking to many whānau members, and those involved in the campaign to have Manahi's VC restored, although they all seemed initially satisfied with the ceremony, and conceded that it was almost certainly the end of the line as far as the campaign for the restoration of Manahi's VC was concerned, some expressed privately the sentiment that there was still unfinished business, and always would be until the VC was granted to Manahi. In their eyes, there was no substitute for this.

From what is known of the long and considered deliberations of the Palace, the chances of Manahi ever receiving his VC appear remote, particularly after the events of March 2007. The Queen appears to have moved as far as possible to accommodate wishes of Te Arawa and the Manahi VC Committee, and the New Zealand Government lobbied to the extent that any government in the foreseeable future is likely to. Yet, as long as a mood of grievance exists among some members of Te Arawa and some servicemen over Manahi's treatment, one thing history reveals is that this feeling that he was 'short-changed' by the Crown will remain, and it is possible that a future generation might pick up the challenge to seek the restitution of his VC.

A subtle reminder of this sense of unfinished business can be found in physical form in the carved tekoteko of Manahi in Tamatekapua that was dedicated on 17 March 2007 – the same day as the ceremony and gifting of the altar cloth, sword and letter from the Queen. The idea of the tekoteko was instigated by Hamuera Mitchell, and carved by the tohunga whakairo Rakei Kingi. Among many other reasons, is momentous because it 'is the first time in New Zealand that a significant and ancient ancestral meeting house has permitted a modern ancestor to be placed inside its walls'.[2] Mitchell had proposed to Ngāti Whakaue that the carving be placed in Tamatekapua as the iwi's acknowledgement of Manahi, which Rau eventually agreed to with some reticence. Rau was insistent, however, that his father's photograph would not be placed in the meeting house, 'as the old people had forbidden this practice from the outset'. For this reason, the tekoteko was agreed on as the most appropriate memorial.[3]

It appears largely as a traditional carving of a representative figure of a person. However, there are differences – some subtle, and some more noticeable. First, the face – unlike the faces of all the other carvings in the meeting house – has no moko. The reason for this is that the figure 'represents a person of today', rather than some ancient ancestor.[4] Then there is an actual Second World War helmet resting on his head, depicting the fact that Manahi's status derives chiefly from his exploits during the war. In his hands is a carved rifle, also representing his feats in battle, while on his chest are impressions of the medals he earned during the war. However, rebated into the butt of the rifle is a replica VC – an enduring reminder of what might have been, probably what ought to have been, and what just possibly might be. At first, Kingi intended to rebate the VC on the underside of the rifle, but Mitchell argued that it would not be seen in that position, and the intended message would therefore be lost. The marae trustees, the Manahi whānau, and Ngāti Whakaue all agreed on the final form of the tekoteko as the iwi's way of commemorating Manahi.[5]

While there may be the occasional mumble about how justice was not done for Manahi, a more common view that has gained prominence since the ceremony in March 2007 is that the greatest testament to Manahi's bravery is not the medal he earned (or even the one that he was granted), but knowledge of his triumph at Takrouna. As long as this is kept alive, not only among Te Arawa, but for everyone else in the country as well, Manahi's reputation will remain his highest honour.

In 1983, Manahi gave his only full interview about the events at Takrouna four decades earlier. The interviewer was Sir Charles Bennett, and also present was Ruhi Pene, who was at Takrouna in 1943. Throughout this discussion – which was filmed – Manahi remained humble in his demeanour, understated about his achievements, and betrayed nothing of his feelings regarding the episode for which he was eventually recommended for a VC. He related the main stages of the two-day ordeal to capture the feature (pointing at times to a picture of Takrouna that was mounted in the room) and concluded with the moment when other troops from the New Zealand Division finally occupied the former enemy stronghold. The interview finishes, but the camera keeps running. Everyone is silent. Manahi stares at the picture of Takrouna and his chest heaves as he takes in a deep breath and lets out a barely audible sigh. The seconds pass, the camera is still filming, but he seems transfixed by that image. It is possible to imagine him recalling in his mind some of the scenes of the battle, and the loss of so many close colleagues and whānau members. The corners of his mouth droop slightly his eyes lower for a moment and then return their gaze at Takrouna. For this short period, he is lost in his thoughts. Ironically, it is in this silence that Manahi reveals the most about the effects of Takrouna on him, and at last it is possible to see why the memory of that time was so much more precious for him than any medal he was awarded.

## NOTES

1. S Campbell on TV3 News, 17 March 2007.
2. Te Puni Kōkiri, *Haane Te Rauawa Manahi 1913–1986*, p. 8.
3. H Mitchell to P Moon, 1 February 2010.
4. Te Puni Kōkiri, *Haane Te Rauawa Manahi 1913–1986*, p. 8.
5. H Mitchell to P Moon, 1 February 2010.

# GLOSSARY

**Ariki** - *Paramount chief, leader, lord, first-born in a high-ranking family*
**Hākari** - *Feast*
**Hapū** - *Sub tribe, clan, kinship group*
**Hongi** - *A greeting made by pressing noses*
**Hui** - *Meeting, assembly*
**Iwi** - *Tribe, extended kinship group, nation, people*
**Kai** - *Food, meal*
**Kāinga** - *Village, settlement*
**Karakia** - *Prayer*
**Kaumātua** - *Elder*
**Kuia** - *Elderly woman, grandmother*
**Marae** - *Courtyard in front of a tupuna whare or wharenui, buildings associated with a marae*
**Mate** - *Death*
**Mate Pākehā** - *Illness or death attributed to causes of Pākehā origins*
**Pā** - *Village, fortified village, stockade*
**Pākehā** - *European*
**Rangatira** - *Chief, leader, master*
**Taina** - *Younger sibling*
**Tapu** - *Sacred, prohibited, restricted, prohibition, ban*
**Tekoteko** - *Carved figure on a meeting house – often on the gable*
**Tohunga** - *Expert, priest, spiritual leader, sage*
**Tohunga Whakairo** - *Master carver*
**Tūāhu** - *Sacred place for ritual practices carried out by a tohunga*
**Tupuna whare** - *Meeting house*
**Tūrangawaewae** - *Place where one has rights of residence*
**Urupa** - *Cemetery, burial ground*
**Utu** - *Revenge, restitution, avenge*
**Waka** - *Vessel, canoe*
**Whakapapa** - *Genealogy, ancestry*
**Whakataukī** - *Proverb, saying*

**Whānau** - *Family, extended family, family group*
**Whanaungatanga** - *Relationship, kinship, sense of connection*
**Whare** - *House, building, residence, dwelling*
**Wharenui** - *Meeting house, large house, main building in marae*

# INDEX

Bold type indicates photographs between the numbered pages. There may be more than one relevant photograph in the block. References in the form 8n16 are to information in chapter endnotes, showing page and note number.

## C



## D



## E



## F



## G



## H

## S



## T



## V

## W



## Y